D. H. Lawrence
and
Nine Women Writers

D. H. Lawrence and Nine Women Writers

Leo Hamalian

Madison • Teaneck
Fairleigh Dickinson University Press
London: Associated University Presses

© 1996 by Associated University Presses, Inc.

All rights reserved. Authorization to photocopy items for internal or personal use, or the internal or personal use of specific clients, is granted by the copyright owner, provided that a base fee of $10.00, plus eight cents per page, per copy is paid directly to the Copyright Clearance Center, 222 Rosewood Drive, Danvers, Massachusetts 01923. [0-8386-3603-9/96 $10.00 + 8¢ pp, pc.]

Associated University Presses
440 Forsgate Drive
Cranbury, NJ 08512

Associated University Presses
16 Barter Street
London WC1A 2AH, England

Associated University Presses
P.O. Box 338, Port Credit
Mississauga, Ontario
Canada L5G 4L8

The paper used in this publication meets the requirements of the American National Standard for Permanence of Paper for Printed Library Materials Z39.48-1984.

Library of Congress Cataloging-in-Publication Data

Hamalian, Leo.
  D.H. Lawrence and nine women writers / Leo Hamalian.
    p. cm.
  Includes bibliographical references and index.
  ISBN 0-8386-3603-9 (alk. paper)
  1. American literature—Women authors—History and criticism.
  2. American literature—20th century—History and criticism.
  3. English literature—Women authors—History and criticism.
  4. English literature—20th century—History and criticism.
  5. Lawrence, D. H. (David Herbert), 1885–1930—Influence.   6. Women and literature—History—20th century.   7. American literature—English influences.   8. Influence (Literary, artistic, etc.)
  I. Title.
  PS151.H36   1996   95-43987
                                                                                                CIP

PRINTED IN THE UNITED STATES OF AMERICA

For Linda

Contents

Foreword Mark Spilka	9
Acknowledgments	23
Introduction	25
1. Katherine Mansfield: We are *Unthinkably* Alike	35
2. H.D.: Bid Me to Love	45
3. Rebecca West: We Must Choose Life	63
4. Meridel LeSueur: Passion on the Prairie	75
5. Anaïs Nin: A Spy in the House of Lawrence	86
6. Kay Boyle: Venus Agonistes	101
7. Sylvia Plath: The Lost Girl	111
8. Margaret Drabble: Cassandra in the Kitchen	123
9. Joyce Carol Oates: The Playing Fields of the Id	133
Epilogue	146
Notes	150
Sources Consulted	161
Index	175

Foreword
BY MARK SPILKA

There are signs that we are now in a new phase of the feminist movement, when modifications and concessions can be made without fear of political reprisals. Attacks on masculinist writings over the past few decades have given way to measured revisions and qualified defenses. The time is ripe for modest and immodest exposures of the vital interplay between masculinist and feminist writings.

Leo Hamalian's latest study, *D. H. Lawrence and Nine Women Writers,* is a handsome contribution to this promising shift in critical attitudes. It follows hard upon such major feminist contributions as Carol Siegel's *Lawrence among the Women: Wavering Boundaries in Women's Literary Traditions* (1991), Carol Sklenicka's *D. H. Lawrence and the Child* (1991), and Elaine Feinstein's friendly biography, *Lawrence and the Women: The Intimate Life of D. H. Lawrence* (1993). In one way or another, all such studies have turned upon the paradoxical notion of an apparently chauvinist male writer who seems nonetheless attractive to many women readers, writers, and critics.

Carol Siegel's working premise, that Lawrence believed that women held the truth and saw himself as a priestly mediator of that truth, is the most radical version of that paradox. Her brilliant study of Lawrence's mediating position between precursors like George Eliot, Charlotte and Emily Brontë, and Olive Schreiner and modernists like Virginia Woolf, Katherine Mansfield, H.D., and Anaïs Nin, sets the most impressive precedent for Hamalian's more extensive focus on such modernists. Carol Sklenicka examines Lawrence's oddly parental portraits of children, and particularly of young girls like Anna and Ursula Brangwen in *The Rainbow* and Winifred Crich in *Women in Love*; she also singles out Lawrence's extraordinary stress on male responsibility for raising children in *Fantasia of the Unconscious* and *Psychoanalysis and the Unconscious*. Elaine Feinstein applies sympathetic understanding to Lawrence's controversial relations with the women in his life, and occasionally praises controversial works like *Lady Chatterley's Lover* which have suffered from previous feminist disfavor.

Signs of these changing attitudes have been registered meanwhile in the annals of the D. H. Lawrence Society of North America. The appointment in 1987 of Judith Ruderman, author of *D. H. Lawrence and the Devouring Mother* (1984), as the first woman president of the Lawrence Society was an historic recognition of the importance of feminist critiques to the ongoing validity of Lawrence studies; and the panel presentations of such critiques by scholars like Ruderman and Margaret Storch suggests their absorption into the very fabric of the society's proceedings.

On 26 June 1993, however, at the International Lawrence Conference in Ottawa, Canada, the now *de rigueur* panel on feminist approaches took a more positive turn. Carol Siegel herself contributed a paper on Lawrence's "Journey Toward Cultural Feminism" in *St. Mawr*; Elizabeth Wallace offered surprisingly positive readings of "The Woman Who Rode Away," *The Virgin and the Gypsy*, and *The Man Who Died*; and Virginia Hyde commented favorably on Lawrence's struggle with "Gender and Salvation" in *The Plumed Serpent*. All these texts have been under feminist fire since 1970, when Kate Millett made her famous attack on Lawrence in *Sexual Politics*.

These startling new approaches were appropriately followed, in the Fall/Winter 1993–94 issue of *The D. H. Lawrence Society of North America Newsletter*, by Earl Ingersoll's illuminating report on radical novelist Doris Lessing's sanguine view of Lawrence. Thus, in response to Ingersoll's questioning, Lessing acknowledged that she had begun to read Lawrence as a teenager in Southern Rhodesia, that he was among the first of the modern writers that she read, and that she continued to prize him for his immense "vitality":

> His writing had an enormous effect on me because of the vitality of the man. I've just reread *Sons and Lovers* and *Lady Chatterley*, and I cannot describe the enormous pleasure and shock of that prose. It was so vivid! That was the main thing. Everything comes alive when he talks about it, doesn't it?" She said that she "never read him for his ideas," but "for his vitality" and for "unforgettable scenes, one after another." (3)

When Ingersoll went on to express surprise at her admiration for *Aaron's Rod* and *Kangaroo*—novels that might be considered "anti-women" or "politically incorrect"—Lessing responded sharply:

> "... I don't approve of this way of looking at Lawrence. I don't see the point of it. I think you should look at what a writer has to offer and take what is offered"—not complain that he's not doing something else...." She went on to say that "this political correctness business" is "so silly" and "bound to pass." She added, "Probably I shouldn't say this, because I'll be lynched, but your country is an extremely hysterical country." (3)

The difference which Lessing here establishes, between her own friendly responses to Lawrence as a woman novelist, and those of feminist and/or politically correct opponents, seems to me instructive. As research by Hamalian and others seems to indicate, women novelists have not on the whole participated actively in the strong feminist case against Lawrence introduced by Simone de Beauvoir in 1953 and Kate Millett in 1970. The most concerted feminist attack has come from academic and political opponents, not from women novelists. Lessing's working premise above—"I think you should look at what a writer has to offer and take what is offered"—is a writer's sentiment in spades; it only becomes a critic's sentiment, and even then a misleading one, when she adds—"not complain that he's not doing something else." It is, in fact, what Lawrence *does* in the way of defining the truths women hold that feminist critics rightly question. Lawrence's "ideas," which Lessing dismisses, are grist for that mill, especially as they become attitudinal and enter into novelistic doings. But even with that qualification, most feminist opponents are not too concerned with the novelist's "attractive vitality" except perhaps as a seductive hazard for women readers. Their concerns are primarily ideological, and, like most cultural theorists in recent times, they tend to take anti-aesthetic stands against white male novelists like Lawrence.

Not surprisingly, even the newly positive feminists reflect or stress such cultural concerns in their favorable responses to Lawrence. Carol Siegel is an especially skillful and sophisticated ideologist in her case for Lawrence's mediational role; Carol Sklenicka also confronts such issues directly. By contrast, Hamalian approaches his nine women writers with something like Doris Lessing's sentiment for what each writer makes of and takes from Lawrence's artistic offerings. Indeed, the great strength of his book comes from his careful concern for what Lawrence means—so far as he can tell—to each woman writer.

He is not a competitive ideologist, like Siegel and her recent predecessors, but rather an appreciative appraiser, diffident rather than assertive, respectful of differences, and responsibly open to a variety of divergent creative outlooks. His deft delineations of those outlooks are accordingly the textured substance, the veritable warp and woof, of his balanced case for Lawrence's impact on women novelists and poets in our time.

My purpose, in this light, is to act in Hamalian's stead as a descriptive if not competitive ideologist, and to provide something of the recent cultural context—academic and political as well as novelistic—which helps to place his handsome contribution in contemporary perspective. It has been my good fortune to read earlier versions of this manuscript as well as the present carefully honed and selected version; and I must confess that I've been impressed from the first by its merits and possibilities and have followed its development and improvement with a strong conviction of its importance. In my view, for instance, the first version of the manuscript offered a surprising demonstration of the range and variety of Lawrence's influence on fourteen women writers: three who knew Lawrence personally (H.D., Katherine Mansfield, Rebecca West); five contemporaries and early moderns who never met him (Dorothy Richardson, Elizabeth Bowen, Anaïs Nin, Kay Boyle, Meridel Le Sueur); and six post-Lawrenceans who responded strongly to his example (Denise Levertov, Sylvia Plath, Carson McCullers, Doris Lessing, Margaret Drabble, Joyce Carol Oates). At least eight of these women had figured importantly, moreover, in the new feminist histories of women writers, a fact which added considerably to the first version's "attractive chauvinist" paradox.

But inevitably some of these early essays were more richly developed than others, and some were tantalizingly skimpy. In the present version Hamalian has wisely trimmed down his hostages to three representatives for each category: acquaintances (Mansfield, H.D., West); contemporaries (LeSueur, Nin, Boyle); and postmoderns (Plath, Drabble, Oates). These representative selections from the original range and variety of influence have also improved with revision, and now stand before us as remarkable proof of Lawrence's mediations. It is the paradoxical nature of those mediations, mentioned above, that I now wish to address on more or less ideological grounds.

In the introduction ahead, Hamalian will explain Lawrence's influence much more variously: by stressing that Lawrence was, like most women writers, a marginal figure, an outsider to the cultural Establishment excluded by class and provincial education; by stressing also his dissenting view of patriarchal collectivities and his preferred focus on individual relations; by observing further how Lawrence "put women and their plight in a male-dominated world close to the center of his mature later fiction"; by opposing his "more spontaneous, less willful, more authentic sense of interaction with life" to rationalist aggrandizements of meaning; by praising his refusal of entrapment in predetermined roles for his women characters; by praising also his views on rich passional life and the "attainment of being" as options for women, as opposed to traditional masculine preoccupations with deeds and doings; by noting briefly his dialogic rather than monolingual model of narration and, more expansively, his creation of a liberating and empowering "ethos of eroticism"; by noting also his charting of "emotional and psychological states of mind" in fiction that no one had probed before him, and his exemplary replacement of Eliotic stasis in poetry with raw feeling and "wind-like transit"; and finally, by citing also his unique collaborations with women, and his openness to women's influence, in writing his novels and tales, and his independent discovery of what Julia Kristeva has called "the stranger in ourselves."

Running through these varied explanations is the persistent theme of sexual and emotional congruities with women's narrative concerns. Writing often from the point of view of women characters, emphasizing spontaneity, being, passional and erotic life, Lawrence had indeed affected women writers as various as Kay Boyle, Anaïs Nin, Sylvia Plath, Margaret Drabble, Meridel LeSueur, and Joyce Carol Oates, in the present study, and Doris Lessing, Carson McCullers, and Elizabeth Bowen, in previous versions. As Hamalian himself notes, many of these same writers were specifically attracted by Lawrence's rebellion against sexual repression and his experimental forays into sexual expression.

The issue of sexual repression and what to do about it is a recurrent theme among modern women novelists. Consider in this light Virginia Woolf's historic complaint in an essay called "Professions for Women" (1930) about her own diffidence in handling direct sexual expression in her fictions, and her view of the problem as one affecting women writers still under the spell of the Angel in the House. As I've elsewhere observed, that angelic lady sounds strangely like Virginia's mother, Julia Stephen, who didn't or couldn't mention sexual matters publicly because men like Virginia's father (the implicit Tyrant in the House) would frown on it and hold it against her.

As I've also noted, while relating Lessing to Lawrence, the same problem recurs at a later stage in feminist fiction, in *The Golden Notebook* (1962), where Lessing claims that men write more analytically about sex than women, and often brashly explain how women feel or should feel about sex. But when Lessing goes on to show how women really feel, she unwittingly borrows a watery metaphor and a few ideas from Lawrence to illustrate her points. It seems evident, here and elsewhere, that Lessing has ironically fallen under that male writer's spell in writing about sex in this novel. Her chief heroine, Anna Wulf, is passionately drawn to "real men" like the philandering if compassionate George Hounslow, whose powerful and dominating sexuality seems to her a sweet and beautiful thing; and, like a true Lawrencean artist, Anna's fictional alter ego, Ella, even finds erotic satisfaction vital to her artistic creativity, if dangerous to her selfhood. Still more ironically, Lawrence seems warmer, more passional, less analytical in his sexual prose than Lessing, though wittingly or unwittingly, she draws heavily on his example in all these passages.

In her interview with Earl Ingersoll, cited above, Lessing herself had touched inadvertently on these ironies while speculating about "why some women might object to Lawrence's writing":

> "All I can make out is that they complain that he has a very amateur attitude toward sex—he certainly has. But his basic attitudes toward sex, I like: he has got an enormous reverence for sex; he doesn't dismiss it and diminish it."(3)

Here Lessing confirms my thesis about her unwitting reliance on Lawrence's "ethos of eroticism" in *The Golden Notebook*. She also indicates a familiarity with his ideas that belies her separation of his art and thought.[1] Lawrence expressed reverent

---

[1] Lessing's stress on Lawrence's "vitality" is another instance of her familiarity with the "vitalist" view of his writing. Her incorporation of that conceptual view into her own supposedly concept-free enthusiasm is also undermined by her interesting choice of terms of admiration for *Sons and Lovers* and *Lady Chatterley*: first, "Everything comes alive when he talks about it, doesn't it?" then praise for his "vitality" and for "unforgettable scenes, one after the other." In *The Love Ethic of D. H. Lawrence* (1955), I early focussed on the sequence of such unforgettable scenes as being a kind of ritual and emotional form, a series of nurturing or depleting interactions by which wholeness of being was

attitudes toward sex not only in his fictions but in his letters, from which biographers like Harry Moore and critics like F. R. Leavis have been quoting for the last sixty years. Lessing is not only familiar with such sources; she has picked up the similarly old idea of appreciating Lawrence for his art rather than his thought which Frances Fergusson first proposed in "D. H. Lawrence's Sensibility" in 1933 and Richard Aldington echoed in *D. H. Lawrence: Portrait of a Genius But . . .* in 1950. In *The Golden Notebook*, moreover, Lessing herself had consciously critiqued as well as raptly absorbed Lawrence's ideas, as in the Yellow Notebook where Ella not only prizes erotically induced creativity, but also criticizes the sexual sleep which leaves her hopelessly dependent on indifferent men. Similarly, as the novel ends, Anna's long sexual struggle with Saul, which supposedly releases each of them to write new novels, is ironically undercut by the more mundane direction of mere boulder-pushing for Anna in the "Free Women" section which actually concludes the novel; and of course the novel which Lessing/Anna goes on to write is *The Golden Notebook* itself, with all of its paralyzed checks and imbalances.

Lessing's complicated response to Lawrence, which Hamalian also wrestled with in his first version of this study, was rich, varied, and both critical and profoundly admiring. Her qualified reliance on his exemplary eroticism confirms what many other women writers also found there: ways of expressing erotic experience congenial to their varied sensibilities. It was Lawrence, then, and not Virginia Woolf, who seems to have given women writers vital access to sexual expression by his exemplary mediations. What Woolf called for he in fact supplied—so much so that latter-day semioticians and proto-feminists like Stephen Heath and Robert Scholes have accused him of stereotypically and misleadingly encoding sexuality early in this century and so defrauding us all.

In *The Sexual Fix* (1984), Heath makes this devastating case against Lawrence's destructive influence on writers of both sexes, and so confirms, at least negatively, the widespread nature of that influence. It was Lawrence, he claims, who almost singlehandedly got us into the "sexual fix" which characterizes our erotic ways in the late twentieth century. His "rigidly formulaic"

---

either furthered or dissolved in Lawrence's male and female characters. I argued so as part of my proof that Lawrence's ideas at their best were very much a part of his art, as with most great writers—Lessing now included.

descriptions of sexual experience, especially in *Lady Chatterley's Lover*, have been slavishly followed by men and women writers alike, and even more slavishly practiced by actual lovers. To prove his point Heath quotes passage after passage from male and female imitators which bear the Lawrence stamp, then recommends the more imaginative and gender-free variations of recent writers on lesbian love like Kate Millett.

Heath's case for the multiple orgasms available to lesbian lovers is pursued on other grounds by Robert Scholes in *Semiotics and Interpretation* (1982). Here Lawrence, Freud, and John Cleland are classed as literary encoders who have joined the more widespread social and physical attempts to eliminate the female clitoris as a rival to phallic hegemony. Scholes traces these centuries-long attempts at real or imagined clitoridectomy to the male fear of being overwhelmed by female sexuality; then, anticipating Heath, he too offers the prospect of multiple orgasms for women by other than heterosexual means.

I have elsewhere complained about the lack of historic focus in these late-century attacks. There is no reference in either case to the discourse of sexual repression in late Victorian times and its impact on heterosexual unions, whereby the achievement of a single orgasm for women was for some time thereafter quite a triumph. Nor is there any acknowledgement of the kind of cocktail sexuality of the early modern period which Lawrence and others amply satirized. In *Lady Chatterley* Lawrence focuses on this double bind, this complicated sexual fix of the early twentieth-century; and his then liberating and empowering sexual descriptions were designed, on the one hand, to help free his readers from the repressive discourse of the past that consigned orgasmic love to prostitutes and allowed no lady to enjoy it; and, on the other, to help free them from the false liberations of trivializing and diminishing views of sexuality. Lawrence's semiotic braveries here are forgotten or dismissed by these new academic semioticians, who enjoy still another historic advantage they also fail to mention: a scientific confirmation of the clitoral source of all orgasms, first developed by Masters and Johnson in America in the 1960s and only then made available to literary and academic discourse.

It was in fact to such scientific findings that Doris Lessing was responding in *The Golden Notebook*, where male doctors are satirized for confidently prescribing new sexual wisdom about the clitoral source of orgasms to women clients. Since Lessing suspects this clinical, analytical approach to sexual union as being somehow diminishing and manipulative, she falls back upon Lawrence's reverence for sexuality and emerges on the "politically incorrect" side of the debate about vaginal vs. clitoral orgasms in the 1960s and '70s. Thus, again like Lawrence, she makes an emotional case for the connective power and importance of vaginal orgasm, which for her is the "only . . . real female orgasm," and can only occur "when a man from the whole of his need and desire takes a woman and wants all her response." What she describes, as I've said before, is "an act of *love*, an emotional experience in which men and women are as they say *one flesh*, in which E. M. Forster's phrase, 'only connect,' applies in physical, emotional, creative, even procreative ways"; but it is, as with Lawrence, a puritanical act, in which "Integrity is the orgasm," and in that sense it resists the polymorphous perversity of the love generation of the late '60s and after, and the gender liberations of still more recent times, by which love works in more various if less mysterious ways its wonders to perform.

Nonetheless, what sexual puritans like Lessing and Lawrence wanted to keep alive, and to protect from dismissal or diminishment, remains crucial to love's survival. Both writers at their best were attracted by and committed to the possibilities of sexual mutuality, and to those tenuous connections between sex and affection which Lawrence engaged in his late call for "warmhearted fucking," and to the engagement also of selfhood in that necessary and inevitable battle between lovers by which any permanent union is achieved. And of course it was Lawrence who brought these problems to Lessing's attention, and whose vitality as their scribe so commanded her admiration in an age far better characterized by the male taboo on tenderness, and the male fear of dispossession, than by the male fear of sexuality. As Lessing seems to have recognized, it was not Lawrence's fear of sexuality, nor of dispossession, but his greater fear of possessive affection, and his courageous attempts to overcome it, which made his struggle with heterosexual conflict so attractive, whatever his lapses into sexism and/or political incorrectness.

My point in summarizing these attractive aspects of their puritan pact is to suggest that such vital concerns and their inscriptions might continue to engage lovers of whatever genders and practices. After a century of sexual revolution, tenderness and selfhood seem to me the wild cards of sexual conflict which earlier players like Lawrence and Lessing have arranged so intriguingly, and which Lawrence as one of the prime inventors of modern sexual politics first arranged and rearranged. This is not to deny that Lawrence moved at times in contradictory directions, that especially during his middle phase he gave himself permission to indulge in games of sexual domination and biblical usurpation of life-responsibility—responsibility, that is to say, for the quality and direction of one's life—by making it a male monopoly and denying it to women, and by pursuing accordingly the breaking of women's wills by all possible imaginative means—including the imagination of some bizarre forms of domestic violence. But throughout those perverse games he also used the strength of female characters to resist his own worst propensities, and eventually overcame them. He is like so many white or black male moderns a mixed case, when it comes to sexism and political correctness, and that tends to explain why so many academic and political feminists attacked and dismissed his works in recent decades, and why others are moving now to reclaim them.[2]

Since reclamation is my theme, let me close this argument by suggesting that we are all mixed cases, whatever our genders or sexual preferences, in meeting individual responsibilities. I think also that women novelists were more early aware of that contradictory condition in their collectively victimized sex as one shared with their collective male victimizers, that they accordingly saw male writers as individuals like themselves, and were especially attracted to those like Lawrence whose concern with male default was like their own, whose preoccupation with the modern marriage crisis brought them onto common ground, and whose identifications with women characters were often profoundly relevant to their own concerns.

In the pages ahead, for instance, Kay Boyle will observe that Lawrence had a great influence on her "because of his tremendous humanity" and his "great feeling about people." And like

---

[2] Another such mixed case, for instance, is William Butler Yeats, quite recently the subject of a similar neo-feminist attempt at reclamation. Thus in *Gender and History in Yeats's Love Poetry* (1993), Elizabeth Butler Cullingford argues compellingly in behalf of her middlenamesake: "If a male poet cannot produce an 'authentic' female voice, he can adopt a female subject position that contests and in [some cases] defeats his own prejudices." She has in mind such anti-patriarchal poems as "Crazy Jane and the Bishop," for which she posits a ventriloquil approach by Yeats that other neo-feminists find in Joyce's Molly Bloom. It seems to me evident that a great many Lawrence characters— e.g. Hannele in *The Captain's Doll*, Kate Leslie in *The Plumed Serpent*, Ursula Brangwen in *The Rainbow* and *Women in Love*, Connie Chatterley, the resistant March in *The Fox*, and so on—belong in this ventriloquil procession of female voices and points of view created by influential male moderns.

Lessing when confronted with the feminist view of Lawrence as a male chauvinist, she will say: "I don't agree with that at all. I think there are male chauvinists on the literary scene, and obviously Norman Mailer is one, but Lawrence was a true artist and a very complex man."

Meridel LeSueur will similarly acknowledge that it was Lawrence who enabled her to break with her own anti-sexual puritanism in her early stories into themes and descriptions of sexual awakening. In a more complicated and ambivalent but no less surprising way, Sylvia Plath will also look to Lawrence for her own early sexual awakening, and will carry her conflicted sexual attitudes into her ultimately tragic marriage to the Lawrencean poet Ted Hughes. More positively, Anaïs Nin will observe, when asked if she too agrees that Lawrence was chauvinistic and dogmatic about women:

> No, I don't feel that way. I think we have to take from Lawrence the great contribution he made in trying to find the language for sensations and emotions and instincts. He tried to understand woman . . . [and] gave me a great deal as a woman.

Elsewhere she will even take Kate Millett to task for not being subtle enough to see that, whatever Lawrence asserted ideologically, " . . . in his work, which is where the true self is revealed, he was very concerned with the response of women."

These samplings from the pages ahead reflect my own ideological concerns. Hamalian is more broadly concerned, to his credit, with *all* that women writers take from Lawrence and make use of in their original arrangements: animal and landscape imagery, for instance, parental conflict and its childhood ramifications, the condition of England or America in wasteland times, uses of myth and symbol and of strong lyric rhythms in both poetry and fiction, as well as the more central focus on the modern marriage crisis and its sexual and passional expressions. But the very term "original," as applied to such writerly arrangements, raises a final ideological concern.

What Hamalian offers to his readers is an old-fashioned influence study placed without apologies in a postmodern context. At an earlier point he wanted to accommodate that context by including "Real Presence" and "Intertextual Study" in his working title. But these are contradictory phrases, according to current ideology, since intertextuality now implies a totally verbal world where language codes determine narrative patterns, where authors and characters alike are absences rather than presences, and where creation is replaced by repetitive and interwoven encodings. Indeed, the deaths of authors and characters and the determining powers of language are among the more excessive claims of semiotic and poststructural theory. Thus Hamalian's earlier desire to speak of Lawrence as a "real presence" for responding women writers decidedly runs against the intertextual grain.

One of the more welcome aspects of the new phase of the feminist movement is the relaxation and/or modification of such claims. As Robert Scholes has pointed out, they are claims of the collective consciousness and as such endemic to much current cultural theory. As I've noted myself, they are also opposed to the old-fashioned claims of the individual consciousness, which however battered are still extant and, like the proverbial baby, should not be thrown out with the bath. In practice, happily, the tensions between these clashing claims are still being honored. Feminists have begun to insist on the importance of human agency in the faceless face of collective victimizations. Author studies continue to flourish bravely under new cultural management. And the culture at large has begun to adjust the newly fashioned claims of collective problems like sexual harassment and domestic violence to old-fashioned claims of personal responsibility and public accountability. It is within the refreshing context of such adjustments that Hamalian can now speak appropriately to Lawrence's "real presence" as a source of literary influence. In the introduction ahead Hamalian will speak more modestly of Lawrence's "temporary" or "permanent" presence as a literary influence. But even under these descriptive modifications Lawrence himself, and the women novelists who respond to him, retain their claims to human agency and creativity.

In his introduction Hamalian will also speak, as indicated, of Lawrence's dissenting view of patriarchal collectivities. He has in mind the industrial machismo of Gerald Crich in *Women in Love* and the oppressive conduct of other industrial, military, or professional figures: Clifford Chatterley and his cronies, Skrebensky in *The Rainbow*, the Prussian officer, the silver-mine owner from whom "The Woman Who Rode Away" rides away. In our own time women and minorities, gays and lesbians, have created new collectivities to oppose these old configurations. Though these new creations continue to foster exciting new forms of knowledge, their antiaesthetic and anti-individualistic biases, and even their understandably anti-heterosexual intolerances, have begun to hamper further development. It seems to me evident, in such respects, that the too-easy encoding of an ongoing male fear of female sexuality does not in itself account for centuries of real or literary clitoridectomies; or that the too-easy encoding of "rigidly formulaic" sexuality in Lawrence does not account either for his varied impact on generations of "imitators" or for codeless orgasmic flexibility in his aptly chosen successor, Kate Millett, or in her presumably flexible successors.

Similarly the feminist claims which stem from Beauvoir and Millett, that male writers are disqualified by gender and temperament from speaking fairly of, for, or through their women characters, must carry as their hampering correlative the view that women writers are also disqualified from representing male characters—or black and white writers from crossing ethnic boundaries. In short, creation itself—with its obvious stake in human agency and imaginative inclusions—is hamstrung by these disabling propositions.

And of course with language and its assumed totality of textual control where only partial determination seems reasonable, extremism is again needlessly disabling. One has only to recall Roland Barthes's reduction of a Balzac tale, for example, to a tissue of interwoven encodings, and his niggardly allowance for the postmodern reader of his own "jouissance" in playing with such codes and stereotypes, to realize that human agency has crept into these early arguments unawares: for surely "jouissance" is akin to the babbling period in childhood, without which children could not learn to speak—to go on, that is to say, to recognize and organize significant sounds into meaningful thoughts and utterances, and so exercise human agency. But if Barthes has unwittingly fallen back to where all love of literature begins, it seems reasonable to hope that the rest of us can now resume, with equal pleasure, our interest in how literature continues and where it leads.

If, in that spirit, we do restore the concepts of human agency and of imaginative inclusions across gender boundaries, and if we do allow writers to control and shape language as well as to be shaped by its repetitions and encodings, then Hamalian's influence study can itself be included among the proofs for new collective knowledge. In a recent contribution to *Novel: A Forum on Fiction*, for instance, D. M. Thompson argues that Lawrence's collaborations with women in writing his novels and tales suggests his expansive relaxation of the bounds of individual authorship and of gendered creativity. In the same vein it could be argued that the principles of authorial and gendered expansion could be applied also to Lawrence's frequent ventriloquil use of women characters as points of view, and to his impact through such procedures upon a wide range of women writers. In these several ways Hamalian's brave imaginative grasp of such expansive mediations helps enormously to bring men and women together again as creative and androgynous agents in our commonly uncommon literary lives.

Sources Cited

Aldington, Richard. 1950 *D. H. Lawrence: Portrait of a Genius But . . .* New York: Duell, Sloan and Pearce.
Barthes, Roland. 1972. *Critical Essays.* Trans. Richard Howard. Evansville: Northwestern University Press.
———. 1975. *The Pleasure of the Text.* Trans. Richard Miller. New York: Hill and Wang.
Beauvoir, Simone de. 1953. *The Second Sex.* New York: Knopf.
Cullingford, Elizabeth Butler. 1993. *Gender and History in Yeats's Love Poetry.* New York: Cambridge University Press.
Feinstein, Elaine. 1993. *Lawrence and the Women: The Intimate Life of D. H. Lawrence.* New York: Harper Collins Publishers.
Fergusson, Francis. 1948. "D. H. Lawrences' Sensibility." In *Forms of Modern Fiction.* Ed. William Van O'Connor. Bloomington: Indiana University Press.
Heath, Stephen. 1984. *The Sexual Fix.* New York: Schocken.
Ingersoll, Earl. 1993–94. "Doris Lessing on Lawrence." *The D. H. Lawrence Society of North America Newsletter.* 24 No. 3: Fall/Winter.
Lessing, Doris. 1981. *The Golden Notebook.* New York: Bantam.
Masters, William H. and Virginia E. Johnson. 1966. *Human Sexual Response.* Boston: Little, Brown.
Millett, Kate, 1970. "D. H. Lawrence." In *Sexual Politics.* New York: Doubleday.
Scholes, Robert. 1982. "Uncoding Mama: The Female Body as Text." In *Semiotics and Interpretation.* New Haven: Yale University Press.
Siegel, Carol. 1991. *Lawrence among the Women: Wavering Boundaries in Women's Literary Traditions.* Charlottesville: University Press of Virginia.
Sklenicka, Carol. 1991. *D. H. Lawrence and the Child.* Columbia: University of Missouri Press.
Spilka, Mark. 1955. "The Religious Dimension." In *The Love Ethic of D. H. Lawrence.* Bloomington: Indiana University Press.
———. 1992. "Lessing and Lawrence: The Battle of the Sexes." In *Renewing the Normative D. H. Lawrence: A Personal Progress.* Columbia: University of Missouri Press.
———. 1980. "Mrs. Dalloway's Absent Grief." In *Virginia Woolf's Quarrel with Grieving.* Lincoln: University of Nebraska Press.
Thompson, D. M. 1994. "Calling in the Realists: The Revision and Reputation of Lawrence's *Sons and Lovers' Novel: A Forum on Fiction* 27 (Spring): 233–56.
Woolf, Virginia. 1967. "Professions for Women." In *Collected Essays,* Vol. 2. London: Chatto and Windus.

Acknowledgements

I wish to thank Mark Spilka, my wife Linda, and my colleague James V. Hatch for reading my manuscript and making valuable suggestions about what to exclude and what to include in it. I am also grateful to the editors at Associated University Presses whose sharp eyes caught errors that slipped past mine. Any remaining in the printed text are, of course, my responsibility. I am obliged to Patricia Lawrence, Jane Augustine, and Edward Butscher for permission to quote from their letters to me. The photograph collection at the New York Public Library proved to be an invaluable source of material and the gracious librarians at the Morris Library of Southern Illinois University, the Lilly Library of The University of Indiana, the McFarlin Library of the University of Tulsa and the Queens University Archives were very helpful in tracking down the photographs I needed.

Credit and thanks are due to:
  Mark Gerson for his photograph of Margaret Drabble.
  Lyle Silbert for her photographs of Meridel LeSeuer, Anais Nin, and Joyce Carol Oates.
  Perdita Schaffner and New Directions Publishing Corp. for the photograph of H.D.
  The Queens University Archive and The John Johnson Agency for the photograph of Katherine Mansfield.
  The McFarlin Library of the University of Tulsa for the photograph of Rebecca West.
  The New York Public Library for the passport photo of D. H. Lawrence.
  The Lilly Library of Indiana University, Bloomington, Indiana, for the photograph of Sylvia Plath.
  The Morris Library of Southern Illinois University for the photograph of Kay Boyle.

I owe thanks to the following publishers for their permission to reprint material from their books or archives:

Black Sparrow Press to quote from *The Hostile Sun* by Joyce Carol Oates.

Harcourt Brace & Company and The Anais Nin Trust for an excerpt from *Delta of Venus* by Anais Nin, copyright 1977.

Houghton Mifflin Company for an excerpt from *H.D.*, c. 1982, by Janice Robinson. Reprinted by permission of Houghton Mifflin. All rights reserved.

New Directions, to quote from *Collected Poems of H.D. 1912–1944*.

A shorter version of the chapter on Syliva Plath appeared in *North Dakota Quarterly* of Winter 1991 and a version of the chapter on Anais Nin appeared in the 1995 number of *Anais: an International Journal*, edited by Gunther Stuhlmann.

Introduction

What do we really mean when we use the much-vexed term "influence"? Elusive, slippery, it exists—writers themselves freely acknowledge that almost everything they create is shaped by everything they have read. Most writers at some point, it could be argued, are either witting or unwitting imitators. For instance, we have Eliot making "The Waste Land" into a poem "full of Pound and fury," Galway Kinnell in a *Book of Nightmares* revealing an intimate familiarity with Rilke's *Duino Elegies,* and both Alice Walker and Adrienne Rich paying homage to the influence of Emily Dickinson.

Thus one may reasonably assume that a writer's thought, theme, or style can be modified by a powerful predecessor. Harold Bloom informs us that such influence is not only inevitable but also the source of profound anxiety—and originality—because writers occupy a battlefield where the younger are trying to slay the older; that is, rid themselves of influence so their own voices may emerge. Diane Wakoski also acknowledges the important role of influence in the development of the writer: "Part of coming to terms with yourself is fighting off the influences that have made you as good as you are."

Elizabeth Bowen views literary influence as "transient, ending with a period of apprenticeship—indeed, being a form of apprenticeship in itself. The writer will shell off, one by one—he may even react against—the influences which have up to a point fostered his growth" (Bowen 1962). According to Bowen, literary influence brings past and present into a quarrelsome but loving dialogue. Similarly, Paul Zweig sees the writer as a "mosaic of vanished others who have blurred into our voices, and haunt our laughter. They may be what the Sufis mean by 'the Friend'; the layered otherness which inhabits us, and is ourselves"(1983, 285). Pierre N. Laval, among the most perceptive of our federal judges, recently argued from the bench that "all intellectual creative talent is in part derivative. There is no such thing as a wholly original thought or invention. Each advance stands on building blocks fashioned by prior thinkers."[1]

As we may infer from the foregoing discussion, influence takes the form of arguing with or accepting the ideas, attitudes, and/or philosophy in another's work. It may be a conscious rethinking or reinterpretation of a published text (as in the case of Joyce Carol Oates). Influence may be revealed in imitating, invoking, parodying, or otherwise being affected by the syntax, recurrent imagery, tropological devices, or dominant themes of a predecessor. It is a critical interaction between two writers of either thought or style, a form of intellectual intimacy that often reveals the source of the affected writer's literary origins. A good writer takes (or steals if he is T. S. Eliot) from other writers whatever is useful, whether or not those writers arouse his or her sympathy. Eliot, Pound, and Yeats influenced an entire generation of poets, many of whom disliked their politics, and Gertrude Stein was not always admired by those who learned from her. Amy Lowell is another case in point.

In tracing Lawrence's influence on the nine women writers included here, I have tried to distinguish between his "temporary presence" and his "abiding presence."[2] To some of these writers Lawrence was an inspirational guest who offered temporary guidance—or misguidance—while for others he remained an active reality much longer. However, either through what he thought or through the way he wrote, his spirit touched all nine of these writers.[3]

* * *

Certain other questions arise at this point. First: why did Lawrence's contemporaries, with the exception of Virginia Woolf, have such little direct influence on the subsequent generation of writers? One answer arises from the very nature of English class structure. Lawrence's contemporaries, mostly men, were members of the cultural Establishment, assured of what Woolf called "middle-class art and expensive education" while the English Establishment still counted as a world power. Lawrence knew the extent of that power, being excluded from it by class, as Woolf was by her sex. Precisely because he was an outsider ("he echoes nobody, continues no tradition")[4] he was positioned to perceive his country's situation with ruthless lucidity.

Furthermore, many women had learned early a lesson known to Lawrence: that power, creative work, or happiness has always been available to women with the cooperation of individual men, while *collectivity*—the state, religion, or patriarchal institutions—has been the main source of discriminatory treatment

(Johnson 1992, 13). Thus when a writer working on the margins needed succor, she most likely would turn to the dissenter, whether male or female, who scorned the collectivity and actively opposed it. Lawrence, who regularly ran afoul of officialdom, served in that role better than any other writer of the time.

By conscious intent Lawrence put women and their plight in a male-dominated world close to the center of his mature later fiction. Perhaps tutored by Frieda, he also advocated their advancement.[5] Like Ibsen, Lawrence condemned the social code that directed women into a life of decorative dependency and boredom. If his women characters are not always shown dealing with the strenuous aftermath of liberation, it is because they are too preoccupied with the process of self-assertion itself. But his women are not predetermined by fixed inherited sensibility, a condition that would preclude change and transcendence—the very conditions that many women identify with liberation itself. Lawrence's women do not accept their uneventful lives as inevitable not do they feel doomed by "temperament."

Even when we recognize that the women in his fiction are characterized "exclusively in utopian sexual terms" that ignored real-life predicaments (Lodge 1992, 30), these women emerge as real, appealing, and forceful. They fight, fiercely and blindly at times, to be free from male domination. By 1912, Lawrence had the nerve to boast that he would "do [his] work for women better than suffrage" (*Letters* 1:490)—and perhaps for writers like Anaïs Nin and Meridel LeSueur he succeeded. Even when he wrote about men, Susan Schweik shrewdly observes, he could advance women's work: to the extent that "The Man Who Died" invites allegorical reading as a Great War novel, the resurrection might be said to signify "a vision of a masculinity demilitarized through the spiritually sensuous touch of a woman who knows that real men didn't need to lend themselves to the war." (1991, 280).

Lawrence may have been important to women writers for yet another reason. Partly because he had earned the detached perception of the outsider, he could sense that English tradition had aggrandized the meaning of life over life itself, in a sort of overassertion of consciousness and intentionality that he thought was an Establishment distortion of reality. His rejection of these "rationalist" values arose from a desire to recover a more spontaneous, less willful, more authentic sense of interaction with life. His attitude toward Being could be characterized as pious, as a genuine reverence for that which may lie beyond consciousness and purely intellectual grasp. He never failed to accept and to appreciate the unruliness, the unpredictability of life in a time when the traditional constraints had not yet fallen before the anarchy of impulse. The openness of outlook, the loose, intuitive structure of his novels, so counter to the currents of his time, must have encouraged and in some instances inspired writers like Meridel LeSueur and Anaïs Nin who were struggling to articulate their anarchic discomfort with the stereotypes of female behavior that either excluded them or forced them to find their own mode of expression.

Thus, for example, through reading Lawrence, a woman could re-conceive the unconscious fantasy structures that govern desire, opening up and making explicit heretofore repressed imaginary experiences, including the possibilities of a rich passional life alongside the usual constrained existence. The sexual awakening of Lawrence's heroines (especially of Constance Chatterley) is endowed with an unrestrained carnal lyricism that sanctifies the experience without excluding them from that experience. Constance is not merely a vehicle for Mellors's sexuality: she is a passionate participant in her own right. This "ethos of eroticism" preoccupies the heroines of Margaret Drabble and culminates in the novels of Erika Jong, who uses a passage from Lawrence as an epigraph to *Fear of Flying*. Her wise-cracking protagonist in *Parachutes and Kisses* feels that it is her right to divert herself with a "Connecticut Yankee Mellors-the-Gamekeeper" (1). She speaks for more than one post-Lawrence woman writer when she candidly jests, "O sweet sex, Lawrentian waterfalls ... it's you that Isadora longs for!" (60). But emphasizing "sweet sex" can obscure the breadth of Lawrence's appeal, and Nona Balakian defines his power in broader terms: the women characters of his novels are "released from bondage into conventional patterns of human relationship. Lawrence's composite heroine with her sharp self-awareness, her healthy sensuality, and her insight into 'unknown modes of being' was bound to extend or change the portrait of the conventional heroine" (1991, 29).

In *Genres in Discourse*, Tzvetan Todorov defines romance as a narrative that has to do with "being and not with doing," with the attainment of knowledge as opposed to the recounting of deeds, the deepening of it as the most fundamental aspect of experience. Although Todorov does not mention Lawrence in this connection, he unwittingly describes the source of Lawrence's strength and illuminates an important aspect of his discourse. Many women writers in our time have made this "attainment of being" (Todorov's term) central to their work in contrast to the more masculine recounting of deeds. These writers, like several others who are not part of this study, could not have moved as freely in their medium had not Lawrence helped to validate for them the pure attainment of knowledge—particularly knowledge of the heart and the passions—as the real work of the novelist.

The traditional novel of the time was "monolingual" (the term is Bakhtin's); that is, the characters were usually interpreted through a single evaluating consciousness. Lawrence, like Dostoyevsky, experimented with a "polyphonic" approach to character. No single voice is identified with a definitive truth (Birkin, who speaks for Lawrence, is called a stuffed shirt by another character who also speaks for Lawrence). This open-endedness permitted a variety of voices to be heard equally in discourse. Lawrence presented with the greatest possible conviction even those views which he probably found disagreeable (those of Loerke, Gerald, Cipriano, even Clifford Chatterley). Lawrence was exploring a creative method that Bakhtin calls a "dialogic penetration" of character. Consciously or not, Lawrence worked toward creating a model for narrative transmission that seemed capable of subverting the patrimonial mode of literary transmission. For a woman writer who could read Lawrence but not Bakhtin, a scene of conflict in which the response of the man and woman is equally stated may have had greater appeal than the technique of authorship typical of the nineteenth-century novel.

Lawrence was determined to uncover the true nature of the sexual relationship. He believed that most generalizations, both in fiction and in psychological analyses, about the way men and women behave sexually, were more expressions of hope or the venting of criticism or the attempt at propaganda than reliable statements of truth. The ramifications of this perspective lent his work a provocative polemic edge. Lawrence refused to accept the conventional wisdom about sex and instead tried to show how it was experienced in actuality by participating individuals. He sought to capture the sensation of being in love, of what it was like, how it felt. His intuition led him to believe that ultimately the mind, "the top of the tingling spine" (the phrase is Vladimir Nabokov's) is the organ of orgasm: during the bodily act of love, a mystery invades, touches, and shakes the soul. That fusion of feeling is apparently what Lawrence meant by "The Rainbow," "The Crown," or "The Holy Ghost." Lawrence insisted that human essence springs from this erotic experience, not from rationality, and he sought to dramatize in his writing what Kierkegaard calls "a psycho-sensual synthesis." An instance of it is the passionate mating of Mellors and Constance, which for the prominent anthropologist Melvin Konner is "suffused with an almost unreal grace and tenderness" (1990, 26).

Yet Lawrence never tried to obscure the extent to which his characters experienced being in love as a loss of power or as a form of enslavement. Erotic experience was for him inseparable from soul-wrenching struggle and surrender. Although Lawrence may strike us as innocent or dated in some matters, in these perceptions he was sophisticated. It was in all likelihood these pivotal insights that spoke to women like H.D. and Joyce Carol Oates, who aspired to explore their own experience in their own way, without dictation from patriarchal voices from the past. They saw eventually that they did not have to accept the prevailing wisdom as gospel any more than Lawrence did, with his inner eye on another reality.

In this radical shift, Lawrence "pushed into" (Robert Creeley's phrase to describe his mental energy) emotional and psychological states of mind that no English novelist before him had attempted to chart—the terrain that Freud had staked out for study. Thus, at least two of Lawrence's journeys into the interior, *Sons and Lovers* and *Women in Love*, helped bring the English novel into the age of psychoanalysis. In a sense, he rejuvenated the genre by showing that it had the power and the scope to interpret the dynamics of male/female relationships in a new light, one that seemed to offer fresh and perhaps lasting insights into human behavior.

Another liberating force was the "rediscovery" of Lawrence's poetry. As a poet, Lawrence was not interested in escaping from personality. On the contrary, his poetry almost bristled with raw feeling and moved with a "wind-like transit" (Lawrence's own phrase) to catch the fleeting moment of sensation. By providing a counterforce to Eliot's dicta, he redirected the flow of poetic energy into open forms that writers such as Denise Levertov, Sylvia Plath, and Joyce Carol Oates would later find congenial. One can hear the music of Lawrence's voice in their work.

In her book about the women who loved Lawrence, Emily Hahn is astounded by H.D.'s enduring attachment to the rambunctious Lawrence. Why, she wonders, did women like H.D. and Katherine Mansfield love him and permit him to enter their lives? (1975, 1). Sandra Gilbert asks herself a similar question:

"How do you reconcile your work as a feminist critic with your admiration for the art of D. H. Lawrence? In other words, how can you be a feminist and a Lawrentian?" By understanding that even when he was being overtly masculine, Lawrence did not quite fit into what Gilbert calls "the masculine mode" in which she had been educated. Instead, he *attended* with a sort of mystical passivity to the flux of experience and the fluidity of language. On one hand a sermonizer, on the other he was a being with a "wonderful, desirable life-rapidity," who himself submitted "joyously to the forces of otherness in all creatures and things" (1991, 94).

In *D. H. Lawrence and the Women*, Elaine Feinstein explores his relationship with women in his own life and his tendency to see the world through their eyes. The list of women who collaborated with him or guided him includes Jessie Chambers (Miriam), whose notes and commentary proved to be useful in the final version of *Sons and Lovers*; Helen Corke, whose diaries provided material for Lawrence's first two novels; Mollie Skinner, the Australian writer who invited Lawrence to collaborate on *the Boy in the Bush*; Louie Burrows, who encouraged his interest in the suffrage movement; and of course his wife Frieda, whom Martin Green credits with co-authoring certain works. That Lawrence was so open to the influence and advice of women of every class was not lost on his women readers.[6] It seems likely that Catherine Carswell, Dorothy Brett, Mabel Dodge Luhan, Cynthia Asquith, and even Ottoline Morrell all contributed a share to Lawrence's cultural and intellectual development and possibly to his style.[7] As Martin Green says:

> What these women saw in Lawrence was a man devoted to his idea of male-female relationships; an idea of religious scope and intensity and an intelligent passion. When he talked about his experience, and to others about his experience, his idea made itself felt as something extraordinarily far-reaching, illuminating every corner of privacy, every stretch of history. His own service of it (and mastery) showed itself extraordinarily sure, subtle, penetrating and inflammatory. (Green 1975, 7)

If this aspect of Lawrence has lost its magic, nonetheless many of his insights about our relationship to the human cosmos are confirmed by contemporary wisdom. Julie Kristeva says that in order to abide the strangers around us, we must first recognize the stranger in ourselves. In almost everything Lawrence wrote there is implicit the same conviction: one must struggle to discover and embrace those aspects to the self long hidden in the deeps. The struggle to integrate the stranger with the functioning ego is re-enacted over and over again in the fiction and poetry of the nine writers studied here whose response to Lawrence helped shape the modern literary sensibility.

D. H. Lawrence
and
Nine Women Writers

Katherine Mansfield. Photograph reproduced courtesy of Queens University Archives—Antony Alpers Foundation.

1
Katherine Mansfield: "We Are *Unthinkably* Alike"

In *Women in Love*, Gudrun Brangwen (modeled on aspects of Katherine Mansfield's character)[1] gets along peacefully with Rupert Birkin (broadly based on Lawrence). This fictional representation draws upon the relationship between Lawrence and Mansfield, but hardly hints at its tumultuous reality.

The actual friendship between Lawrence and Mansfield oscillated from genuine affection to furious bickering. At one point Mansfield thought that Lawrence was losing his sanity, and after a disastrous experiment in shared living during Lawrence's Cornwall period, wanted nothing further to do with him. Writing to Ottoline Morrell (17 May 1916), she says: "It is really over now—our relationship with L. That 'dear man' in him whom we all loved is hidden away, absorbed completely, lost, like a little gold ring in that immense german christmas pudding which is Frieda" (1984, 267). Yet just prior to her last meeting with him in 1918, Mansfield would confess, "I am more like L. than anybody else. We are *unthinkably* alike, in fact" (Mansfield 1927, 146). And while they were seeing each other frequently in London with Murry and Frieda absent, she wrote, "For me at least, the dove brooded over him, too. I loved him" (1984, 1 191).[2]

Two years later on Capri, "out of who knows what twinge of pain, what sinking of the stomach, what cataclysm of irritation" (Hahn 1975, 210)—Lawrence flared out at Mansfield. She had tried the climate of the Italian Riviera for her illness, but had preferred Menton in France. In February of 1920 Lawrence wrote that infamous letter, saying "I loathe you. You revolt me stewing in your consumption . . . The Italians were quite right to have nothing to do with you."[3] That letter put Mansfield in a towering rage and may have touched off her savage attack on Lawrence's *The Lost Girl*, dismissing it as a "pack of lies . . . [with] not one memorable word" (1927, 156–57).

Thereafter the relationship mellowed somewhat. When *Aaron's Rod* appeared in 1922, Mansfield pencilled a note on a page of her *Novels and Novelists* (1939, 308), likening the novel to "a tree firmly planted, deep thrusting, outspread, growing grandly, alive in every twig." She concludes, "All the time I read this book I felt it was feeding me." Lawrence, visiting her native New Zealand, sent her postcard with a single poignant word, "Ricordi." If their vision of life diverged unalterably on many crucial questions, they managed to maintain an interest in one another's work until her death in 1923.[4]

Their rocky relationship began in 1913, right after Lawrence sent a story from Italy entitled "The Soiled Rose" to the Murrys for the May issue of their publication, *Rhythm*. The following month, when Lawrence and Frieda returned to England, they met the Murrys in their three-room London flat which also served as an office for the magazine. Lawrence first glimpsed Mansfield sitting beside a bowl of goldfish on the floor of a bare room (Moore 1974, 184). Lawrence took an immediate and personal interest in the Murrys, which evolved into a close but difficult relationship between the couples (Baker 1972, 184). During a holiday at Broadstairs with the Lawrences, the Murrys were given a gift of *Sons and Lovers* to read on the train back to London. When they had turned the last page, both of them realized at once that they were in the presence of a great and powerful novel, a masterpiece of its kind.

In fact, the impression made on Mansfield was so strong that, within days, on 2 August, she wrote out a thirty-five-chapter outline for an autobiographical novel, apparently to be called *Maata* (probably after her Maori schoolfriend, Maata Mahupuka), and began working on it immediately. "There can be little doubt that it was her reading of *Sons and Lovers* that inspired her to plan a Bildungsroman of her own," Claire Tomalin asserts in her brilliant biography of Mansfield,

> in which a central autobiographical character is shown undergoing formative experiences through various friendships and love-affairs ... One or two touches suggest that Lawrence had put a fingerprint on her imagination: Maata's skin "flames like yellow roses" when she undresses, and when Rhoda leans out of her bedroom window in the morning, "A-ah," she breathed in a surge of ecstasy, "I am baptized, I am baptized into a new day," which certainly does not sound like anything else in Mansfield (1988, 120).[5]

In drawing attention to these likenesses, Tomalin has the good sense not to hold Mansfield hostage to Lawrence.

In 1915, Mansfield's beloved brother, Leslie Beauchamp, was killed in France by the premature explosion of a hand grenade. The shock of the news, which left her stunned and "submerged in grief," broke off any further work on the autobiography of her adolescence. In the tragic circumstance of her brother's death, perhaps the enterprise may have seemed to her self-indulgent and may have involved some painful recollections of Leslie. Lawrence wrote "with sensitive understanding of her inner sickness" (Berkman 1951, 69) and encouraged her not to be sad, but to recognize that her own spiritual life would arise from the ashes of her brother's tragedy. Perhaps thinking of his own grief after his mother's death, he identified with her profound sorrow and urged her to believe that "for us there is a rising from the grave, there is resurrection, and a clean life to begin from the start, new, and happy. Don't be afraid, don't doubt it, it is so."

This tragic episode precipitated a shift in Mansfield's attitude toward love and sex. She grew more conservative, even skeptical. She developed a distaste for open portrayals of sexual matters. Murry's account of her reaction to *The Rainbow* is interesting: "Katherine hated parts of it—in particular the scene where Anna pregnant, dances naked before the mirror. That Katherine said to me, was 'female'—an apotheosis of the 'female': a sort of glorification of the secret, intimate talk between women, the sexual understanding of the female confraternity, which Katherine could not abide" (quoted in Hankin 1980, 191). She managed to praise it with faint damns.

But Lawrence continued to espouse Mansfield and she in turn remained loyal to him. In September of the following year (1916), Mansfield was sitting in the Cafe Royale in London in the company of Koteliansky and Gertler, two friends of Lawrence, when she overheard the novelist Michael Arlen ("Michaelis" in *Lady Chatterley's Lover*) and composer Philip Heseltine "maliciously reading and publicly ridiculing" Lawrence's new book of poems, *Amores*. Mansfield took the volume from their hands, marched out of the cafe with it, and "symbolically rescued her friend from their scorn" (Meyers 1978, 92)—an action that Gudrun replicates in *Women in Love* by snatching Birkin's letter away from Halliday and walking out of the Cafe Pompadour. When Mansfield used the Cafe Royale incident in her story, "Marriage a la Mode" (1921), she substituted a letter for the poems as the object of ridicule. William, who has been abandoned by his wife Isabel for a group of decadent admirers, returns to London after visiting her, and sends her a love letter in the hope of winning her back. But Isabel reads it aloud to her friends who mock the letter and become hysterical with laughter.

If Lawrence's affirmative feeling for Mansfield failed to lift her low spirits, it coincided with the positive mood that informs his own work in progress, *Women in Love*, which took its final form during the Cornwall summer of 1916, when Mansfield and Lawrence were in daily contact (and finished when they were apart but still friends). As most readers of Lawrence know, Hermione Roddice is drawn largely from Ottoline Morrell, Rupert Birkin from Lawrence himself, Ursula Brangwen from Frieda, Gerald Crich in part from John Middleton Murry, and Gudrun from Mansfield. However, Murry denied any resemblance to himself or to his wife, and detested the book as mean-spirited. He may be right about himself, but clearly Gundrun's case is another matter. Lawrence used Mansfield as an inspiration rather than a precise model for Gudrun. Whether or not she emerges in a negative light is moot. Some critics think it is a portrait of a sex-obsessed, sadistic, tough-as-nails bohemian (Mansfield herself declared that Gundrun was repellent),[6] but in the opinion of other critics, Gundrun emerges as a woman who defies Victorian conventions and who challenges the sexual status quo. Because she is so determined to live her own life (as Mansfield herself was), she comes across to some readers as too aggressive. Lawrence's fearlessness in defining one configuration of a liberated woman reminds us that Mansfield created characters, especially Kezia, her "seeing eye and focus" (that phrase is Gordon's in his "Introduction"), who express a curiosity about life and a human sympathy similar to Gudrun's.

During the fall of 1918, while Mansfield was living at No. 2 Portland Villas in Hampstead, Lawrence came down to London hoping to find employment that would exempt him from war service. "Lawrence has been running in and out all this week," she notes in a 22 October letter (1987, 282). Five days later she writes, "Lawrence and Frieda have been in town. I saw a great deal of Lawrence. I loved him. He was just his merry, rich self, laughing, describing things, giving you pictures, full of enthusiasm and joy in a future where we were all 'vagabonds'" (284). About that time Mansfield was writing a story called "Psychology" (Alpers 1984). It describes a daytime meeting between two people both in their early thirties who have been nourishing a relationship that threatens to become an affair. The woman wants to get the most out of "this extraordinary absolute chance which made it possible for him to be utterly truthful to her and for her to be utterly sincere with him" (319). As her would-be lover departs for another engagement, she observes (ironically?), "He was superior to it all. He—with his wonderful 'spiritual' vision" (322).

Alpers thinks that the story provides a glimpse of Mansfield and Bertrand Russell in 1916 (Alpers 1984, 30–31). But the age difference between Mansfield (n. 1885) and Russell (n. 1872) would be sixteen years. The visitor solicits an opinion on a literary matter: "I've been wondering very much lately whether the novel of the future will be a psychological novel or not" (321). We infer that the pipe-smoking visitor must be a novelist: "Weren't his novels to be big novels?" she thinks to herself (319). Details from Russell's manner may have contributed to the portrait of the novelist, but a more likely model for him would be Lawrence, who was only three years older than Mansfield and a frequent daytime caller at Portland Villas while the story was gestating. Though the woman is attracted to the visitor's charisma, Mansfield may be implying that the sexual consummation of the relationship would have led to a boring affair.[7]

In the spring of 1919, right after finishing *Women in Love*, Lawrence wrote what Emile Delavenay describes as a "curious sequel" (1972, 249), a play called *Touch and Go*, which was to be the first in a series for a people's theater. It shows him reworking material that had preoccupied him earlier: the mining community of his youth and his friendship with the Murrys. With the exception of Ursula, the main cast of *Women in Love* takes the stage almost unchanged. Gerald Crich becomes Gerald Barlow, a mining magnate; Birkin becomes Oliver Turton, the spokesman for Lawrence; and Gudrun is transformed into Anabel Wrath, who tutored Gerald's sister Winifred before leaving Gerald for an affair with a foreigner. She leaves partly because she is jealous of Oliver, whom she thinks Gerald loves. However, she has returned with the intention of reviving their relationship on a firmer foundation. She marries Gerald and stands by him valiantly in the showdown with the striking miners. If, as Meyers says, Lawrence represents the negative aspects of Mansfield's character in *Women in Love* (*Spirit*, in *Touch and Go* he presents the positive side of it. Sylvia Sklar argues (1975, 203), persuasively, I think, that Anabel shares more attitudes with Oliver, the Lawrence figure, than with Gerald, the Murry figure. Oliver burns with the conviction that "every man [ought] to live and be free" (385).

The imagery of flame, fire, or sun that rejuvenates or even impregnates occurs frequently in Lawrence, especially in the early poems. The sun imagery is often associated with masculinity, alternately a creative or destructive force. This imagery is also important in his prose. In the unfinished fragment "The Flying Fish," Gethin Day is leaving Mexico for his ancestral home in England. Lawrence describes what had happened to him in Mexico: "something in the hard, fierce, finite sun of Mexico ... had made the ordinary day lose its reality to him ... He was ill" (*Phoenix* 784). In chapter 26 of *The Plumed Serpent*, Cipriano, Kate Leslie's Indian husband, who requires her to make love in the "frictionless" native style, is identified with the Morning Star (the sun). Kate Leslie senses that she must submit to him totally if she is to share that glory. She can never truly be free as long as she remains in Mexico, enthralled by the sun. In the novella "The Man Who Died," the sun seems to be associated with masculine power. At the climax, the resurrected man exclaims, "I am risen!" ("his own sun dawned, and sent its fire along his limbs," Lawrence adds).

While living in Sportorno on the Italian Riveria, Lawrence wrote a story called "Sun," about a woman who is resurrected spiritually and physically by the healing touch of the sun (as he thought Mansfield would be, when he beckoned to her). Here the fiery orb is vital to the process of renewal, but it is no longer indisputably linked to male puissance alone. It stirs sexual tides that originate in the depths of womanhood. "By some mysterious power inside her, deeper than her known consciousness and will, she was put into connection with the sun, and the stream flowed of itself, from her womb. . . . The true Juliet was this dark flow from her body to the sun." She is convinced that the sun knows her in the biblical sense of the word (thus making it masculine), but its symbolic associations remain ambiguous. The healing powers of the sun also seem to be linked with the feminine principle, as in one of Lawrence's late works, *Apocalypse*. Lawrence may be suggesting that the sun combines both male and female principles.

Mansfield's choice of imagery suggests a remarkable parallel to Lawrence's mode of perceiving and connecting. As C. M. Hankin has noticed, there is in her juvenilia a clear correlation between the sun and masculine potency. The sun is depicted as a lover in two early poems, "The Rangataki Valley" and "The

Awakened River." In the former, she writes: "O mystical marriage of Earth / With the passionate summer sun!" In the latter, the river "lies on silver pillows, the sun leans over her." The author warns the river: "Be careful, my beautiful waking one! You'll catch on fire!" In the prose fragment, "Radiana and Guido," the sun apparently has lost its power to ignite. Radiana tells her lover, "My soul is like a great stretch of sand on which the sun has shone all the long day—it is dried up, parched, hot." But the Promethean fire in Guido is life-giving. He replies, "It is as though I had a great torch in my heart that leaps up and flames and burns all over my body ... Let me pour into you the fire that is consuming me." In the 1918 story, "Sun and Moon," she named the male protagonist "Sun."[8]

In a subsequent Mansfield story, "At the Bay," the motif of sun-potency is central to the meaning of almost every episode. Mrs. Harry Kember not only exposes her body to the sun, but in contrast to Lawrence's Juliet, allows herself to become "burnt out and withered ... When she was not playing bridge ... she spent her time lying in the full glare of the sun. She could stand any amount of it; she never had enough. All the same, it did not seem to warm her." (Mansfield 1956, 111). She turns into a "horrible caricature of her husband." Both the patterning of incidents and the attitudes of the characters suggest a correlation between male and solar power—neither is warming any longer (this late story which Alpers calls "a response to Gudrun's creator" (*Life*, 341) was written while Mansfield was fighting various ailments).

The very title of the story, "The Daughters of the Late Colonel" (1921), indicates that Mansfield may have wanted to explore and restructure the territory of an early Lawrence novella, "Daughters of the Vicar" (1914). The families of both stories are similar in their poverty, pretensions, and subjugation to a tyrannical father. In the Mansfield story, the children are terrorized into unthinking obedience to the authoritarian paterfamilias. Both Constantia and Louisa occupy a hazy and directionless world where time has no meaning. For Constantia, hope of release is somehow linked to the presence of the sun and the inscrutable Buddha figure on the mantelpiece.[9] But the sun is mostly absent, and it is the moon that is a potent presence. The big pale moon makes Constantia do strange things to express her real passional self. In sunless families where tyranny has displaced affection, where sex is a hidden, dirty little secret, even the astral bodies are altered in their courses.

Was Mansfield truly responsive to either the central message or the innovative nature of Lawrence's prose? Anaïs Nin thinks not. She remarks (*The Diary: Volume Four* 385): "She [Mansfield] failed to understand Lawrence" or "realize sex. She was not modern enough." This criticism is not altogether accurate. More than one of Mansfield's observations in *The Collected Letters I* suggest convincingly that she had absorbed important aspects of Lawrence's new aesthetic: identifying totally with her characters, whether fish, flesh, or fowl, she was "transforming herself into someone else on one long sustained lyrical note" (Moss 1986, 223). For instance, in a long and interesting discussion addressed to Dorothy Brett, Mansfield describes how it feels to identify with a duck as experienced by Kezia in "The Prelude": "When I write about ducks, I swear that I am a white duck . . . In fact, this whole process of becoming the duck (what Lawrence would, perhaps, call this 'consummation with the duck or apple') is so thrilling that I can hardly breathe." That reduction of distance between author and character is a technique that Lawrence devised as an alternative to stream-of-consciousness, and in turn, Mansfield may have studied and modified this technique for her own ends. This may be what she meant by her cryptic remark in *Novels and Novelists* (321): "All the time I read this book [Lawrence's *Aaron's Rod*], I felt it was feeding me."

However, the other half of Anaïs Nin's statement contains a disturbing truth. If Mansfield did understand sex in the sense that she welcomed it as one of life's highest pleasures, she rarely committed that sense of it to print. Her heavy reliance on metaphor (sun, flame, and fur) in her writing on sensual themes suggests a cautiousness and encumbrance in such matters that seems far more Victorian than modern. Admittedly, she was constrained by a censorious moral code, but in the later stories, sexual relationships loom as something to be endured like a physic or observed in others. It is not reserved for her sensitive young heroines. It is never a Taj Mahal. Elizabeth Bowen, in her introduction to Mansfield's *Stories* (1956, xxii), reinforces Nin's skeptical insight: "Staking her life on love, she was least happy with love in fiction. Her passionate faith shows elsewhere. Finesses, subtleties, restless analysis, cerebral wary guardedness hallmark the Katherine Mansfield lovers." A laconic and unsentimental evaluation of her work comes from Lawrence himself, not always a generous judge of his contemporaries: "She was a good writer they made out to be a genius," he said in 1925. "Katherine knew better herself but her husband, J. M. Murry, made capital out of her death" (Tomalin 1988, 240).

In a late journal entry, when Mansfield surveyed what she hoped for in her remaining life, she expressed an aspiration that Lawrence would have shared:

> I want to be all that I am capable
> of becoming so that I may be . . .
> a child of the sun. About helping
> others, about carrying a light
> and so on, it seems false to say a
> single word. Let it be that. A
> Child of the Sun.

It so happened that on the day Mansfield made out her will, shortly before her death at Gurdjieff's Institute of Harmonious Living (a place which, she said, Lawrence and Forster would understand), Lawrence was visiting her birthplace, Wellington, en route from Australia to New Mexico. Although there had been silence between them ever since he had wished her dead in the notorious letter from Capri, he decided to send her the postcard mentioned earlier—"how like him," Mansfield commented (*The Letters of D. H. Lawrence* 4. 283). Though Lawrence never learned about it, Mansfield had willed her books to Murry but asked that he give one to Lawrence. As Anthony Alpers says (*The Life*, 366), "Thus the two made their parting gestures, the one a little more generous than the other's, on the same date, at opposite sides of the earth." When Lawrence learned of her death in 1923, he said, "I always knew a bond in my heart. Feel a fear where the bond is broken now."

Sylvia Berkman is right in saying flatly that Mansfield felt a greater affinity with Lawrence than with any other writer of her generation, including contemporary Virginia Woolf.[10] While Mansfield despised what she described as the "pretentious, snobbish, schoolmaster" vein in his work (1987, 2:219), she admired the honest passion which charged his writing and his rare gift of vigorous poetical realism. Lawrence, to her mind, was "obsessed [with sex], but at least he believed in and battled for his obsession, and that among the 'half-female, frightened writers-of-today,' distinguished him as a real creator" (Berkman 1951, 136). Mansfield sensed that they were akin not only in their mercurial temperaments, in their prematurely precarious health, but also in their determination to capture on the printed page the sensuous feeling of life.

Elizabeth Bowen cannily observes (1956, ix) that Mansfield, "ever on the move, has left us no 'typical' Katherine Mansfield story to anatomize." For the raw material, she tapped into her own dreams and disappointments, and for information about how the unconscious functioned, like Lawrence, often turned not to Sigmund Freud but to her own rich imagination that enabled her to transform her often drab daily reality into heartbreaking stories of loneliness and anarchic emotions struggling into articulation. At the top of her fictional form, she is no less skillful in the short narrative than Lawrence. "She employed all the resources of art to disguise, distance, and shape her themes," one critic writes. In that process, she created a wide range of characters whose emotions she examined with exceptional sensitivity under the magnifying glass of her art (Hankin 1980, x). Although interest in her life has overtaken the work itself, she is, as Howard Moss recognizes, (1986, 222) the only important writer of the century who was devoted exclusively to the difficult art of the short story.

2
H.D.: Bid Me to Love

By the time of Lawrence's death in 1930, Hilda Doolittle had acquired a coterie reputation based on a body of brief, intense lyrics identified with the literary movement called imagism. Her first *Collected Poems* (1925), which brought together the first three volumes of her work, was greeted by muted praise. In the next half dozen years, she published a novel that went almost unnoticed (*Palimpsest*) and two more books of poems that created only a ripple of interest. Although her poetry made a powerful impression on Ezra Pound (who urged her to use her initials as her signature—the reverse of Lawrence's—instead of her name), and later on Amy Lowell, her writing remained virtually unknown during the thirties and forties. Up to World War II, most critics saw her as "an intriguing but minor poet, whose 'crystalline' talents had been refined under Pound's brilliant tutelage" (Fuchs 1990, 542) as part of his effort to forge a new poetic movement.

Her reputation began to blossom after World War II. She produced two long masterpieces: *Trilogy* (1944–46) and *Helen in Egypt* (1960), based on a revisionist myth which has Helen living in Egypt, not in Troy. Four other works in particular enhanced her reputation: a final sequence of poems, *Hermetic Definition*, published posthumously by New Directions (1972); *End to Torment* (1979), her version of the Pound liaison; *The Gift*, an autobiographical account of her Moravian heritage; and *HERmione*, a collection of prose pieces dealing with explicitly lesbian themes.

As her work was attended by a fresh wave of appreciation, she emerged from under Pound's shadow to become a major focus of interest in recent literary criticism. In her autobiographical fiction, she explored the theme of "culturally forbidden love of woman for woman" in language that was radically "explicit, not coded, celebratory" (Friedman 1990, 206). A number of contemporary writers, both poets and critics, have acknowledged her as

H. D. Photograph reproduced courtesy of Perdita Schaffner and New Directions Publishing Corp.

their mentor. Even though she has been called "a man's poet" (Rasula 1983, 162)[1], Denise Levertov has expressed almost unreserved admiration for her struggle against the masculine mythmakers of Western culture while Alicia Ostriker has remarked that she abandoned whatever she had learned about imagism in order to read H.D. afresh. Robert Duncan lauded her as the most original poet of her milieu, a voice which exerted a lasting effect on his own.[2]

This appeal to the recent generation is not hard to understand. She invented an interior landscape where the complex, sexual, and spiritual polarities of her nature could work themselves out. Much of her poetry deals with the collapse of faith during great crises and the resiliency of the human spirit faced with such conditions. Writing most productively during the two world wars, H.D. "rejected the nightmare of history, substituting for it a personal, spiritual quest for resurrection" (Gilbert & Guber 1985, 1457) similar to that which animated the ideals of the counterculture during the sixties.

At the outset of this quest, her thinking was influenced by Lawrence (as the countercultural poets like Michael McClure, Lawrence Ferlinghetti, and Gary Snyder would be). At a significant point in her development he came to represent the possibility of rebirth and renewal—while she was a young expatriate on the edge of English literary circles, he was a brilliant, magnetic writer who offered her not only encouragement but also a vision of a world based on humane values and the exercise of the free spirit.

The story of their meeting has become familiar literary history which requires a brief rehearsal here if the complex interrelationship between them is to be comprehended. Through Amy Lowell, a moving force in the imagist movement, H.D. and her husband Richard Aldington were introduced to Lawrence in August 1914 when they were all invited to Lowell's dinner at the Berkeley Hotel in London (a year later their work would appear in Lowell's anthology, *Some Imagist Poets*). In *Tribute to Freud*, H.D. recalls that she had expected to meet a smooth-faced man who resembled her father (she knew him from a photograph, "the only time I saw this unbearded manifestation of Lawrence"). Instead she was introduced to a red-bearded, bushy-browed figure who "looked taller in evening dress" (1974, 140).

Before long, Lawrence was acting as her literary adviser, a role H.D. accepted with mixed feelings. About twelve years after Rilke had published his *Sonnets to Orpheus*, H.D. wrote "Eurydice" a poetic version of the autobiographical impulse manifested in her novel *Bid Me To Live*. In contrast to Rilke's sequence, where Eurydice is nothing more than an abstraction, in H.D.'s reading she is the sole speaker, portrayed as eager for life but angry at Orpheus for disturbing her peace. The Orpheus behind H.D.'s poem seems to be Lawrence, who apparently persuaded H.D. that she should make the dominating voice the one she knew best, her own, leaving out the voice of Orpheus altogether and making Eurydice the central heroic figure of the poem—a very original interpretation of the Greek myth (Goldensohn 45).

Despite differences in background, she and Lawrence liked each other almost immediately. That following year (1915) Aldington was conscripted into the British infantry and H.D. moved close to his training camp. When Lawrence saw her again in 1917, she had suffered a debilitating stillbirth and her marriage was breaking up.[3] Aldington accused H.D. of frigidity toward him, a charge which may have been true because by 1915 she apparently had been smitten with Lawrence. Partially in retaliation—the events of these years are not clear—Aldington started an affair with a close friend of H.D.'s, Brigit Patmore (the Morgan of *Bid Me To Live*), though the affair has been dated at a later time (Doyle 1989, 122).

Meanwhile, accused of spying for German submarines off the coast, Lawrence had been unceremoniously run out of Cornwall. Unintimidated by such officiousness, H.D. invited Lawrence and Frieda to use her rooms while she moved temporarily into the attic of 44 Mecklenburgh Square with Dorothy "Arabella" Yorke, a young American artist whom Aldington would later wed and who would appear as Bella in *Bid Me to Live* and as Josephine Ford in *Aaron's Rod*. Near the end of *Kangaroo*, Lawrence recalls the occasion and through the voice of Richard Somers repays H.D. handsomely for her hospitality: "The American wife of an English friend, a poet serving in the army, offered him room in Mecklenburgh Square, and the third day after their arrival in London Somers and Harriet [i.e., Lawrence and Frieda] moved there . . . the young woman tossed the rooms to them, and food and fuel, with a wild free hand. She was beautiful, reckless, one of the poetesses whose poetry Richard [Somers] feared and wondered over."

During the fall of 1917, Frieda and Lawrence stayed at H.D.'s quarters, close to their new friends (the H.D.-Aldington-Yorke triangle Lawrence would later transform into the Julia-Josephine-Robert contremps that occurs in the first part of *Aaron's Rod*).

During those months, a desperate H.D. apparently turned to Lawrence for consolation and comfort. Her impressions of his physical appearance at the time are revealed in her portrait of Rico in *Bid Me to Live*: godlike with his "archaic Greek beard and the fire-blue eyes in the burnt-out face that she had seen, an Orpheus head, severed from its body."[4] Rico "was the only one who seemed remotely to understand what I felt when I was so ill" (from the stillbirth). On page 81 of the novel—a book that may be granted more autobiographical authority than usual because it was written under advice from Freud who thought she should depict her life rather than fictionalize it—there occurs the famous paragraph where Julia seeks physical confirmation of the "track between them, written in the air" (Doyle 1989, 66).

Lawrence thought H.D. was charming, though she occasionally exasperated him. ("She is like a person walking a tight-rope. You wonder if she'll get across.") Even after Frieda tried to poison H.D.'s image of Lawrence by telling her that he cared only for men, their friendship deepened into intimacy during the ensuring dark months of the war. They had suffered a shattering loss, Lawrence of his mother, H.D. of a child, and that loss linked them in tragic awareness. They exchanged manuscripts and clearly appreciated each other's work. (The same point is made in "The Letters of H.D." in *Contemporary Literature* 581.) According to Janice Robinson, "H.D. read the very early poems he had written but not yet published when he met her and was enormously affected by them." This influence was both immediate and fairly long-lasting, because H.D. instinctively sensed that for Lawrence as for herself it was the poem that always mattered and that he had hewed for himself a way to bring all of his history and anger to his Georgian verses without allowing structure to inhibit the energies of his language.

From the outset of the relationship there existed a psychological attachment between them, seemingly no less intense for Lawrence than for H.D. Christopher Pollnitz reads the poem "Medlars and Sorb-Apples" in *Birds, Beasts and Flowers* as Lawrence's covert admission of that attachment (Kalnins 1986, 127). Just before writing this poem, Lawrence had decided to spend time alone in Fiesole away from Frieda. As read by Pollnitz, the poem mentions the possibility of "a new partner, a new parting, a new unfusing into twain." Pollnitz doubts that there was a new partner in Fiesole, and thinks there Lawrence may be referring to his relationship with H.D., more specifically responding to H.D.'s "Eurydice," with its bitter lines: "So you have swept me back / I who could have walked with the live souls / above the earth" (H.D. 1988, 51–55). Yet the nature of the relationship leaves unanswered vexing and vital questions for some critics: Was the attachment purely psychological? Did they become more than close platonic companions? Why did they have to communicate in poetic code? Like all unsettled romantic mysteries, this one has its fascinating twists and turns.

On the evidence of H.D.'s roman-à-clef, *Bid Me to Live*, Harry Moore suggests (1974, 283) that Frieda encouraged Lawrence to make love to H.D. so she herself could have an affair with Cecil Gray, the Scottish musicologist and composer with whom H.D. would later run away. Before Aldington went overseas, Lawrence had sent H.D. to Corfe Castle a poem he had written about his mother.[5] The final phrase may make more sense if interpreted in the light of a sexual liaison between Lawrence and H.D.: "You went your ways / Unnoticed among them, a still queen lost in the maze / Of this earthly affair[sic]."

In *Bid Me To Live*, Julia says to Rico, "You sent out a flare to me that time at Dorset before Rafe [who is modelled on Aldington] went. Couldn't you have at least waited until he was gone?" The "flare" may refer to Lawrence's poem hinting at a possible affair already in full swing. Julia, seemingly the voice of H.D., states in *Bid Me To Live* that it "was not she who had started out to lure him. It was himself with his letters and last night his open request for this relationship." In her homoerotic autobiographical novel, *Paint It Today*, Midget, the spokesperson for H.D., tells a friend: "I have a lover—not Basil [the Aldington stand-in]. I don't see him very often, but I know he is there. He is a distinguished poet. We simply meet by accident in the woods, or in the little house in the woods." This mis-en-scène for clandestine passion inevitably recalls the sexually alive woods in *Lady Chatterley's Lover*; hence, H.D. may be creating a fiction based on an earlier fiction rather than revealing personal history.

Lawrence's attitude toward H.D. underwent a significant change. Just before Aldington returned from France where he had seen combat, Lawrence wrote to Amy Lowell: "Hilda Aldington is very sad and depressed, everything is wrong. I wish things would get better" (*Letters*, 1984, 105). Lawrence says nothing about the cause of her depression, but according to Charles Doyle, "at least part of the explanation is a rebuff from himself" (1989, 57) which caused H.D. to depart with Gray for Zennor in Cornwall (Guest 1984, 94), where the Lawrences had spent most of the previous fall. Lawrence disliked Gray and when he learned that H.D. had left Aldington for good, he couldn't control his anger. In a passage omitted from a published letter, he wrote: "Arabella [Dorothy Yorke] has been living with Richard ever since we knew them. They wanted to get married but Hilda Aldington is a cat, and won't give them a divorce, though she herself went off with Gray."[6] Furious with her, Lawrence wrote to H.D., "I hope never to see you again" (H.D. 1974, 134).

In *H.D.: The Life and Work of an American Poet*, Janice Robinson contends that Perdita, the daughter born to H.D. in 1919, may have been fathered by Lawrence, a suggestion that greatly offended Perdita Schaffner. In fact, she has stated emphatically in the introduction to the Virago edition of her mother's novel (ix) that her father was Cecil Gray,[7] who figures in *Bid Me To Live* as Vane or Vanio. At any rate, when Lawrence discovered that H.D. had a baby, he wrote a friend in April 1919, "I hear her baby girl was born last Sunday, and they are both doing very well. We shall be going to London soon and may see her." If he did visit, that was probably their last meeting. But the contact continued.

Despite the abrupt end to their relationship, it was, according to Robinson, the deepest and most passionate of H.D.'s lifetime. To emphasize her point, she calls one of her chapters "D. H. Lawrence Everywhere," which would have served as a subtitle for her book. "How can we prove what [Lawrence and H.D.] meant to each other?" she asks and then embarks upon a controversial piece of detective work to "prove" that they had a tumultuous affair which Aldington tried to "cover up." According to Robinson, the sneaky husband offered himself as consultant to critics and biographers, at one point convincing Harry Moore, an early editor of Lawrence's *Letters*, to take out references to H.D. In the late forties, Aldington wrote his own version of Lawrence's life wherein H.D. appears more or less as a passing reference. Robinson interprets this as a diminution of H.D.'s role and a conscious effort by Aldington to distort the "truth" that had become so unbearable for him. Furthermore, he allegedly discouraged H.D. from publishing any allusions to her liaison with Lawrence.[8]

Aldington's efforts to "block the truth," according to Robinson, proved to be in vain. Both Lawrence and H.D.'s works, she thinks, are full of "textual clues," a kind of secret code, which when interpreted correctly, reveal the true nature of their relationship. H.D. had to keep her feelings for Lawrence hidden from her homosexual companion, Bryher (Winifred Ellerman), who was puzzled when she first met Lawrence in 1926 by his request that she make quite sure to convey his love to H.D. Like Robert Duncan, Robinson reads sections of *The Man Who Died* as "a brilliant metaphoric description of H.D.'s relationships with Pound and Aldington" and *Lady Chatterley's Lover* as essentially "the story of H.D.'s life from 1914 to 1918." Robinson offers a detailed analysis of the correspondences between *Lady Chatterley* and H.D.'s first unpublished novel, "Paint It Today," written about 1921, focusing on parallel scenes of a tryst in the woods. She furthermore suggests that *Aaron's Rod* and H.D.'s "The Flowering of the Rod" share a common source, the phallic imagery of Exodus 7, and that *Pilate's Wife* (unpublished, 1919) and Lawrence's *The Man Who Died* not only tell the same biblical story but also serve as palimpsests for the Lawrence/H.D. "affair." She also confirms beyond any doubt the suspicion that *Bid Me To Live* is a roman-à-clef, primarily about the time in late 1917 when the Lawrences stayed at the Aldington flat in London.

Lawrence, according to Robinson's theory, was as omnipresent in H.D.'s psychic life as he was in her writing. Indeed, H.D. "was haunted" by him. The repressed source of two visions or hallucinations that H.D. experienced during a trip to Greece in 1920 was not her mother, as Freud thought, but Lawrence, "her twin brother."[9] As mentioned earlier, Robinson believes that Lawrence may have been a central figure in the question of Perdita's paternity. Aldington was away in France when the child was conceived and Robinson nominates Lawrence as the father, on the grounds that children of uncertain paternity play a role in many of his works after 1919.

Although the evidence to support Robinson's theory of paternity seems rather thin, some readers find further proof of H.D.'s profound if not sexual attachment to Lawrence hidden among the images of *Helen in Egypt*, the epic poem completed in 1954 but unpublished until the year of her death in 1961. Robinson provides some useful leads but does not press her case sufficiently with close reading. She does, however, show how the poem reflects H.D.'s growth into a poet of much broader aspirations. Just as Lawrence's work outgrew the largely introverted Georgian and imagist phases of his early years and engaged the external world, *Helen in Egypt* evokes a human world more complex and more quantified by history than the archaic purities and dislocated passions of her imagist phase. In its broadest sense, this epic poem stresses multiple, overlaid identities, in the main characters especially. Achilles is the mythic projection of the male ethos and the ideal lover with whom Helen, mythic projection of western woman, desires reconciliation.

On a more concrete level, however, the poem functions as a version of H.D.'s personal history. Her lives and loves are subsumed in the cast of its characters. Stesichorus may be equated with Freud, Paris with Aldington, Ciron with Havelock Ellis, Lawrence with Achilles,[10] and of course H.D. with Helen. "Poem 6" in part 2 lends credence to Robinson's line of speculation. Helen (H.D.) is thinking about her relationship with Achilles (Lawrence) and begins to speak:

> Yet [I am] never forgetful,
> never unmindful of the Child
> Aphrodite sent
>
> War and the sea-enchantment
> I am awake, no trance,
> though I move as one in a dream

The first novella ("Hipparchia") of her twenties trilogy known as *Palimpsest* is set in the Roman Empire at war. The Greek heroine (H.D.), who shares Lawrence's notorious contempt for Romans ("Romans are wine-pressers"—124), loves Philip ("He and my father were in some ways singularly allied though opposite"—18). She envisions herself as Thetis and the handsome and noble Philip as Achilles (54–55). Because Philip appears to embody certain characteristics of Lawrence ("he goaded her fine tempered intellect with his precision, with his flaming subtlety. Philip was her passion, her intellect, her mind which none had broken"—101–2), H.D. seems to be establishing via Philip a connection between Lawrence and Achilles. Lawrence may have paid her back by basing the heroine of *Lady Chatterley's Lover* on H.D., throwing the reader off the track by naming her sister Hilda.

In *Hedylus* (1928), an Athenian beauty named Hedayle (as the name implies, H.D.) loves above all others one Demion or Demon of Olympia who "was the sun and the sun and the sun." When he comes to visit her at Samos, he says of their earlier relationship, "I didn't quite snare Hedayle." She responds, "Is that what (after ten years) you've come back to tell me?" (160). The implication is that they became lovers in 1918, the year that Lawrence and H.D. were most intensely involved with each other. Like the recovered Christ in *The Man Who Died*, Demion having loved her leaves her by sea.

Although some of its poems belong to the twenties, *Red Roses for Bronze* (1931) was published shortly after Lawrence's death. With this juxtaposition in mind, one is tempted to read the concluding lines of "In the Rain" as literal history:

> I was dead
> and you woke me,
> now you are gone,
> I am dead.[11]

In section X of "Choros Sequence" we are introduced to the figure of Achilles, who will assume a central role in H.D.'s later poetry, probably as a mask for Lawrence. The general tone of lamentation suggests that the occasion for the poet's grief may have been the death of Lawrence, like Achilles cut down untimely in his life.

Whatever the nature of their relationship, H.D. apparently admired Lawrence enough to make him the hero of *Bid Me To Live* (1960). It was started in 1921 and not completely assembled until 1949. Set in London during World War I, it is concerned primarily with the period of time that Lawrence and Frieda stayed in the Aldingtons' flat in the winter of 1917 while H.D. was living out of a suitcase between Corfe Castle, where Aldington was stationed, and her rooms at 44 Mecklenburgh Square, where she and Richard returned when he had leave. Among the major characters are Frederick, known as "Rico" (an unusual name, incidentally, that H.D. may have borrowed from Lou Witt's Italian husband in "St. Mawr") whose fiery novels about sexual passion no publisher dares print, and his "great Prussian wife," Elsa. They have been summoned back to England from Italy. When the heroine, Julia Ashton (H.D.) discovers that her soldier husband Rafe (Richard Aldington) has transferred his sexual interest to an earlier mistress, she turns to Frederick, to whom she has been powerfully attracted even though he lives in Zennor, in distant Cornwall. He repels her cautious sexual advances after inviting them. Imagery and events associated with Lawrence (his beloved gloire de Dijon roses, cypress tress, nature itself, his skill at charades, his stay in Italy and Zennor, his mother, his T.B., his hatred of war) are smoothly worked into the plot. And the novel does provide an account of the impact that Lawrence's poems exercised on her relationship with Aldington.

Several of the pseudo-Greek versions in *Collected Poems* take on a new meaning if they are read as though Lawrence were the doomed, beloved, heroic protagonist. For example, part 15 of "Toward the Piraeus" is hardly the kind of poem a woman would address to a philandering husband. It may be directed toward Lawrence, who "skilled to yield death-blows," often satirized the clandestine bed-hopping of his friends and their endless chatter about their affairs:

> It was not chastity that made me cold nor fear
> only I knew that you, like myself, were sick
> of the puny race that crawls and quibbles and lisps
> of love and love and lovers and love's deceit.
>
> It was not chastity that made me wild, but fear
> that my weapon, tempered in a different heat,
> was over-matched by yours, and your hand
> skilled to yield death-blows, might break
>
> With the slightest turn—no ill will meant—
> my own lesser, yet still somewhat fine-wrought,
> fiery-tempered, delicate, over-passionate steel.

In a different vein, Lawrence's "mother" poems in *Amores* were particularly moving, H.D. thought; many of the images in his *New Poems* would invade the structure of *Helen in Egypt*, H.D.'s re-creation in her own terms of the Helen-Achilles myth. For example, the image of "his fingers' remorseless steel" is clearly an echo of Lawrence's "Seven Seals." Robinson thinks that H.D. "plundered" that poem more than once and indeed "the seven arcs," "the seven slats of the ladder," and "the wheel as a seal," all recurrent images in H.D.'s visions, poems, and novel, are anticipated by and perhaps stem from the mystical language Lawrence uses to describe an erotic experience in "Seven Seals." It is as though H.D.'s poem had been dipped in the Greek Orphic mysteries which had absorbed Lawrence's attention for a time.

Analysis by Freud and the experience of the London blitz of World War II helped inspire her long poem *Trilogy*—"The Walls Do Not Fall," "Tribute to the Angels," and "The Flowering of the Rod." Robert Duncan is right in saying that with Pound's *Cantos* and Williams' *Paterson*, H.D.'s *Trilogy* is one of the major works of the imagist genius. Fusing the political with the poetic in a seamless continuity, H.D. condemns World War II as an attack not only on humanity, but also on the claims of poetry. She argues that the catastrophic conflict is an occasion for reasserting those claims. In so doing, she seems to be following the lead of Lawrence, in whom World War I aroused apocalyptic visions similar to those described by H.D. in *Trilogy*.[12]

Duncan throws considerable light on Lawrence's presence in *Trilogy*. He compares Lawrence's *The Man Who Died* to H.D.'s "The Walls Do Not Fall" and brings to our attention decided parallels between them. (Shortly after returning home to San Francisco, Duncan had drifted into the orbit of Kenneth Rexroth, who encouraged him to read deeper into H.D. She was to exert an imaginative and poetic hold on Duncan for the rest of his life.) H.D. first encountered Lawrence's fiction about Golgotha and its aftermath during her psychoanalytic conversion. She notes in the "Advent" section of *Tribute to Freud* (141): "Stephen Guest brought me a copy of *The Man Who Died*. He said, 'Did you know that you are the priestess of Isis in this book?' Perhaps I would never had read the book if Stephen had not brought it to me." As first she was afraid that Lawrence had somehow taken over a similar story she was writing (*Pilate's Wife*, unpublished at Yale University) about a wounded Christ buried alive.[13] After she read the novella, these fears of telepathic transmission were allayed.

When she took up the theme again in her trilogy, the Christ "is not the embodiment of a self-importance or Messianic inflation of the ego." For H.D. he comes as a new Master over Love; but this Christos, like Lawrence's Man Who Died, must be set free from "old thought, old convention," the nausea of His false image, "of pain-worship and death-symbol." Like Lawrence's Christ, H.D.'s passes through this stage to be united with the person of Osiris. In turn, we see Mary Magdala of "The Flowering of the Rod" transformed by the "magic of the daemons of womanhood—Isis among them—like the Priestess in *The Man Who Died*, belonging to the greater day of the human consciousness."

What Duncan thinks H.D. may have found most significant in *The Man Who Died* is what he calls Lawrence's curious turn of vision: the spiritual man is the old dead self, and the physical man, "the indwelling in the body's awareness," is the new. This is also the subtext of *Aaron's Rod*: that a man or a society, cut off from the elemental animal bases—the earth, the sun, true sexual communion—is doomed unless it can find a way to reconnect to these forces. Toward Madeleine, the woman who worships him as the messiah, Lawrence's Christ feels only pity and revulsion, "a nausea of disillusion." In the new life a second figure of the woman appears, the priestess of Isis, who attends not to his image but to the growing sense of her own powers as a woman. The Lady of Isis presses his wounded body to her own in a ritual of healing and restores him to a state of wholeness. She also conceives a child by him.

Dianne Chisholm (1992, 84) argues that there is an important distinction between these two versions of the Isis myth: Lawrence, she believes, is writing an Oedipal mother-son narrative while H.D. is elaborating Freud's highly suggestive notion of a healthier pre-Oedipal mother-daughter relationship. The Isis of H.D., she claims, should not be confused with the "son/sun-worshipping Isis" of Lawrence, who signifies a dark age not yet illuminated by humanist Enlightenment" (85). Yet Lawrence and H.D. are not so far apart as Chisholm implies. Closer scrutiny of Lawrence's final words seem to suggest that the protagonist of *The Man Who Died* is ready to surrender Oedipal authority, bringing him closer to H.D.'s ultimate view. "My public life is over," he says, "the life of my self-importance." Beyond lies the other, Lawrence's version of "the greater day" of the human consciousness (1931, 200) which knows no gender or phallic domination. And in H.D. the empowerment of Helen, descended from Isis, signals the millennium.

In "Tribute to the Angels," the second volume of the trilogy, H.D. revises the Book of Revelations in the *New Testament* according to her own private vision, much as Lawrence did in *Apocalypse.* [A pagan forerunner of the apocalyptic visionary of the Bible,] Hermes Trismegistus of the first stanza, whose province is "thought/inventive, artful and curious," may represent Lawrence. That speculation is supported by the closing lines where Hermes has been displaced, absorbed in, or identified with the figure of John of Patmos. Images of lilies, the rainbow, the flowering rod, feathered objects, the span of heaven, the rose, and the phoenix, favorite Lawrence symbols of resurrection, lace through H.D.'s lines (110):

> *This is the flowering of the rod,*
> *This is the flowering of the burnt-out wood,*
> *where, Zadkiel [an archangel], we pause to give*
> *thanks that we rise again from death and live.* (109–110)

In 1919, Lawrence had published a slim volume of poems called *Bay*, which like "Seven Seals" used mystical language to speak about an erotic encounter. A few of the poems in *Bay*, especially "Shades," rang so true to H.D.'s experience with Lawrence that they stamped themselves indelibly upon her subconscious memory. From the depths of that period long suppressed, images rise to the surface in *Helen in Egypt*, written some thirty-five years later. ("Memory," H.D. writes in *Notes on Thought and Vision*, "is the mother, begetter of all drama, idea, music, science or song.") No poem that she ever wrote suggests more strongly than *Helen in Egypt* the passionate and profound kinship that H.D. felt for Lawrence. As I have pointed out earlier in this chapter, in this version of H.D.'s inner drama where the distances between events are protracted, contracted, and retracted, Lawrence becomes Achilles, "the New Mortal"; Freud is several people including Stesichorus, the inventor of the choral heroic hymn (Horace Gregory thinks H.D. is Stesichorus—"Introduction"); Aldington is Paris, whose envious barb wounds Achilles; and H.D. is Helen, keeper of the Amen-temple, who becomes identified with the priestess of Isis. In this connection, it is interesting to note that she re-read *The Man Who Died* just before embarking on her Helen poem in 1952 (Robinson 1984, 347). Early in this 304-page masterpiece she announces:

> the harpers will sing forever
> of how Achilles met Helen
> among the shades
>
> but we were not, we were not shadows;
> as we walk, heel and sole,
> leave our sandal-prints in the sand
>
> Poem 3, book 1

Helen and Achilles may be mythical, but Lawrence and H.D. were flesh and blood, not shades. In one place, she confesses, "I loved Achilles finally, in Leuke [London?] but I let him go."

This interpretation of *Helen in Egypt* as a love-duet between Lawrence and H.D. is given credibility by another beautiful late poem, a coda to the Helen poem, "Winter Love" (from *Hermetic Definition*), wherein H.D. reveals that during her lifetime she found a Spirit to match her Spirit only when she met Achilles (not Paris), doomed to die young, "in a trance, a dream." The presence of Achilles suggests almost beyond doubt that the real hero of the poem is Lawrence, not Erza Pound to whom it is dedicated. Once more H.D. is Helen of Troy in a dramatic soliloquy:

> O Helen, most blest,
> O Virgo, unravaged,
> but knowing the thirst
> Of the moment un-mated;
> the insatiable thirst
> will lead to Achilles
>
> O Helen, most blest,
> Recall first love and last.

According to Robinson, H.D. was "ever aware that her love for Pound had led to her love for Lawrence and a life in poetry" (1984, 428), but in this poem H.D. seems to be confessing through her dream of Helen the magnitude of that love. The Lawrence/Achilles figure is designated as her "first love and last," implying that none of her subsequent lovers ever quite succeeded in taking his place.

Although the dream-like atmosphere of "Winter Love" is disturbed by images of war ("the forest of masts"), the poem looks beyond immediate violence toward transfiguration. During World War I, Lawrence wrote a poem called "The Attack," about a transformation that occurs in the context of an aerial bombing of London. It describes a mystical experience, an attack on the substance of Lawrence's very self but one that leads to another kind of illumination, a rebirth possibly involving H.D. Another Lawrence poem, "Zeppelin Nights," with its image of death raining from the sky upon London, becomes in the crucible of H.D.'s imagination a tantalizing image of aerial attack which takes place on a stretch of beach. She writes:

> have you seen a gerfalcon
> fall on its prey?
> so my throat knew that day.
> his fingers' remorseless steel,
> when I had strength only to pray
> Thetis, let me go out, let me forget
> let me be lost.
>
> *(Helen in Egypt)*

These poems and others like them may have suggested to H.D. the theme of love "as the eternal reality juxtaposed against the historical reality of a world at war" (Robinson 1984, 113).[14]

When Louis Martz restored H.D.'s projected volume, "The Dead Priestess Speaks" (as part of *Collected Poems 1912–1944*), he added lyrics that seem to belong there, such as the fantasia on Freud in "The Master" and the meditation on Lawrence in "The Poet."[15] Although "the voice [of the priestess] is still recognizably H.D.'s rapt, intense, and toneless idiolect, there is a shift from supplication and exclamation to a more interrogative mode" (Pearson 1984, 447) that may owe something to her analysis with Freud. The poem about Lawrence indicates that he must have been, more than three years after his death, an important presence in H.D.'s sessions with Freud in 1933–34 ("Advent," in *Tribute to Freud*, is a rich narrative account of her therapy). In this poem, she is trying to explain to Freud (whose bearded visage reminds her of Lawrence) that she had to relive her experience of Lawrence fictively in order to exorcise him from her imagination:

> No,
> I don't pretend, in a way, to understand . . .
> I say ,
> "I don't grasp his philosophy,
> and I don't understand,"
> but I put out a hand, touch a cold door,
> (we have both come from so far);
> I touch something imperishable;
> I think
> why should he stay there,
> why should he guard a shrine so alone,
> so apart,
> On a path that leads nowhere

Reminiscent of Lawrence's poetry in tonality and style, this passage depends upon the most delicate touch in the syntactical arrangements, the hint of rhyme, the almost weightless equivalence of phrasing ("I say," "I think"), and an extremely reticent scheme of imagery which plays off tactile gestures against terms implying both arrest and movement (so "understand" can attach its abstraction to the concrete directness of "guard"). These lines take on a poignant, even ironical quality when read against a passage in *Bid Me To Live*. Julia has touched Rico's sleeve:

> She put out her hand. Her hand touched his sleeve. He shivered, he seemed to move back, move away like a hurt animal . . . even this touch (not heavy on his sleeve) seemed to send some sort of repulsion through him. She drew back her hand.

In Robinson's estimation, H.D.'s Moravian understanding of spiritual mysteries came close to Lawrence's religious concepts (113):

> Her unpublished Moravian novel, "The Mystery," is thematically related to "The Attack," as is her poem, "Hymn" (for Count Zinzendorf, 1700–1760). Zinzendorf, like Lawrence, had a vision of a Utopian community to be based upon fulfillment rather than renunciation. Lawrence, like Zinzendorf, believed that it was possible to live in a state of peace in the world but that such peace depended upon the creation of another world of consciousness (as in Rananim). H.D.'s "Hymn" employs the same language of mystical discourse as Lawrence's "Attack."

A contemporary, John Cournos, suggests that H.D. and Lawrence stopped short of physical intimacy. In *Miranda Masters* (1926), also a roman-à-clef, a writer named Gombarov (Cournos) leaves for Russia before Richard Ramsden (the Lawrence figure) arrives in London to visit Miranda (H.D.), but because he had been Miranda's closest confidant at the time, Gombarov is presumably in a position to intuit the nature of her relationship with Ramsden. Still, her revelation that she is in love surprises Gombarov. Before he departs she says to him:

> There is a power in this person to kill me! I mean literally. For the spiritual vision his thoughts, his distant passion, have given me, thank God—because his vision is of God—I thank God. But, Gomby, there's yet another aspect to it. If he comes too near, I am afraid for myself. I do not mean physically—though I do not expect to see him physically.

Gombarov guesses that she is referring to Ramsden, the poet whose beautiful, passionate verses are shocking England by their frank pagan sexuality. He warns her against Ramsden/Lawrence, who is, in his view "a great flame . . . but a disintegrating flame. Everything he touches falls to ashes in the contact" (Cournos 1926, 175–76). Apparently the affair remains platonic.

Among the modern critics, Peter Firchow suspects that Lawrence was never physically intimate with H.D. Other critics not entirely convinced by the Robinson's thesis include Susan Friedman, who argues in her breakthrough feminist revaluation of H.D. (*Psyche Reborn*) that Robinson focusses mainly on images supporting her "case" for Lawrencian intimacy and tends to ignore larger areas of design, thereby misreading the mandala of

H.D.'s work. Friedman proceeds to put far greater emphasis on H.D.'s relation to Freud[16] and Bryher, following the fairly common practice among some critics to diminish Lawrence's influence on H.D.[17] This minimalist interpretation of Lawrence's influence is not altogether persuasive in face of H.D.'s intimate allusions to Lawrence scattered throughout her opus. Indeed, as late as 1948 she tells Sylvia Dobson that she is re-reading him and figuring out his horoscope: "He was born on September 11, 1885, so for my birthday, one day a year, we were twins or are twins" (*Conjunctions*, 2 March, 143).

H.D.'s struggles with Lawrence, dramatized in *Bid Me To Live*, are revisited in *Compassionate Friendship*, an unpublished journal essay written in 1955. When she tries to assign him a rank among her "initiators," she places him fourth in a list of seven, after Pound, Aldington, and Cournos. We shall probably never know the ultimate truth about H.D.'s relationship with Lawrence, since his letters to her, which might have clarified the ambiguities of the affair, were destroyed by Aldington. Whatever the nature of their relatively brief relationship may have been—DuPlessis thinks it was "sexual thralldom"—H.D. saw it as a gift to be cherished. Her sure movement toward growing openness, her struggle to break free from all forms of confinement and to forge her own style in both life and letters, were encouraged by the intellectual and spiritual proximity of Lawrence.[18]

3
Rebecca West: We Must Choose Life

Cicily Isabel Fairfield, the daughter of an English mother and a poor but cultivated Anglo-Irish army officer who had served briefly with the Confederacy during the American Civil War, was born in London and raised in Edinburgh. While living there, she trained for the theater at George Watson's Ladies College, and at the age of eighteen she played Hendrik Ibsen's dark and stormy Rebecca West in *Rosmersholm*. Discouraged by the tendency of the Royal Academy of Dramatic Art to cast her as "a wrinkled old crone," she left the theater and embarked upon a career in journalism. She chose as a pseudonym the name of the Ibsenite feminist whom she admired so much. She knew that when an artist chooses another name for her creative self, she is not merely inventing a pseudonym: she is revealing her innermost identity. Like Ibsen's heroine, the new Rebecca West was determined to protest against the British class system, which in her opinion had suppressed the creative potentiality of women by spawning special privilege and rigid convention.

The young firebrand, reviewing for the feminist journal *The Freewoman* and the socialist weekly *The Clarion*, spoke out for free love and women's trade unions while attacking imperialism and conservative divorce laws. Her amazing ability to argue eloquently for socialism and to review books with incisive wit brought her to the attention of literary men, including George Bernard Shaw, Max Beerbohm, H. G. Wells, and D. H. Lawrence. Before long, her passionate spirit and intellectual vision made her a major force in the radical feminist movement that crested before World War I.

About the time she met H. G. Wells, she was asked by *The Freewoman* (12 July 1912) to review the second novel of a rising young writer from the Midlands. Bowled over by the energy and vitality of *The Trespasser*, she was lavish in praising it: "Mr. Lawrence has conquered. This book is magic," she said (Marcus

Rebecca West. Photograph reproduced courtesy of the Special Collections of the McFarlin Library at the University of Tulsa.

44), though on re-reading it some years later, she would call it "two thirds a mistake" (Marcus 1982 346). Two years later, for the first issue of Wyndham Lewis's *Blast*, she contributed a powerful story called "Indissolvable Matrimony," which demonstrates how deeply immersed she was in the psychological tradition of early Lawrence and the Brontës (Marcus 266). In this blow-by-blow description of the battle of the sexes, the opponents are an intellectual woman of "unfeminine" (i.e., unladylike) sexuality and her cold-blooded husband, who is outraged by her sensuality. On the level of its sexual meaning, this story can be read as a reversal of the Helena-Siegfried scenario that animates *The Trespasser*, as though West were inviting the reader to consider that shocking anomaly, the "sensuous woman," rather than the tired tribulations of the "sensuous man."

Shortly after publishing her first book in 1916, a perceptive and still readable study of Henry James, she again reviewed Lawrence. On this occasion it was his play, *The Widowing of Mrs. Holroyd*, and while she praised it as "very beautifully and subtly written," she compared it negatively to *Sons and Lovers*, which she thought it paralleled too closely, and advised Lawrence to stay with the novelistic genre where his genius lay. The realistic drama, she observed shrewdly, was not hospitable to his "special gift of drawing the development of an emotional situation" (Marcus 348).

Possibly under the prompting of Wells, she decided to write fiction seriously. Three years after the war ended, bored with Wells and determined to carve her path independently as a novelist, she left him in Capri and moved by herself to Italy where Lawrence and Frieda had chosen to live. By then she was the author of a highly lauded novel (*The Return of a Soldier*)[1] which exposed sham relationships and the desexualizing of traditional marriage. Moreover, she had another novel in the press (*The Judge*), which like *Harriet Hume*, exploited her Scottish childhood. Hardly unknown to the English literary circle in Florence, she was immediately befriended by Reggie Turner, a kindly old homosexual who had known Oscar Wilde. Turner introduced her to other English expatriates, including Norman Douglas, the author of the celebrated *South Wind*. One day while lunching together at a trattoria, the three of them decided that they should call on Lawrence, who had recently arrived alone in the city by "a slow train that crawled up from Rome laden with poor folks who could not afford to pay for speed" (West 1977, 388).

Years earlier, in addition to reviewing Lawrence favorably on at least two occasions, West had spoken out on his behalf when Henry James, in an article for *The Times Literary Supplement*, had dismissed Lawrence as a minor writer. She retorted with some heat that Lawrence was "the only author of this young generation who has not only written but also created, and created with such power that he would be honourable in any generation" (Moore 1974, 196). Turner and Douglas, sensing that she was impatient to meet her hero, took her to his quarters in an inexpensive pensione overlooking the Arno, where he was typing his next novel, *Aaron's Rod*, the second half of which takes place in Florence. When it appeared the following year, she dismissed it as a "plum-silly book" by a man of genius (Glendinning 1987, 77). Later, in an unpublished piece (1929), she would light into him for saying in "Good Boy Husbands" that English men were grown-up babies because in their tenderest years they were delivered over to the care of women (Scott 1990, 584).

Nonetheless, she and Lawrence liked one another immediately. Although he was seven years her senior, he made friends like a child, she said, or like a "wise old philosopher at the end of his days," thus catching the combination of the innocent and the sage that created wherever he went "a spiritual drama." On the following morning, the first warm day of spring, she and Douglas went for a walk in the countryside with Lawrence, who, she observed, "moved quickly and joyously" (1977, 390). As he told her about the hardships of his travels to the abbey of Monte Cassino and his life among the malicious Sicilian peasants, she realized that he was a kind of wandering saint who went on journeys with a spiritual rather than a geographical destination. "Lawrence travelled, it seemed, to get a certain Apocalyptic vision of mankind that he registered again and again and again, always rising to a pitch of ecstatic agony" (Moore 1974, 334–35). In one of their conversations, she must have mentioned that Secker's refusal to give her a review copy of *The Lost Girl* had angered her, because shortly thereafter Lawrence warned Secker to be sure that she got a copy of his next novel. As they walked and lunched at a little Italian inn, she discovered that she and the coal-miner's son had more in common than she had supposed: like him, she opposed war, imperialism, and conservative divorce laws; argued for free love; and showed an uncommon sympathy for oppressed women. Lawrence became for her at that moment "the embodiment of the renascent quality of the day. He was made in the angelic colors" (1977, 390). This would be the only time they would meet, although she would maintain communication with him.

Her opinion of him as a craftsman vacillated, however. Compared to Proust and Joyce, the other two major authors who were to influence her fiction, in her eyes Lawrence was a writer "who had rejected all modern technique, who could use realistic devices and subject-matter only so long as he simple-mindedly pursued the aim of fictionalizing his autobiography." With a remarkable lack of sensitivity to the nuances of Lawrence's language and the subtlety of his mind, she also asserted that his intellect was "not fully developed enough" to work out in words the significance of his insights—a "failure" that flawed the description of Gerald's icy death in *Women in Love*[2] and the love scenes in *Lady Chatterley's Lover*, commonly regarded by other critics as the most memorable passages in those novels. This, she guessed (wrongly), resulted from his failure to revise (1984, 27). She asserts that he deserved the notoriety for "the troublesome mettle of his judgements," adding that it was difficult "to learn from him lessons suitable to one's own developing career." Despite the real reservations that she had about the risks of emulating Lawrence, she was drawn to him instinctively as an artist "of great humanity whose sense of commitment to life rather than art shone burningly through all his works" (Orel 1986, 66). She regarded Lawrence "as a creature that passed among ordinary human beings like an angel, sometimes with a sword, sometimes with a blessing." She praised his *Etruscan Places* extravagantly: "It is a book," she wrote, "which, if only for its description of the grey sea at Ladispoli, must be read by anybody who cares for living words" (Scott 1990, 591).

During the formative years of her career, she had already allowed Lawrence's style and insights to percolate through her sensibility. Indeed, as Gordon Ray points out (1974, 86), the theme of her first novel, *The Return of the Soldier* (1918), "owes as much to D. H. Lawrence as its technique owes to Henry James." It describes the hypocrisy and sexual emptiness of traditional marriage, a theme akin to one of Lawrence's chief preoccupations. In spirit it is close to Lawrence's antiwar stance that so angered the English reading public. When the returned soldier's amnesia threatens to break up his marriage, his wife Margaret summons a famous mental specialist, who diagnoses Baldry in Lawrencian language.

> There's a deep self in one, the essential self, that has its wishes. And if those wishes are suppressed by the superficial self . . . it takes its

revenge. Into the house of conduct erected by the superficial self it sends an obsession (1918, 162)

Her second novel, *The Judge* (1922), infuriated Wells, who took it as a rejection of his own critical values: "She splashed her colours about, she exalted James Joyce and D. H. Lawrence, as if in defiance of me." Although Wells may be exaggerating, the energy and richness of her language reminds us more of Lawrence than of those writers to whom she was allegedly closer in spirit. Indeed, this novel might be read as a version of *Sons and Lovers* seen from the woman's point-of-view. Ellen Melville, a beautiful young woman who works in an Edinburgh office, falls in love with Richard Yaverland and he with her. West makes Richard's domineering mother a powerful presence in the novel, possibly because she was not convinced that Lawrence had explored the Oedipal situation thoroughly enough from the point-of-view of the two women involved. Mrs. Yaverland thinks to herself: "He loves me, his mother, so far beyond all reason. Because he thinks me perfect, the queen of all women." (242) On the other hand, while she wants her son to marry "the right woman" and be normal, she fears Ellen just as Paul Morel's mother feared Miriam and regarded her as a bad influence on Paul: "It was true that Richard adored her [Ellen], but then no doubt this kind of woman knew well how to deceive him" (245). At the end, when Richard cannot tear himself free of his mother, Ellen muses, "Her love hadn't been able to reach Richard across the dark waters of his mother's love. And how like a doom that love had lain on him" (490). Ellen is much harder in her judgment of this Oedipal web than Paul Morel is, no doubt because the mother in West's novel is a ruler as well as a more obvious rival for the son's affection.

After *Women in Love* appeared in 1921, West wrote three columns about it in a July issue of *New Statesman*, most of which she distilled into the opinions expressed in "Elegy"—the only other reviews to greet the book were by Rose Macaulay. When invited some years later to contribute a literary essay to *The Quarter*, West promised to write an article in praise of Lawrence. For some reason, her projected piece failed to materialize. Lawrence wrote immediately from Bandol in France to say that he understood and sympathized with her dilemma, closing with a burst of exasperation: "Of course if you felt like doing it you'd have done it; and why bother about a thing if you don't feel like it!" What Lawrence probably never learned is that in *The Strange*

Necessity (1928), a collection of critical essays and reviews, West had slipped him into her essay on Willa Cather, comparing the two at some length to Lawrence's advantage. Referring to his famous poem "Snake," West comments admiringly on his willingness to follow the snake, even to identify with it, "to become the whole caboodle"—unlike Cather's temerity in such matters. In the context of its time, when many readers associated Lawrence's name with pornography and Cather's with the new American regionalism, her conclusion is unexpected. But most important, it suggests that what she had found illuminating in Lawrence's writing had become a model for her own aspirations:

> Does not such transcendental courage, does not such ambition to extend consciousness beyond its present limits and to elevate man above himself, entitle his art to be ranked as more important than that of Miss Cather? (243)

Lawrence, flattered to know that by then she respected, championed, and even imitated him, asked if there was anything he could do on her behalf, and even though he was seriously ill, took the trouble to send her an embroidered picture of a panther which he had been working on (he must have heard, possibly from Wells himself, with whom he had a cordial relationship, that Wells's affectionate nickname for her was "Panther").

When West learned how grave this illness was from a friend with whom she had attended the dramatization of *Point Counter Point* in London, she responded, "Oh, I don't believe that, it's quite impossible"—for the world without Lawrence, Dame Rebecca believed, would be like Huxley's play without Mark Rampion [Lawrence]: the best thing would be gone (1977, 387). West made up for her failure to produce the promised article before Lawrence's death by composing as a substitute the elegiac obituary piece cited above, which first appeared in *The American Bookman* and was reprinted as a pamphlet entitled *D. H. Lawrence: An Elegy* (1930) and later in a second collection of critical essays, *Ending in Earnest* (1931).

In this piece, she describes their only meeting and states his claim to "our reverence and gratitude." The forces which moved Lawrence, she states, seemed to her generation to be "the best part of our human equipment." Among those forces was human passion. "He laid sex and those base words for it on the salver of his art and held them up before the consciousness of the world ... and prayed that both might be transmuted into the highest that man could use" (1977, 394). If his prayer remained unfulfilled, at least his life was "a spiritual victory." He had the courage to oppose a "Puritan morality of a disagreeable, flesh-insulting kind the horror of which we today forget" (1931, 8)

Many readers wish with Victoria Glendinning that Rebecca West, "who often wrote sharply about the ways in which men and women fail one another" (1986, 293), had devoted more of her own genius to describing the release of passion that she recognized as essential to a happy physical life. She can write about the passions with power and candor when she chooses to do so; as, for example, in the closing passage of chapter 7 in *Cousin Rosamund*, the unfinished third novel of her projected trilogy: "It seemed certain that I must die when he touched me, but instead of course I lived" (233). There is here an echo of Gudrun's "Shall I die?" when Gerald plunges into her body (*Women in Love*), but one wonders whether West, despite her intellectual fearlessness, suffered from the same temerity about such physical matters that she attributes to Willa Cather, so cryptic is this scene.

To preserve the memory of Lawrence, she had his embroidered picture and his letter to her framed (the only other letters she ever framed were from George Moore and Virginia Woolf). Although she didn't always like his work, she remained steadfast in her loyalty to him. Outraged when the exhibition of his paintings in London was closed down, even though her interest in his paintings as art was minimal, she rushed to his defense. Some years later she tried to re-create his image from memory in her portrait of Laurence Vernon, "with his fine short pointed brown beard, which he never fingered, his clear brown eyes which never sparkled, his trim body in his formal and unnoticeable clothes" (1936, 16). Isabelle, the tragically widowed heroine, loves Laurence, and when her industrialist lover asks her where she would like to dine, she replies, in a kind of inside joke, "Laurent's. His place I regard with affection, since something of importance happened to me there" (353). In the early 1950s, she and her husband Henry Andrews paid homage to the memory of Lawrence by visiting Frieda in New Mexico. As though visiting Frieda had conjured up his spirit, she recalls Lawrence in her next book. Lawrence, she notes, "invented a new kind of novel which appeared to be realistic but was actually an exercise on symbolism." Although the dialogue of *The Rainbow* and *Women in Love* struck her as unnatural, she pinpointed the greatness and originality of both novels with unerring accuracy: the "incredible actions and speeches declare the progress of the characters' inner lives with the clarity of poetry" (1957, 221).³

According to West, Lawrence and Joyce were the two great writers of their time, but the writing of both suffered a serious flaw: it was not concerned with power(!). Both were "prepolitical" and that gave their writing a peculiar feeling of detachment from reality, a "lack of feeling for developed society." On the other hand, West contends, Lawrence could not be guilty of the charge that critics (including Bertrand Russell) leveled against him, especially during the fifties:

> It is absurd to accuse him, as some have done, of sympathy for fascism on the basis of *The Plumed Serpent*. That book represents not support of Hitler but hostility to Rousseau. Lawrence too thought that man was born free and was everywhere in chains, but he considered this to be the source of all man's sorrows; and he was proposing a new sort of social contract in which the individual would not be forced to alienate his right to passionate being. (1957, 222)

The last part of this statement would seem to apply to West's aspirations in her own writing. She sought to reinterpret realistic discourse into a more poetic idiom as it unfolded the passionate drama of the individual's journey toward liberation. Although many readers would agree with Peter Wolfe that "her freshness and vigor place her much closer to D. H. Lawrence" (1971, 160) than to Henry James (to whom she had often been compared), she lacked Lawrence's gift of the poetic idiom (the results of her few attempts to write poetry are largely disappointing) and his eye for the memorable metaphor that express the flow and ebb of passion.

In 1960 she appeared as a witness for the defense in the most notorious trial of the decade—or as she put it, "said a good word" for what seemed to her "poor, sincere, dated, dowdy *Lady Chatterley's Lover*." That comment may sound self-contradictory to anyone familiar with an important scene that occurs near the end of *Sunflower*, a novel which she had planned to finish writing around the time the first *Lady Chatterley's Lover* appeared ("Afterword," *Sunflower* 273). Sybil Fassendyll, the actress "known for her blonde beauty," is shown "something that she might like to see in her garden by her butler Parkens (*pace* the gamekeeper Parkin of the first *Lady Chatterley*). In a passage that appears to jump right out of a famous scene in Lawrence's "dated, dowdy" novel, West writes, perhaps as a parting act of homage to a writer to whom she owed a debt:

> She bent over the hedgehog and cried out, in animation that was not feigned, because now the whole of life was so lovely that she had only to bend her attention to any part of it to become immediately enchanted. (254)

Of all the male writers who had influenced her—including Proust, Bennett, and Joyce—Lawrence seems to have affected her the most. She had her eulogy of him reprinted twice after its first publication (Deakin 1980, 61), and despite an occasional disparaging remark more kindly than malicious, West's life-long appreciation of Lawrence's unorthodox genius is best characterized by a statement that might be applied to her own ambitions as well: "Lawrence was in fact no different from any other great artist who has felt the urgency to describe the unseen so keenly that he has rifled the seen of its vocabulary and diverted it to that purpose, and it took courage to do that in a land swamped with naturalism as England was when Lawrence began to write" (1931, 76).

Although Dame Rebecca was influenced to some degree by the plot, setting, and characters in Lawrence, she responded most wholeheartedly to the lyrical energy of his language, his gift of startling intuition, his readiness to attack taboos (especially in matters of sex), and the spirit of freedom and life-affirmation that animated his work. Like Lawrence, she was a moralist, a preacher against death. Her *Black Lamb and Grey Falcon*, a minor masterpiece that describes her travels in Yugoslavia as she examines Balkan politics and culture, shows how well she had learned to translate the techniques and insights of fiction into sophisticated travel writing, a genre that Lawrence had refined into an authentic art. Her gripping reports on the Nuremberg trials of the Nazi war criminals, *A Train of Powder*, read like a novel by Lawrence or by West herself.

Her method of composition was as unorthodox as Lawrence's. She refused to limit the imagination to conventional literary forms. "In seeking to discover what she knew," says Faith Evans (1980 11), "she would take off on all kinds of tangents, reverting to the original point only when most people had quite forgotten it. She would not be bound by the structural formulae of literary conventions." Like Lawrence, she wrote as though she were composing a piece of music, with "hardly a thought of how it will make up into a shape" (H. G. Wells, quoted in Evans 1980 11). In an earlier time, this spiraling style of writing was often faulted as undisciplined, but a contemporary critic might commend it as a technique adapted to existential explorations, one that was perfectly appropriate to West's probing imagination.

If there are not many passages in Rebecca West's work that can be traced back to specific sources in Lawrence (the one above is an exception), nonetheless at times he seems like such a presence that he might have been included as a character in more than one of her novels. West, working against the vulgarizing process of a blatantly commercial age, strove to save the lines of communication, to purify its signs and signals so that the honest artist could continue to communicate a valid experience to an honest reader. As Bonnie Scott notes, she still has power as an iconoclast (1990, 568). Although she readily admitted that Lawrence had his faults,[4] he exemplified so much that was important to her that she loved him and admitted him into her soul. In *Ending in Earnest*, she proclaimed him to be "perhaps the greatest genius of his times," and in a punning line from *The Thinking Reed* (1936, 17), she may have slyly paid him the highest tribute: "Laurence [sic] is what I would have been if I had been a man."

Meridel LeSueur. Photograph reproduced courtesy of Layle Silbert.

4
Meridel LeSueur: Passion on the Prairie

During the early 1930s, a Minnesota social activist named Meridel LeSueur achieved modest success when she published sixteen stories about the political and sexual awakening of working women in the Bible Belt, not exactly a hot subject in a Depression America concerned chiefly with economic survival. Although these stories would be reprinted or cited in Edward O'Brien's annual collection of best short stories, a rare distinction for a woman writer of that time, in the following decades the repressive literary and political atmosphere of the Cold War and the prevalence of McCarthyism silenced her voice and confined her writing to children's stories—about Abraham Lincoln, for instance, and Native American–white relationships. It was the liberal political climate of the sixties combined with the supportive attitudes of a more sophisticated reading public that made it possible for her to be heard again: Dale Jacobson believes her work was helped to a good extent by the advent of the women's movement "which provided her with an audience that was looking more at sexism than classism" (1992, 205). Out of relative obscurity, she was elevated into a cult figure (Duncan 1982, 25), who, still in good health and lively spirits as of this writing, jokingly refers to herself as "Lazarus" because she feels as if she had been "resurrected from the death of McCarthyism."

When LeSueur embarked on a career as a writer during the late 1920s, she intuitively sensed that an imaginative treatment of a woman's life could not be very penetrating or complete unless the writer was willing to ride the theme of sexual awakening deep into the interior of the psyche. As her need to express her version of the truth compelled her to confront this virtually forbidden subject, LeSueur discovered that she knew no American writers who could give her direction. Kate Chopin had not yet been discovered; Edith Wharton, like Henry James, wrote about upper-class manners and morality. Edna St. Vincent Millay was composing poetry about a flamboyant life-style that had little pertinence to LeSueur's rural sensibility. For a time, she took the Wisconsin author Zona Gale as her mentor, but Gale's timidity and caution in matters of sexual passion hardly encouraged LeSueur's determination to break out of the Puritan inhibitions that she had acquired from her family while living in a small midwestern town.

The writer who pointed her in the right direction, as it turned out, was not an American nor another woman. She says simply that D. H. Lawrence saved her life (1982, 6). Although she would later suspect that his influence had not always been beneficial (in swallowing Lawrence whole, she also blinded herself to his irritating lapses into sexism), she leaves no doubt about his importance to her at this juncture of her career. "I'd never have gotten out of that Puritanism without Lawrence," she told Elaine Hedges in an interview (1982, 6). This breaking out is the crucial preoccupation—one might say the central theme—of LeSueur's fiction, and the title of one of her strongest stories, "The Ripening Seed" (with its slant allusion to "new germination" in the final paragraph of *The Rainbow*) places emphasis on the creative process bursting out of confines.

Prior to her liberation, LeSueur's early experiences could not have differed very much from Lawrence's in the Midlands. While she was growing up in Minnesota, the stricken copper mines, the ranks of the unemployed, and the poverty that attended both were familiar sights, and the bleakness of that environment, where she encountered stereotypes of women in the role of tending to household chores and men in the role of working outside the home to earn money for the family (Pennings 1988 154), must have encoded itself on her memory as similar Midlands scenes had on Lawrence's. LeSueur understood only too well Lawrence's vital concern that both men and women break with their past and transcend these role-stereotypes. Like Lawrence, she sought the vehicle of escape and transcendance in a sexual passion that had the power to elevate the individual out of the old self. Sexual communion came to symbolize for her, as she knew it had for Lawrence, especially in "The Man Who Died," a form of physical resurrection, a rising out of the grave.

The presence of Lawrence—sometimes as a weighty hand—is reflected in the themes of several short stories that LeSueur completed during the 1920s and in the imagery of her poetry ("the agony of the bloody roses"). Lawrence's theories of sexual repression may have persuaded her that sex was, in the words of Elaine Hedges, "a central and transforming experience for women—and one that is achieved through the agency of the male." Although the first part of that insight hardly seems startling today, it was a radicalizing discovery for LeSueur during a time when the legs of a piano had to be decently covered. Often in her stories, innocent and essentially compliant young women acquire "some essential but previously unavailable knowledge of themselves through their first sexual experience" (Hedges 1982 7), much as Lawrence's women characters are initiated into enlightenment through the lineaments of physical gratification.

An important theme at the heart of Lawrence's work is the myth of Persephone—that is, the presence of dark demonic energies in nature that have the power to regenerate us. In one of his early novellas, "The Ladybird," this myth of Persephone is central: Count Psanek reveals himself to be a "lord of the underworld" disguised as a Czech prisoner of war, who has come to claim the sexually slumbering Lady Cynthia as his bride. Bathed by sensual presence and perhaps physically gratified by him, she has the possibility of renewing herself, like Persephone.

The Persephone motif surfaces also in Lawrence's poetry. Holly Laird traces this motif as it is modified to fit new crises arising in the writer's life (1988, 122–23). In an early unpublished poem called "Letter from Town: The Almond Tree" (not the same poem of the same title in *The Complete Poems*, vol. 1), the poet is urging a young woman to celebrate spring with him, to be his springtime Persephone before she misses her chance to identify with the life-giving forces of resurrection: "you said you would be my Persephone—you would not / Persephone has passed through the town, fastening her girdle knot."[1]

In "Autumn Sunshine" (*The Complete Poems* 177), Persephone is no longer equated with the reluctant maiden pursued by the callow poet. With the passage of time, she has unveiled another aspect of her persona to the poet, and he discovers that the death of his mother has a new meaning when associated with the "hell-queen" from whose "pale cups of mould" all must drink. Having drunk, the mother figure herself becomes transformed into the newly crowned queen of the underworld. Here Lawrence is deploying the myth of Persephone to mitigate the hard unacceptable fact of his mother's death. Thus we see Lawrence, toward the end of his life, interpreting the Persephone story more broadly as a personal metaphor standing for the resurrection into an after-life. Through acceptance of and association with the self-renewing Persephone, he symbolically rescues his mother, and possibly himself, from the Nothingness of death.[2]

Although it is unlikely that LeSueur knew Lawrence's unpublished poems, she did know his early published poetry as well as "The Ladybird." In her early work, she alludes repeatedly to the Persephone myth, as if drawn to the same shaping source for her ideas. Her female protagonists move dazedly in the grip of urgent and potentially transforming forces at the very core of being, forces that they cannot easily identify—what Lawrence refers to in *Studies in Classic American Literature* as "the dark potency of blood-acts . . . which obliterate the mind and the spiritual consciousness, plunge them into a suffocating flood of darkness" (1961, 85). While Lawrence imbues the Persephone myth with a shadowy otherworldliness, LeSueur treats it as if it represents a potent living energy. In her work, Persephone should be understood as symbolic of the latent transforming powers of a woman's fertility which links her to the earth.

LeSueur's first exploration of that myth occurs in the story called "Persephone," about three itinerant people: a woman named Freda, her daughter, and the narrator, a bearded man named March (since March in "The Fox" is described as "the man about the place," a faint tribute to Lawrence may be intended here) who has apparently abducted Freda from her husband Franz. In the following two passages of charged biblical idiom and rapturous rhythms from *Ripening* (1982, 80), LeSueur evokes the "blind ecstasy over the earth" they once felt:

> Freda and her husband seemed intimate with the fields, and the half-mystical rites of panting and reaping . . . The very lay of the land with its dark rich color was strange as was the magic they had with the earth and with natural things.

Then again in this passage:

> So that it came about that the country people as they dreamed over their work in the spring and autumn, were half consciously touched by the mystery of their tasks—a mystery between their own action and the secret of what they acted upon, by virtue of which alliance everything they did prospered and yielded in the field, the vine, the flesh.

Here is a parallel passage from chapter 1 of *The Rainbow*, where Lawrence is describing "dark potency" of the Brangwens' Marsh Farm:

They knew the intercourse between heaven and earth, sunshine drawn into the breast and bowels ... Their life and interrelations were such; feeling the pulse and body of soil, that opened to their furrow for grain, and became smooth and supple after their plowing. (2)

LeSueur took from Lawrence what she needed and adapted it to her own intent—to show that women related to the land no less passionately than Lawrence's menfolk. She upholds the romantic belief that the act of connecting vitally to mothering earth must remain a significant experience for all humanity, an ongoing experience of renewal rooted deep in human need. On another scale, she is writing about people who have become rootless and who must forge new connections to the nurturing earth. They can do so only by relating to the earth as if it were a living, pulsating force. Of those who do, LeSueur writes: "Their life is one with the life of the sky, the earth, the beast of the field, and its vegetation." She assumes as Lawrence did that these atavistic feelings and beliefs are more authentic and worthwhile than the commonly held values of contemporary society. Freda and Franz are "surcharged with living nature, its rhythms of fertility, of harvest, of accumulation and inertia" (Kinkead-Weekes 1986, 23). LeSueur wants her readers to perceive, through concrete and rhythmic language, what Lawrence urged us to recognize: that a vital unity exists in life, a togetherness of man and woman with the whole of earthly nature. This view of the world may have been re-enforced in LeSueur's mind, as it may have been in Lawrence's, by the study of the religious beliefs of Native Americans (a subject that deserves extended attention).

LeSueur gives the theme of communion with the earth the dimensions of a personal myth. In "The Wind," the young protagonist is terrified by her first sight of a storm that blows up with a "tangy smell of the sea and smell of spring coming from the earth." Her terror is transformed mysteriously into a kind of ecstasy and she is excited to a sexual consummation that originates not from her husband but from the lightning that "pierced her body" and "the freshening wind" that blows over and through her. (While writing "Wind," LeSueur may have remembered Lawrence's poem, "The Song of a Man Who Has Come Through," which opens: "Not I, but the wind that blows through me." The poem envisions the wind as a phallus, as "a wedge-blade inserted.") The young wife's initial ambivalance toward wedlock suggests that LeSueur probably sympathized with the

Brangwen sisters' attitude toward marriage as "the end of experience" (1961c, 1–3). In the opening section of the story, LeSueur compresses this skepticism into a telling image: "When he left [in the mornings], he kissed her as neatly as if he sealed her forever as his wife, in a little nutshell" (1982, 97). Later on, the "freshening wind" that "blows through them" in the "exciting windy darkness" cleanses the air and joins the man and wife together for the first time. This experience recalls those charged moments of highest passion and mystery that Lawrence described variously as The Crown, the Rose, or the Holy Ghost.

In LeSueur's short story, "Harvest," the farmer's wife has an overwhelming sexual obsession for her husband, but she embraces her pregnancy and identifies with the fertility of the fields, reminiscent of Anna Brangwen's concurrent attraction to Will and her sense of oneness with the earth in *The Rainbow*. The farmer himself, interested in "rational" and technological methods of cultivating the land, brings to mind Gerald Crich and his obsession with soul-killing efficiency in the mining of coal. In both Lawrence and LeSueur, it is the woman attuned to "instinct" who carries the flame of life.

LeSueur's "Annunciation" (1935) is generally regarded as her most successful story of this period. A fictionalization of her own experience, the story conveys the impressions and feelings of a starving pregnant woman waiting to deliver, alone and heavy-bellied, watching a pear tree. "I've never heard anything about how a woman feels who is going to have a child," the protagonist of the story muses, but Lawrence—LeSueur may have forgotten this—had devoted several pages in *The Rainbow* to Anna Bragwen's reactions to impending motherhood while carrying Ursula. Standing naked before a mirror, she exults in the flowering of her womanhood. LeSueur's narrator also stands naked regarding her reflected image, but she wonders how she should relate to its changing contour. In Anna, pregnancy creates a sense of security; in LeSueur's protagonist, a sense of anxiety. How will she care for the child when she can barely feed herself? LeSueur was one of the first American writers to break the puritanical restraints that discouraged a woman from depicting her own body or her relationship to it. In defying this taboo, she may have taken her cue from Lawrence's sometimes clumsy efforts to do so through the experience of his female protagonists.

Another story by Lawrence that seems to have affected LeSueur is that little masterpiece, "Sun." A dissatisfied American wife, Juliet, sheds her clothes, inhibitions, and intellect under the genial fructifying power of the Italian sun. She identifies wholly with nature, especially the cypress tree nearby, a "proud tongue of gloom" sent up by the phallic earth to communicate with her (in *Aaron's Rod*, the cypresses of Florence also communicate mystically). In LeSueur's "Annunciation," the narrator says to herself, "Lie in the sun with the child in your flesh shining like a jewel. Dream and sing, pagan, wise in your vitals." She, too, communicates with the trees as she sits in the pale sunshine. She thinks, "The tree has spoken to me with its many tongued leaves, speaking through the afternoon of how to round a fruit. And I listen through the slow hours. I listen to the whisperings of the pear tree, speaking to me, speaking to me." Her trees, like those celebrated by Lawrence in *Birds, Beasts and Flowers*, have an implausible life of their own that presumably unfolds to sympathetic eyes. Like Lawrence, LeSueur related to nature in a sensual way, seeing all living forms as sexual energy (in contrast, say, to Sartre's "stupid trees" in *Nausea*).

LeSueur's novel *The Girl* (1939), actually a collection of short stories woven together, takes up a situation similar to the opening scene of Lawrence's "The Fox" and dramatizes it in the context of midwestern poverty and violence. Two young unmarried girls in a sisterly relationship—the narrator, simply known as The Girl, and her friend Clara—work as waitresses in a place called The German Village. A virile young man, apparently a vagabond like Henry, unexpectedly comes into the narrator's life:

> Something kind of exploded in my eyes and I saw him . . . I got up and ran to the open door and down the stairs and I looked at his long face lean like a fox.

Just before the narrator falls asleep, she "could see Butch's serious fox head leaning to her." She dreams that he dies a violent death by gunshot. The identification of the young man with the fox, the death of the threatening animal by gunshot . . . both have parallels in Lawrence's novella. In "The Fox," March shifts her sexual loyalty from Banford to the reincarnated fox (Henry) while The Girl chooses the ideal of sisterhood over virile manhood by naming her baby after Clara.

In *Salute to Spring* (1940), a young school teacher starts out on an auto trip to San Francisco and enroute picks up a young man named Thom Beason, who fairly exudes sex appeal. His physical proximity hypnotizes her, almost exactly as Henry in "The Fox" casts a spell over March ("she could at last lapse into the odour of the fox . . . his brush was on fire"—Lawrence 1951, 125–26). Like March, the teacher literally doesn't know what hit her. She is overcome by

> the enormous glow of his presence, wonderful as if he had turned naked, roasted in the oven. You could smell his sunburnt flesh. And you could smell the earth turning on its spit under the mighty sun. (74)

When the sun falls on her body, "it was as if all her blood sprang warm out of her" (76). Nothing else happens during the journey—Thom gets off at his destination and the teacher continues her journey, troubled, like March at the end of "The Fox," by the promising potential of forbidden passion. LeSueur associates fiery imagery with the flesh and candidly describes blood desire, acknowledging its potency. These feelings swell the significance of this passage until sexuality seems to be empowered with suggestions of mystical cosmic importance, much as it is in Lawrence.

Related to this identification with nature, there is Lawrence's curiosity about human contact with the animal world and all other forms of life. In the novella "St. Mawr," Lawrence invokes the presence of a savage stallion to suggest sexual virility. LeSueur adapts this analogy to her own ends in "The Horses," where a young woman is physically attracted to a stallion and rides it with increased abandon. Although LeSueur is less explicit than Lawrence, her story is charged with feelings that recall the experience of Lou with St. Mawr—an inexplicable attraction which she can barely control.

During the seventies, a small collection of LeSueur's work was reprinted under the title of *Corn Village*. Then three collections of her stories and reportage along with her previously unpublished novel, *The Girl*, were brought out again, this time by West End Press. Another collection of her stories and articles from 1940 was re-issued under the title of *Salute to Spring*, and many articles and interviews with her have since appeared in a number of Left and feminist journals. In 1982, to celebrate the revival of interest in LeSueur's work, the Feminist Press published an anthology of her writing entitled *Ripening: Selected Works, 1927–1980*, edited by Elaine Hedges.[3] More recently, several of her children's stories have been reprinted to quiet acclaim, and with increasing frequency her work has been finding a place in general and feminist anthologies and school texts.

About this same time, while Erika Duncan, one of her early supporters, was expressing the fear that LeSueur was becoming a cult figure (1982, 25), she produced—or reproduced—a volume of verses called *Rites of Ancient Ripening*—a collection of assertive, drumming chants, "renderings" of Native American oral poetry into English. As Blanche Gelfant (1984, 75) sees it, this project radically opposed the modern "male" poetry that LeSueur traces back to T. S. Eliot. It was a quest for a "feminine" form of expression, inasmuch as LeSueur imputed to the Native Americans a timeless and perennial quality which she believed they shared with women. Gelfant seems to think that LeSueur was the first poet to adapt the Native American tradition of the chant for English readers, but it is possible that she found encouragement in *The Plumed Serpent*, where Lawrence created chants (the hymns of Quetzalcoatl) based on those of the Aztecs. Lawrence had attempted to compose, not "hymns for a revival of Methodism, but Indian hymns as a way of pre-Columbian salvation" (Clark 1964, 90).[4]

In 1987, The Holy Cow Press of Stevens Point, Wisconsin, launched a project called "The Meridel LeSueur Wilderness Book Series." It reprinted the five children's books that she had written during the 1940s and 1950s for Alfred Knopf. The first two books of this series suggest that she had not lost her feeling for Lawrence while she was composing them. *Little Brother of Wilderness: The Story of Johnny Appleseed* develops the Lawrencian theme of the individual seeking integration with the earth. The title character is portrayed as someone in complete harmony with nature, his life devoted to strengthening that unity. In the second book, *Sparrow Hawk*, the integration between individual and earth is stressed also, but as part of integration on other levels of life as well—between individuals, between societies, and in the function of the individual within society. *Sparrow Hawk* is the more readable and sophisticated of the two. In the words of one reviewer, "we can see LeSueur's powerful poetic writing style unleashed from the early restrictions put on vocabulary and phrasing in children's books" (Spaeth 1989 24). In *River Road*, even young Lincoln seems to have read Lawrence: "He knew that he was part of his country—of the paths, trees, man, woman, animal, great beasts and tiny deer. He knew a man who becomes part of his people, of animals, land, cannot be discouraged or destroyed."

There are other aspects of Lawrence that apparently drew LeSueur to his work. Born and brought up in the Midlands mining village of Eastwood, he was one of the few indisputably major British writers whose roots were working class. If he suspected that subscribing to any political ideology in a country as organized as England would be pointless (he never joined either the communist or socialist parties, as one might have expected him to), his gut sympathies remained with the poor miners and factory workers of his youth. In *Lady Chatterley's Lover*, which LeSueur read in a pirated or paperback edition during the late 1920s, Mellors's political radicalism is not very explicit until Connie says that Mellors should be pleased that the Tevershall miners have become "bolshevists" and Mellors replies, "Yes, I am." And for LeSueur, his letter to Connie must have struck a heroic note, condemning as it did the cash nexus of capitalism and warning about a future of death and destruction for the industrial masses. Reading *The First Lady Chatterley* when it was finally published in 1944 could only have reinforced LeSueur's positive feelings about the gamekeeper's creator. He pictures his hero Oliver Parkin as a determined Marxist willing to give up middle-class values and habits that he regards as damaging to the psyche. As secretary for the Communist League, he is disillusioned, as was LeSueur, with bourgeoise democracy and a suffocating class system trying to disguise itself as "individualism."[5]

Aaron's Rod also fired her imagination. Lawrence's protagonist expresses his disenchantment with the disintegrating mercantile civilization of Europe and his need to belong to a vital, living community of like spirits. Similarly fed up with what she saw as the backwash of exploitive capitalism, LeSueur declared in "The Fetish of Being Outside" that she could "no longer breathe in this maggoty individualism of a merchant society" (Nekola 1987 301). In its place she wanted to enter what she describes as the "dark chaotic passional world of another class, the proletariat, which is still perhaps unconscious of itself, like a great body sleeping, stirring, strange and outside the calculated expedient world of the bourgeoisie" (303).

If at times she seems to echo the English novelist, LeSueur's voice is nevertheless distinctively her own. Appropriating Lawrence's great cycle of birth, mating, procreation, and death, she turned toward pagan spirituality of ritual attuned to natural cycles. What is striking in her fiction is the way she metamorphosed his male assertiveness into her own female vision of the natural world. She transformed Lawrence's energetic prose into rhapsodic rhythms grounded in the midwestern earth, committed to challenging the world of political presumption whose formulations excluded the imperatives of that vision. Her voice enlivened the everyday existence of rural, working-class Americans who were the first to read her. Perhaps the most fitting tribute to her genius comes from Carl Sandburg: she was, he said, "an original artist beautifully reverent, with a high solemnity, gravely achieved affirmations of life, and an approach too infrequent among the realistic and naturalist schools of writers" (Duncan 1982, 26).

5
Anaïs Nin: A Spy in the House of Lawrence

Twenty years ago, in his foreword to the *Anaïs Nin Reader*, Philip Jason noticed something that appears to be quite obvious now, even though it received scant attention then or since: that "any Nin student [would] benefit from determining the direction in which Nin's reading of Lawrence headed her" (1973, 15). Few writers have left us more illuminating signposts to their development than Anaïs Nin. While yet a young woman intent on becoming a writer, she had already saturated herself in the work of modern literary giants. As writers who affected her thought, she names Jean Giraudoux, Pierre Jean Jouve, and Djuna Barnes of *Nightwood* (Nin 1976a, 366) and calls Dostoyevsky and Proust "her gods of the deep" (1969, 256). But the writer whom she valorizes as the one who launched her career is D. H. Lawrence.

Although his influence on Nin has been noticed[1] and deplored by some feminist critics), there has been little systematic study of it. To appreciate the relationship between her texts and his, we must recognize her approach to assimilating and then disgorging his novels and tracts. She entered into a kind of ongoing conversation with the dissident voices in Lawrence's work and converted them into points of departure for her own narrative journeys.

At a crucial period in her life, Lawrence's novels and poetry with their subtle and penetrating recognition of the "dark gods" within (which she took as a metaphor for an instinctual but enlightened unconsciousness) helped her to clarify and to define her awakening femininity. "My first passionate love for a writer," she told an interviewer, "was for D. H. Lawrence. Reading him was a discovery for me. His descriptions of emotions, sensations, instincts, ambivalences, all the obscure parts of experience, were an illumination of the path I wanted to follow" (1976, 36). Waverly Root in "The Femininity of D. H. Lawrence Emphasized by

Anaïs Nin. Photograph reproduced courtesy of Layle Silbert.

Woman Writer" lists several reasons that she felt more attracted to Lawrence than to the French novelists[2]: he was authentically feminine, fundamentally intuitive as women are alleged to be, and sensitive in a woman's way to the world about him—feeling, that is, before comprehending (cited in Snyder 1976, 37). Lawrence, she felt, had bequeathed to her a sense of womanhood that Lucy Irigaray describes in broad terms as multiple, decentered, and undefinable (Moi 1987, 147)—a legacy radically different from anything that her predecessors could give her.

In the year of Lawrence's death, Nin contributed a piece entitled "D. H. Lawrence Mystic of Sex" to *The Canadian Forum*, signed Melisendra ("he restated mysticism in modern terms"). By 1932, two years later, she had expanded that first short appreciation of Lawrence into a book which she hoped would create a bridge between the oppressive if "beautiful prison" of her antique house in the Paris suburbs and the rest of the world (Scholar 1944, 6). While immersed in this study of Lawrence, the twenty-eight-year-old Nin met Henry Miller, then drafting his own essay on Lawrence. Like Lawrence, both Miller and Nin envisioned themselves as trailblazers in a sexual revolution, and although she soon rejected Miller's male perspective, she converted Lawrence's commitment to sexual liberation to her own by writing fiction about the nature of eroticism and the relationship between identity and sexuality (Gilbert and Gubar 1985, 1686), a vast territory that would be explored and charted energetically by her successors.

Lawrence's novels raised issues that reverberated in Nin's imagination. For example: in *The Lost Girl*, the central figure, Alvina Houghton, marries an Italian itinerant actor who expects complete submission from her. Her willingness to undergo such submission suggests masochism and complicity in the subjugation. Is Alvina consenting of her own free will? Or is she driven to that consent by outside cultural forces? Just what is a woman's role in her own subjugation, if indeed it is subjugation? Nin was obsessed by these questions. The two novels that she produced before *The House of Incest*, her first published fiction, were "bad imitations of D. H. Lawrence" (Freeman 1972, 30) that dramatized a woman's struggle to be free. The others were better. On 20 January 1930, she notes in her diary that she has written several stories resembling those of Lawrence (1985, 277). About two months after his death, she confesses to her diary: "Finding him has only given me the courage of my own writing; it has made me feel less blind." On 23 January 1931, she exclaims,

"Lawrence, Lawrence. My God, it has meant more to me to explain him than to do my own creation. The more I read him the more I found in him" (1985, 379). After reading his *Nettles*, she wrote Lawrencian poems of her own which she called "Nettles."

There is little doubt that Lawrence's sensibility is present in the themes, tonality, and general outlook of her fiction as well, even though Henry Miller contends that her style is not contaminated by an ounce of "man-made culture." Indeed the imaginative power of Lawrence's writings created a refuge for her where she could escape the outside world not of her making. In her own words, he "create[d] a reality in which you could live" both as a woman and as a writer (Snyder 1976, 103). For a time completely captivated by this abstract reality, she had the good sense to see that imitation was not necessarily a sign of impotence but a necessary exercise in emulation which writers must work their way through rather than evade or deny.

Although Nin is not noted for the strength of her critical writing, she first gained attention when she published the first serious, sympathetic appraisal by an American—certainly by a woman—of Lawrence's work, entitled *D. H. Lawrence: An Unprofessional Study* (1932) at a time when his reputation was starting to decline. According to her own account, this book, written in sixteen days as a partial response to John Middleton Murry's attack of the previous year, was "really an act of love" (1975, 87). It was Lawrence, she confides, who had wakened her and for whom, out of gratitude, she had decided to write her first book. The result alienated her family and helped Edward Titus to go bankrupt. The book never got properly distributed to reviewers until Black Manikin Press took it over and it became one of the most sought-after books on their list (Ford 1975, 158).

As a text written by a feminist, it is perhaps unorthodox. Nin accepts Lawrence's phallic consciousness as "not only invigorating for men but also unthreatening, even liberating, to women" (Balbert 1989, 9). Not until Hilary Simpson's impressive *D. H. Lawrence and Feminism* (1982) would this view be reiterated by a feminist critic. Guided by a writer's perspective rather than that of a critic or scholar, her observations are more enlightening about her own aspirations than about Lawrence's. She uses Lawrence to talk about herself, much as Lawrence used the classic American writers as a springboard for his own views.

Rather than explicating Lawrence's work, Nin quotes phrases and passages from it without identifying them and uses them to express her own ideas about writing. This aspect of the book led

Kingsley Widmer, veteran Lawrence critic, to dismiss the study as "a dithyrambic little book" marked by "narcissistic obtuseness." The usually reliable Widmer misses the mark. In her appreciation of Lawrence's sympathetic portrayal of feminine sensuality, she shows herself to be a remarkably insightful observer, determined to reinterpret whatever she finds useful while shaping her own vision. Indeed, what started out to be a critical study ended up as an essentially creative experience which became the genesis of her later work—Nin herself assigns it this central position in her canon. In her groundbreaking *The Mirror and the Garden* (the title comes from a line in Nin's "Prologue" to *This Hunger*), Evelyn Hinz takes this text as an invaluable entry to the labyrinth of Nin's sensibility.

In the preface to her pornographic potboiler, *Delta of Venice* (1977, xiii), Nin describes the powerful appeal of Lawrence's language at its most sensual: "I had a feeling," she writes,

> that Pandora's box contained the mysteries of women's sensuality, so different from men's and for which men's language was inadequate. The language of sex had yet to be invented. The language of the senses was yet to be explored. D. H. Lawrence began to give instinct a language, he tried to escape the clinical, the scientific, which only captures what the body feels.

On 5 August 1930, she exults in her diary: "Lawrence's language, mine, through which understanding flows like a force, rushing us into intimacies, silent communications, electric currents of livingness." We owe Lawrence a "tremendous debt," she reiterates, for his patient, unending struggle "to find the language which was not the language of ideas, of our mind, of our concepts—but the language for feelings, instincts, emotions, and intuitions—the hardest language to gain" (1975, 82). She describes his writing as "interlinear"—a term intended to mean that he strives "to make conscious and articulate the silent subconscious communications between human beings" (1932, 6). His crowning achievement, she concludes, was fusing the reflective mode of the traditional novel with the concern for sensibility in the stream-of-consciousness novel, and presenting both simultaneously.

Nin's narrators often use a similar "interlinear" technique to tell their stories. As Hinz explains succinctly, "Nin's narrative voice is really a duet, the product of the tension between two modes of apprehension," the reflective and the sensuous (1971,

51–52). Hinz seems to be suggesting in this important observation—rightly, I believe—that Nin was experimenting with a technique that would resolve the "dissociation of sensibility" that T. S. Eliot pinpointed as the modern writer's inherited affliction.

For Lawrence "the flow of sensibility" of both men and women was drenched in sex (1976, 22). He was "the first [writer] to acknowledge that woman has a sexuality, a life of her own, and that lovemaking can originate with the woman." Yet, Nin notes approvingly in her preface to *Little Birds*, he never falls from eroticism into pornography, even in *Lady Chatterley*: "It is one thing to include eroticism in a novel or a story and quite another to focus one's whole attention on it. The first is life itself. It is, I might say, natural, sincere, as in the sensual pages of Zola or Lawrence" (1976, x). In *The Four-Chambered Heart*, the third volume of *Cities of the Interior*, Nin demonstrates this distinction through the relationship between the main character, Djuna, and Rango, a wandering Guatamalan musician with whom she falls in love. He recalls Lawrence's primitives. His body had not been "chiseled like a city man's" but "modeled in clay more massive, more formless, too, cruder in outline, closer in primitive sculpture, as if he had kept a little of the heavier contours of the Indian, of animals, of rocks, earth, and plants." A simple man, he is stupefied by civilization. His rejection of the urban environment and his uncontrolled jealousy eventually separate them. Here the erotic component of the novel is fused with the plot (the reflective level).

But in *Little Birds* and *The Delta of Venus*, instead of being guided by her insight about Lawrence and Zola, Nin focuses wholly on the sexual and succeeds in producing a "soft porn" which diminishes the reflective voice. The following passage from "Hilda and Rango" *(Little Birds)* sounds at times like an unintentional parody of *Lady Chatterley*, or *The Virgin and the Gypsy*. Rango, a gypsylike Mexican painter, is making love to Hilda (the name of Connie's sister):

> That night he took her, in the candlelight. He was like a demon crouching over her, his hair wild, charcoal-black eyes burning into hers, his strong penis pounding into her, into the woman whose submission he first demanded, submission to his desire, his hour. (108)

Although Nin could occasionally lapse into this kind of overenthusiastic evocation of Lawrence's most purple prose (brought on by her need to pay the rent), Lawrence's determination to treat sexual relations candidly, to abolish "dim half-lit truths" and "popular lies," and to integrate the contraries in our psyche appealed powerfully to her. She not only admired his integrity but also respected what she thought was his refusal to use sexual intercourse to socialize the female figures of his fiction and poetry into accepting inferior status. Rather than accept such a status (as his mistress), Gudrun leaves Gerald, Kate Leslie turns her back on the Mexican leader who seems devoted to her, and Hannelle will chuck Hepburn again in "The Captain's Doll" if he does not shape up. In her own work, Nin would reflect upon this phenomenon from a perspective not unlike Lawrence's, though hers, according to Hinz, is more "subtle and far-reaching."

Her theorizing in The Novel of the Future notwithstanding,[3] Nin by contrast to Lawrence does not have in any primary sense a philosophic or speculative cast of mind. But like him, she believes that "the absolute need which one has for some sort of satisfactory mental attitude towards oneself and things in general makes one try to abstract more definitive conclusions from one's experiences" (1932, 161). For both writers, experience meant not only meetings in the world of the everyday but referred also to encounters in a world of literature.

Hinz points out that such personal stock-taking arose from the modern artist's awareness that in our time science and psychology rather than religion and ethics provide the données upon which most people rely. Consequently, the old moral and aesthetic values no longer correspond directly to practical experience, while the cultural environment provides inadequate sanctions for either art or life. In such a milieu, says Dorothy Van Ghent in her study of the English novel, two things follow: the search for values becomes introspective; and second, the search for order becomes aesthetic; that is, a search for new ways of expression. "The artist, his artifact, and his world become inextricably related; the respective questions, who am I? what is art? what is life? are answered simultaneously" (Hinz 1971, 7). Nin's affinity with Lawrence in theme and tone becomes increasingly apparent as we watch her engage these issues and quarrel with most traditional practices and their supporting epistomologies.

Encouraged by Lawrence's intention in The Rainbow, Woman in Love, and The Lost Girl, Nin narrates most of her own fiction from a feminine point of view, dramatizing the conflicts that underlie a woman's struggle to liberate herself from unsought restraints of convention while she tries to discover her most profound reality. Harriet Zinnes (1963, 283) says, "Like Lawrence, Anaïs Nin is one of the few writers to understand modern women's striving" and like him "is particularly interested in today's neurotic woman" who has not yet accepted her own sensuality. This acceptance opens up into another kind of language.

As her characters awaken to that new sensual reality, Nin lets her style go forward to embrace and embody the "changing rainbow of our living relationships" (the phrase is Lawrence's, cited by Nin 1947, 20). In defining her aim, Nin paraphrases Lawrence's definition of poetry as "quivering momentaniety." She writes: "Life is so fluid that one can only hope to capture the living moment, to capture it alive and fresh . . . without destroying that movement." The fragile, almost ephemeral quality of her prose owes something to Lawrence's concept of poetic style.

Her characters take their cue from the words of Gudrun, the artist who feels threatened by the moral and social suffocation of ordinary life: "one must be free, above all, one must be free." Craving freedom, her protagonists set loose passions they cannot control. For Lawrence's women in love, the way is clear: for instance, Ursula and Gudrun and Alvina Houghton give up their old lives in England without much regret or conflict. For Nin's women, this decision is far more agonizing. The metamorphosis is painful, and overcoming the sonamabulistic state in which they are often immersed requires more insight and will than their previous experience has granted.

Often the freedom attained is provisional, a staging ground for something more enduring. In *Solar Barque* (which became part three of *The Seduction of the Minotaur*), Lillian Beye is a woman of unbounded, restless vitality and voracious but buttoned-up appetites whose marriage has failed. She makes futile attempts to find herself in affairs with other men. Finally, like Kate Leslie in *The Plumed Serpent*, she goes searching in Golconda, Mexico, "where the sun painted everything with gold" and the natives, like children, lived completely in the present. Amid these new surroundings, she feels a sense of freedom and renewal ("already she felt incarnated, in full possession of her own body"). It is a faltering movement toward releasing her true nature, an opening to a new state of being. Nin's Mexico is more benign than Lawrence's.

Through the words of one or another of her characters, Nin suggests that love, like the various stages of childhood and adolescence, consists of a series of states (Hinz 1971). Lovers should transit these states together. "Each year, just as a tree puts forth a new ring of growth, she should have been able to say, 'Alan [her husband], here is a new version of Sabina, add it to the rest, fuse them well, hold onto to them when you embrace her'" (Nin 1968, 108). In her critical study of Lawrence, she singles out his empathy for feminine sensuality and sensibility, and adds,

> In marriage, more than in any other relationship, the question of oscillation is crucial. Over a certain number of years, people undergo changes of many kinds, but because of a certain moment two individuals stood together on the same peak, we mistakenly believe that they always grow in the same direction." (59)

For Nin, as for Lawrence, growing together and growing apart belong to the same process. Lawrence was convinced that the pitfalls of marriage could be conquered by a monogamous relationship based on the admission of two integrities, each recognizing the ultimate independence of the other:

> Lawrence put it in a beautiful way, I think, in his metaphor of star equilibrium. He said the possibilities for relationships are like a five-pointed star, with the ideal relationship being one in which two individuals balance each other at all points. (1975, 62–63)

In "The Sealed Room" section of *The Children of the Albatross*, the second novel of *The Cities of the Interior*, this concept of the ideal relationship is reworked by Djuna, the main character, as she thinks to herself: "To dance each keeping to his own self . . . a deft dance of unpossession" (1959, 24). She looks for this kind of relationship in Paris with a series of young men, among them Lawrence, with his red-gold eyes and red-gold hair ("He moved propelled by sheer impulse and was never really still"). The prospect of achieving this state proves to be a powerful aphrodisiac for many of Nin's questing women. When it is attained, it has the potential to "become monogamous, in the sense that it is self-fulfilling" (1975, 63). The "sexually radical" Nin seems to lean toward a marriage-like heterosexual relationship as superior to any other. Here she is in accord with Lawrence, who declares in *Lady Chatterley* that Christianity's greatest contribution to Western civilization has been the invention of the monogamous institution of marriage.

It should be noted here that Lawrence's protagonists in such tales as "The Fox," "The Captain's Doll," and *Aaron's Rod* resist a monogamous relationship as confining, but the idea of individual responsibility, beginning with *The White Peacock*, developed in *The Rainbow* and *Women in Love*, and articulated clearly in *Lady Chatterley*, becomes urgent until it attains an apotheosis in the bonding ritual of the Christ figure with the priestess in *The Man Who Died*. Nin is more concerned with the cause of marital incompatibility and less with a "solution" to it as Lawrence was. But she also saw individual responsibility as the primary force in any sexual relationship, marital or otherwise.

Using dreamwork to enrich plot texture is an important device in both Lawrence and Nin. Lawrence was among the first English novelists to deploy dreams in the Freudian sense, to interpret the past rather than to predict the future. In the novella, "The Fox," March's dreams lead us to understanding her character, her sublimated desires, and her inarticulate unhappiness. Her recurrent dreams can be read as evidence of March's unconscious and inadmissable wish to be rid of Banford—after Henry has killed the fox, in her dream she places the fox skin on Banford's dead body to suggest the triumph of Henry's determination to kill her emotional attachment to the older woman. Lawrence is putting a psychological case history into fictional form, and the uncanny effect of the two passages is not explained away when their psychological meaning is explained (1969 Draper, 82). Henry's power over March is embodied in the language that describes and evokes the fox, making it essentially a mythic creation (the fox sings and his brush burns), generating the peculiarly symbolic sense of a reality beyond everyday experience. In *Aaron's Rod*, Aaron's search for himself is represented by a puzzling dream: he is steering a barque aimlessly on a strange vast watery underground. Aaron senses that it holds the key to his identity. These are but two instances.

As Hinz states in *The Mirror and the Garden*, the search for the self in Nin's fiction may be directed outward or inward: the outward search is conducted through the analysis of one's relationship with others; the inward takes the shape of a dream or reverie. "In "The Writer and the Symbols," Nin says that all her books "end with a return to the dream, not as an escape, but as a key to character. I describe many times, in various ways, the loss of the true self in relationships, and the return to the source where the genuine self lies imbedded." In *The Four-Chambered Heart* (1966, 172), Djuna identifies the dream as "heightened theatre" where the deepest desires are enacted. In the novella, "The Voice," Djuna, a thirty-year-old woman unfulfilled like Constance or March, is rescued from the spell of her crippled father, who functions in the story much as the wheelchair-bound Clifford Chatterley does in the novel. She is saved from benign enslavement by her growing grasp of the powerful myth which has heretofore forbidden her from recognizing its "illusory substance." In "The Sealed Room," Djuna imagines a youthful version of Lawrence as her lover.

For Nin, the dream-reverie can be either an escape from reality or "the seed for the miracles and the fulfillment." (These words recall the closing lines of *The Rainbow*, where Ursula emerges from her state of hallucination renewed.) In the dream, one comes into contact with the "real." In *The House of Incest* Nin writes: "The greatest of all joys is to be able to retrace one's lies, to return to the source and sleep one night a year washed of all superstructure." But persisting in the dream can be perilous: "We cannot stay at the source all the time." Nin's narrator retraces her steps to reality and writes her book which she hopes espouses fertility, fecundity, and creativity—values that correspond to Lawrence's insistence upon wholeness, organicism, and "livingness in life" (Franklin 1979, 11).

In *Under a Glass Bell*, such short stories as "Je Suis le Plus Malade des Surrealistes," "The Eye's Journey," and "Under a Glass Bell" warn us about what happens to those who remain in the "sonambulistic garden": all the characters in these stories who do not invoke their right to freedom are ultimately revealed to be insane or unnaturally cruel. The story "Hedja," most closely akin to Lawrence in method, is an ominous parable on this theme. Hedja escapes the constraints of her Oriental childhood and the "stilted windowless" life she leads with her lover Molnar. But Hedja never truly grows up and by the end of the story, "she is back in the garden of her childhood" (95). Unlike some of her contemporaries who were drawn to the discoveries of psychoanalysis, Nin deploys this material poetically rather than clinically.

Related to dreamwork, the theme of "The Sleeping Beauty" threads through a number of Lawrence's fictions, perhaps best exemplified in *Lady Chatterley*, "The Fox," and "The Ladybird." Constance lives in a kind of limbo, a dream-state from which she must be awakened into a life of responsibility by a virile intruder (in the sense that he is from another social class) who will call to her blood. The absence of the intruder in the first part of "The Fox" and of "Sun," or the failure of the woman to respond fully to his presence may lead to a sterile future, a form of emotional arrest that Lawrence portrays in "The Ladybird" and "The Fox," wherein Lady Cynthia and March each teeter on the edge of death-in-life. March seems destined to escape to a new life in Canada, and Constance may find meaning in motherhood and love, but for Lady Cynthia only the endless English nightmare lies ahead.

Nin also pays major attention to the sleeping beauty theme. In *The Diary: Vol. 7*, she claims that she herself was awakened sexually as a young woman by Lawrence's *Lady Chatterley*, which she read on a train to Switzerland. This revelation is developed into the central moment of a story called "Elena" (Nin 1977a, 85). Elena is going to Montreux:

> None of the men she had singled out as desireable companions for the trip boarded the train. So she opened the book she was carrying. It was *Lady Chatterley's Lover*. Afterwards Elena remembered nothing of this trip except a sensation of tremendous bodily warmth . . . and a feeling of great anger at the discovery of a secret which it seemed to her was criminally withheld from all people. She discovered first of all that she had never known the sensations described by Lawrence and second, that this was the nature of her hunger.[4]

As she emerges from the train at her destination, she thinks to herself: "It was the submerged woman of Lawrence's book that lay coiled within her, at last exposed, sensitized, prepared as if by a multitude of caresses for the arrival of someone." Elena's hunger is the hunger of all Nin's women. The title of one of her books, *This Hunger*, contains the theme of all her work. "Her fictional characters," says William Burford, are hungry for destruction and creation, "their turnings and directions" just as unpredictable as Lawrence's (1947, 10). They have in common a willingness bordering on compulsion to face the unknown. They are propelled by a kind of existential rage to seek new experience. Elena will experiment with bisexuality, just as Ursula does in *The Rainbow* and Birkin does in *Women in Love*.

Edmund Wilson (*The New Yorker* 1944, 56) was among the few critics to appreciate Nin's originality before her work became the vogue: "Though she owes something to Freud, as she does to Lawrence, she has worked out her own system of dynamics, and gives us a picture, quite different, from that of any other writer." Although Nin must be most valued for the uniqueness of her highly personal vision, there is no gainsaying how important Lawrence's spiritual presence was to her when she struck out on her own distinctive course while gradually discarding the dead weight of wornout traditions. Regarding the question of style, Anatole Broyard (*New York Times Book Review* 1987, 14) singles out Lawrence's influence on all novelists including Nin: "Just as Picasso fractured the picture frame, Lawrence fractured the narrative line. 'Women in Love' leaps from symbol to symbol—from that time the novel form was never the same."

Early in her career, she recognized the potential of Lawrence's technique and she, too, in her own way, fractured the narrative line—by both adopting and adapting techniques borrowed from her reading of French literature, especially the surrealists (Wilson 1944, 73). According to Oliver Evans, the author of the first book of Nin criticism, she espoused a new form of the novel, "a form which is closer to that of poetry than to the commercial item with which we have been made unhappily familiar." In the intuitive leap from symbol to symbol, she abandoned the linear narrative for a style that sought to convey the nature of a rich inner life.

As her confidence in her own creative powers developed, she gradually outgrew her mentor. She came to feel that the "priest of love" aspect of Lawrence was too puritanical (although he was violently antipuritanical), too confining, and too domineering to help her any further with her own anarchic voyage of discovery.[5] She needed to travel in her own direction. But her admiration and appreciation of Lawrence's insights never declined, as testified by her ongoing defense of him against feminist critics. One such instance of her continuing allegiance to his ideas occurs in "Eroticism in Women." Nin takes Kate Millett to task for her "unjust" treatment of Lawrence. "Whatever he asserted ideologically, she [Millett] was not subtle enough to see that in his work, which is where the true self is revealed, he was very concerned with the response of women," says Nin. She then quotes her "favorite passage" of prose, Lawrence's depiction of sexual intercourse in *Lady Chatterley,* and juxtaposes it against a similar passage from her own *A Spy in the House of Love,* so that we may observe the differences and similarities (1976b, 7). More than anyone else (1985, 294), Lawrence set loose her tongue and broke down her reticence of expression:

> Over and over again, in his description of women I find myself. In his treatment of language, in the poetic intensity of his prose, I find courage for my own writing. . . . In a way, too, by his own fervor and naturalness, he has uncovered, crystalized my love for Hugo [later her husband].

As an act of homage after she had more or less exhausted the inspirational wellsprings of Lawrence, Nin wrote a sympathetic evaluation of *The Complete Plays of D. H. Lawrence* in 1966 for *The New York Times Book Review*.[6] In 1972, following a lecture at Lewis and Clark University, she was asked whether she agreed with the accusation that Lawrence was chauvinistic and dogmatic about women.[7] She replied:

> No, I don't feel that way. I think we have to take from Lawrence the great contribution he made in trying to find the language for sensations and emotions and instincts. He tried to understand woman . . . Lawrence gave me a great deal as a woman. He was the one who said that women would have to state their own patterns, that they were being created by men. (1975, 99)

By the mid-1970s, after she had become an important speaker for women's rights, Nin encouraged her readers to achieve selfhood "by discovering and honoring the true nature of their wishes and dreams" (Franklin and Schneider 1979, 293), an ideal that she had inherited in part from Lawrence and in part from Dr. Otto Rank. In *A Woman Speaks* (3) she reiterated her version of Lawrence's message to the world: "to give you a center of gravity in your own soul, an axis in an unstable world, a core so that you will build a one-celled world with a creative will."[8] Among her final entries in the last volume of her diaries (1980, 338), Nin narrates a dream in which she shares a memorable moment with the writer who had never ceased to believe that it was possible for a woman to immerse herself in the destructive element and to survive the dangerous experience:

> I found my bed on the top of a great waterfall with D. H. Lawrence. We wonder whether to throw ourselves in or not. We do not jump. We look down and see Lady Chatterley swimming in the ocean. We watch terrified while she swims from one ocean to another.

Kay Boyle. Photograph reproduced courtesy of Special Collections at the Morris Library, Southern Illinois University of Carbondale.

6
Kay Boyle: Venus Agonistes

The reader who is familiar with the fiction of Kay Boyle might well ask what there could have been about the work of a prickly, consumptive son of an English collier that would have appealed to a young woman who had left her midwestern roots behind and who was determined to live the life of a bohemian. Boyle answered this question partially during an interview: like herself, "he had a great feeling for people."

She offered nothing more specific, but might have added that Lawrence was probably the first male English novelist of our time interested in perceiving the world as he imagined a woman must see it, in writing about women as though he himself were a woman. If Lawrence didn't always succeed in something authentic, nonetheless his exercise in empathy opened new vistas of the imagination for women who aspired to write serious fiction. Moreover, known as a notorious rebel, Lawrence also was an unrelenting advocate of personal freedom. Ignoring the conventions of English society, he eloped with the woman he loved and took up the life of exile in Austria before settling at Lake Garda in Italy. The pattern of Lawrence's career must have exerted a strong romantic appeal for a young writer discovering her power as a creative artist and a free spirit, as it did for another writer also born in Minnesota, Meridel LeSueur.

Boyle's first impressions of Lawrence's work were probably formulated while she was a young woman living in Paris during the twenties. In *Being Geniuses Together* (1968, 16), she says that her loving mother sent her a copy of Lawrence's *Studies in Classic American Literature*. Boyle remarks, "These essays, read and re-read, gave me a singular courage as they signalled to me a new and quite ruthless way of thought." The intensity, swiftness, and assertiveness of Lawrence's style apparently encouraged Boyle to cultivate similar tonalities that would lend her own prose its distinctive flavor.

Lawrence's unorthodox and provocative essays on American writers performed a second service for Boyle: they led her to the discovery of his fiction. Among the novels that she read, she liked *Women in Love* the most, but she admired *The Boy in the Bush* tremendously, too, for its warm and rich humanity (Tooker and Hofheins 1976, 30). She seems to have studied both *Sons and Lovers* and *The Lost Girl* with great attention before deciding to write. Moreover, Lawrence's love poetry fascinated her. The most important thing she learned from Lawrence was that poetry and fiction came from the same well, that in fact the poetic sensibility could heighten rhetoric with startling figures of speech, unexpected imagery, and complex symbolism, giving it a richness of texture often absent from realistic fiction.

That texture is woven into her second published novel, *Year Before Last* (1932).[1] This story centers on the romantic relationship between a writer named Martin Sheehan and a married woman named Hannah. Martin induces her to abandon her husband and to run off with him, gambling everything on love. Martin and Hannah enjoy a searingly passionate affair that sweeps everything before it. The couple travels restlessly from hotel to hotel in quest of a place where they might rest, work in peace, and find a cure for Martin's respiratory ailment. They move to the Riviera, within eyeshot of Vence (where Lawrence passed the final weeks of his life). An impoverished Italian poet (based on the figure of Emanuel Carnavali, to whom Boyle dedicated the book and whose autobiography she edited) writes letters to Martin bearing the enticing aroma of Lake Garda (where Lawrence and Frieda spent their first year together). Hannah tenderly nurses her afflicted lover, but in the climactic scene Martin suffers a bloody, possibly fatal hemorrhage. As in a typical Lawrence novel, the conclusion is left indeterminate.[2]

In her "Afterword" to the 1985 reissue, Doris Grumbach develops the connection between the tubercular protagonist and a young poet whom Boyle had loved before his untimely death of tuberculosis at the age of thirty-one, Ernest Walsh. (Hemingway, who didn't like Walsh, says in *A Moveable Feast*, 126–27, that Walsh made a living out of dying). But there is a strong possibility that Boyle drew on another real-life model for some of the details of Martin's life. It is likely, as Grumbach suggests, that she was indeed remembering Walsh, who had died young in 1926 when she began to write the novel, but it seems credible that Boyle's emotional reaction to the death of Lawrence, which occurred while Boyle was completing the novel, took over and provided its sustaining energy. As the novel unfolds, it follows rather loosely the parabola of Lawrence's career. Boyle apparently decided to weave her plot out of the cruel destinies of two writers for whom she cared deeply.

Boyle also may have drawn upon the Lawrence novella, "The Captain's Doll," for some of her material. She assigns her characters Lawrencian names. The main character in "The Captain's Doll," Hannelle, gives her name to Hannah; Alexander Hepburn's wife Evangeline Hepburn becomes Eve Raeburn, Martin's possessive aunt who also collects dolls (1932, 16) and Hannelle's friend, Martin, who has a minor role in Lawrence, lends his name to the major character in Boyle's work. Like Hepburn in "The Captain's Doll," Martin is a veteran of World War I whose postwar depression is cured through a passionate relationship.

Her third published novel, *Gentlemen, I Address You Privately* (1933), is about a self-defrocked priest named Munday who escapes from his abstract spiritual existence to a life of the senses among the provincials of Le Havre. He falls in love with Ayton, a sly, elusive, charming young English adventurer, himself a kind of D. H. Lawrence character viewed ironically. Although he resembles Ernest Walsh, Munday sounds like Lawrence of *The Escaped Cock* (which Boyle read in The Black Sun edition published by her friends the Crosbys in Paris). He combines biblical allusion with animal imagery as he reflects on his past: he had "backed into the Church as into a stable of refuge, backing, backing, a quivering shy stallion" (112). Now rejuvenated in the flesh, "he knew his own perfect manly power, like the burning power that enriched the Levites and gives their spirit even an untamed urgent strength" (14). Reminiscent of Lawrence's resurrected Christ, Munday feels "a wondrous, a mystic sense of his own self, as if in dream he recognized the somnolent and the waking being." Boyle appears to be endorsing Lawrence's message as valid for her own time.

A central episode in Boyle's novel seems to borrow from a famous scene in *Women in Love*, where Gerald Crich subdues the rabbit Bismark with brute force. Boyle turns this incident into the rabbit-skinning scene that leaves Munday, the executioner, disgusted by what he considers to be a violation of innocence: "the rabbit opened its mouth and screamed down the length of its body" (85). In this novel Boyle appears intent on rendering Lawrence's mythic fable into a naturalistic narrative, as though testing in a modern context the Lawrencian notion that one can be resurrected spiritually through the revival of the senses.

Lawrence frequently used the imagery of horses to suggest the idea of raw natural power dominated, caged, or broken by implacable human will (for "will," read "ideas") in such tales as "The Prussian Officer," "The Horse Dealer's Daughter," and "The Rocking Horse Winner" (the last a favorite of Boyle), as well as in *Women in Love*, where Gerald subjugates the Arab mare to his cruel spurs. In one of Boyle's best stories, "The White Horses of Vienna," the imagery of tamed horses plays a central role. Central to that little masterpiece about the early days of Austria's Nazi movement, the Lippizaners of the Spanish Riding School are described as those "still unbroken vestiges of beauty bending their knees." As the horses perform the image of a natural force mastered by a seemingly gentle trainer parallels the submission of the kindly doctor to the idea of Nazism.

Boyle had read Lawrence's "St. Mawr," a novella about an unbroken stallion. "One of the kings of creation," St. Mawr becomes the focus of interest after the marriage between the wealthy Lou Witt and Rico, "a drifting artist sort," falls apart. Rico is described as "more like a horse than a dog, a horse that might go nasty any moment," and at times, identified with a threatening aspect of St. Mawr. At other times, Rico and St. Mawr stand as rivals—and Rico wants to destroy the stallion. Perhaps Janice Hubbard Harris illuminates Lawrence's intention here when she observes that St. Mawr is "a richly ambivalent embodiment of alien life and consciousness [which] helps us to visualize a concept of life and vitality as mysterious and amoral, beyond rational comprehension or ethics ... In himself he is not the miraculous presence Lou should worship. But the miraculous presence is in him" (1984, 193–94).

A story from her first collection, *Wedding Day and Other Stories* (1930), "Episode in the Life of an Ancestor" carries an unmistakable echo of "St. Mawr." In Boyle's story, a grandmother recollects when as a young woman she defied her father's egotistical desire for her to be a submissive female. The conflict between the father and daughter is contrasted to the way she treats their horses—what Suzanne Clarke (in *Twentieth Century Literature* 1988, 325) characterizes as "mastery without egotism." Clearly the wildness of the horse represents some kind of primeval vigor and sexuality that recalls Lawrence's stallion, under the domination of the strong-willed Lou Witt. However, there is an important distinction. As Suzanne Clark notes, Boyle produces by contrast "a heroine who moves through mastery—of the horses, the schoolmaster [who woos her], even her father—to a sympathy which is not identification with a male voice" (326). Boyle makes a point of suggesting that the energy associated with the stallion is "an energy both shared and directed by the woman," while Lawrence is more ambiguous about who exerts control, the woman or the stallion.

In "Summer," from the same collection, Boyle seems to rework another Lawrence story, "The Fox," into a parable of her own. Two unnamed women are staying together in an unnamed hotel. The younger of the two, embittered by her single state, becomes curious about a shadowy young male guest when during the day she overhears "the soft bark of his laughter." One evening she imagines sounds of animal movement in his room: "It began to run in a frenzy in his room. It was a trapped fox barking in frenzy to get out of his room." The following morning when he approaches them, the two women reject his advances, though the younger seems ambivalent about him. While Boyle's story remains ambiguous, it can be read not only as a reversal of Lawrence's version of reality, but even as a mockery of it. The younger woman does not wish to see the older removed, nor when the young man confronts her is she irresistibly drawn to his fake, foxy, animal "magnetism."

Many of the pieces in her second collection, *The First Lover and Other Stories* (1933), satirize those whose overgrown intellects have smothered their capacities for emotion. In the title story, a man "with reverence for art" tells the narrator that she must learn to "quiet" her spontaneous angers and loves, her ferocity of feeling, and "twist it into perfect works of art." But the narrator does not wish to "twist it" or sublimate it, but wants to express the emotion in its most pristine form. For Boyle, the "ferocity" of emotion must remain unadulterated if life or art is to have vitality and vision, and while there is nothing specifically Lawrencian in this view, Lawrence is inevitably associated with it because he voiced it so consistently in a variety of ways, perhaps the most celebrated instance being the witty disquisition that Tommy Dukes delivers on "mental-lifers" and "ferocious" penis painting in chapter 4 of *Lady Chatterley's Lover*. Boyle seems to be reminding her readers that Lawrence's view holds as true for her milieu as it did for Lawrence's, that good art is never tame.

In *The First Lover*, the most skillful story is ironically entitled "The Rest Cure." Boyle had been informed that a well-known sculptor (probably Jo Davidson) had gone down to Vence to visit Lawrence in his last days in the hope of having him sit for a head. In the story, we are introduced to an invalid writer sitting on a terrace overlooking the Mediterranean Sea in the south of France. The ailing man, obsessed with the sun, breaks the heads off the geraniums that block the afternoon light and snaps irritatedly at a visitor standing before him—a publisher whose "solid grey head had served to cork the sunlight." After some bickering with the visitor, the writer closes his eyes and drifts back in time to the "black blank mines" of his English childhood and the "beautiful" year he spent in Cornwall during the war. Aside from the flashbacks to his youth, the writer's goading of the guest, and his expression of distaste for a live lobster his wife purchased for dinner, nothing much had occurred.

The story starts to move when the invalid demands that the lobster be released. Setting it on the rug across his lap, he studies the creature and decides that it resembles his father: "There was the same line of sparkling dewlike substance pearling the *langouste's* lip, the same weak disappointed lip, like the eagle's lip, and the bold, suspicious eye." He falls into a reverie which confuses the image of the beast with the image of the miner who would come home at night "with the coal dust showered across his shoulders like a deadly mantle and beer on his breath, swaying at the door as he fumbled for the latch." After another outburst against the visitor, he discovers that his hand has fallen against "the hard brittle armor of the *langouste's* hide" and he sees its eyes raised to his. "His fingers closed for comfort about the *langouste's* unwieldy paw. Father, he said in his heart, Father help me. Father, Father, he said. I don't want to die." The cantankerousness of the dying man is his only defense, as Sandra Spanier's interpretation makes clear, "a mask to hide his vulnerability from himself as well as from the visiting publisher who had come to exploit him in his helplessness." As the reader by now has guessed, Boyle based her story (as did Tennessee Williams his one-act play *I Rise in Flame, Cried the Phoenix*), on the reports of Lawrence's final hours, which, she says, "had deeply moved her." The wonderful thing about Boyle's story is that she tells it precisely as Lawrence might have told it had Lawrence been describing his own last days.

My Next Bride (1934) also is about expatriates framed against an ambiguous background. Essentially, it is a fictional treatment of the author's experiences in France during the twenties. Victoria John, a midwestern woman, drifts into a Parisian art colony of exiled Americans under the direction of a man named Sorrel (based on Raymond Duncan, in whose commune Boyle lived after 1928.) There she falls in love with Antony Lister, a wealthy, sensitive American expatriate (based on Harry Crosby).[3] But Antony is married to an American named Fontana (modeled on Boyle's good friend, Caresse Crosby).[4] Unlike the egocentric Sorrel, Antony loves other people and possesses an intense passion for the poetic vision of Lawrence (and Emily Dickinson). He believes that poetry has the power to keep the spirit alive and to transcend the differences that keep people apart. On the roadside walls leading to their country home, he and Fontana scrawl the poetry of Lawrence, which they love passionately. The most memorable theme of this novel is Victoria's deadly struggle for emancipation from the age that bears her name. In her quest for selfhood, Victoria, like the heroines of Lawrence's fiction, must pass through the purgatorial fires of imprisonment (like Alvina Houghton), of madness (like Ursula), and of mindless promiscuity (like Constance Chatterley). Paradoxically, she, too, emerges from the experience renewed.

Boyle's collection *The White Horses of Vienna and Other Stories* (1936) contains a cameo-piece entitled "Maiden, Maiden," in which the struggle for liberation ends in entrapment. It concerns an English doctor and his mistress who go to the Alps on a vacation. The woman, tired of her relationship with the doctor, is drawn instantly to a local guide with whom she starts an affair. She is on the verge of leaving the doctor for the guide, when he is killed in a climbing accident and his body interred in the ice. As Sandra Spanier notes (111), it is "reminiscent of the tragic Alpine episode in *Women in Love*," with the fate of Gerald and Loerke reversed. Gudrun comes to the Alps and finds a kind of liberation there ("Gudrun felt free in her contest with Gerald"); ironically, Willa loses hers. The existential freedom that the Brangwen sisters achieve turns sour in the mood of the thirties.

Life Being the Best and Other Stories, though published in 1988, was written during the 1930s and belongs psychologically with her work of that period. In these stories, Boyle appears to have been captivated by Lawrence's concept of "blood consciousness"—that blood exerts a kind of instinctive intelligence upon our behavior. "Peter Fox" is about a young Englishman hiking across the Alps. He meets an Englishwoman vacationing in the Tyrol with her children. Her effect on him is magical: "When he looked into her face, the look of it startled his blood" (87). He tells her that he came from Bolzano, "but his blood was reeling in his body" (89). In another story, "The Meeting of the Stones," a young woman is living on the Riviera with her paralyzed father, who had suffered a stroke when "the blood had whacked the base of his reason from under." He is a powerful force in Coppelia's life. "He could say no word, but in his blood there was ceaseless strong movement weaving" (70). That blood-force mysteriously dominates her until she falls into an infatuation with her English neighbor. In a Lawrencian mood, she is ready to have an affair with him ("she felt her heart gone hard and cruel with ardor laid over with an impervious veneer of wild desire"—73) until she discovers that he is homosexual. At the end, she feels betrayed rather than fulfilled by her blood-urge.

The effects of the will to power on the lives of human beings, especially on the relations between men and women, a dominant theme in Lawrence, is replayed in one of Boyle's most enigmatic works, *Death of a Man* (1936), a title that echoes Lawrence's "Death of a Porcupine." The novel centers on an affair between a pampered, neurotic American woman named Pendennis and an Austrian doctor named Prochaska, who fairly radiates animal sensuality. Although she knows that she is giving up her family and friends by doing so, Pendennis offers herself to the pro-Nazi doctor. Prochaska's reaction to this offering is described in language that recalls the idiom of Lawrence: "a keen and powerful tide of blissful torment [swept] through his blood (80) . . . Dr. Prochaska felt the blood swooning in him (95)." The language here, Hatlen says, suggests a loss of volition and self-awareness: "A loss of will, an ecstatic melting-away of the self, is the form which love takes for a willful, masterful person like Prochaska" (*Twentieth Century Literature* 1988, 356). Boyle here appears to have had in the back of her mind the confused feelings of the doctor who is unexpectedly confronted by a declaration of love in Lawrence's short story, "The Horse Dealer's Daughter."

It should be noted here that an important character in *Death of a Man* is Gerald, the twin brother of Pendennis, who establishes his power by taming a horse with a reputation for being skittish (*pace* the scene in *Women in Love* where Gerald tames his Arabian at the railroad crossing). Boyle reworks that scene again in chapter 33 of *Plagued by the Nightingale*, when the handsome young Luc dominates a filly "who was dancing drunkenly on her hoofs and cocking her wild head at the engine and the string of cars" at a railroad crossing (184). In Lawrence, that scene is an epiphany that takes place between two crypto-sadists, Gerald and Gudrun; in Boyle, it is an incident that reveals very little about the characters involved.

The title piece of *The Crazy Hunter: Three Short Novels* (1940) is a curious story about "complex characters in desperate need of connection" (Spanier 1986, 133). It achieves some of the same effects as Lawrence's novella, "St. Mawr," but goes beyond it in complexity of plot. A young woman named Nan from a horse-breeding family falls in love with a gelding which gradually becomes identified with her father, an artist like Rico. When the horse goes blind, Nan's mother wants it shot (in "St. Mawr," it is Rico who wants the animal shot). The father is determined to save the horse because in his eyes it represents the "the forces of good against the forces of destruction." The animal is more: "he's freak and he's love, he's got something to do with love as it works out against—against this empire-building and the suppression of the native." At the end, as in "St. Mawr," the fate of the horse (representing the blood passion of humans?) is left ambiguous. Some of the situations in "St. Mawr" are reversed and the symbolism is less conjectural in Boyle, but the presence of Lawrence is unmistakable. Like a true artist, Boyle adds dimensions to her Lawrencian tale that make it sophisticated and original.

When Boyle published the collection called *Thirty Stories* (dedicated to Caresse Crosby) in 1946, she included three of the four stories discussed above and appended an afterword that read, "She [Kay Boyle] wishes it stated, simply for the record, that she never at any time met D. H. Lawrence." She is probably referring to when both of them were in Paris at the same time. However, she is not disclaiming influence, When asked in 1976 by an interviewer, "Which writers have influenced you?" Boyle answered, "I would probably have to say different people each year, but I know D. H. Lawrence had a great influence on me because of his tremendous humanity. Lawrence had a great feeling about people." Asked how she felt about the women's liberation attitude toward him, she responded, "I don't agree with that at all. I think there are male chauvinists on the literary scene, and obviously Norman Mailer is one, but Lawrence was a true artist and a very complex man" (*Fiction!* 30).[5]

What is evident throughout her career as a writer and teacher is that Boyle embodied an unwavering courage and integrity, akin to the kind that characterized Lawrence's odyssey through life. Both wrote about the meaning of love in a world of changing, often conflicting values—the Old World of tradition and the New

World of change was the stage for Lawrence, America and Europe for Boyle. Just as Lawrence risked official censure by raising his voice against the insane slaughter in the trenches of World War I, Boyle spoke vehemently against the war in Viet Nam, for many young people on the West Coast, she became a symbol of resistance to unjust authority. Even more vehemently than Lawrence she rejected the myths about the nature of womanhood and shattered the middle-class image of women happily attuned to hearth and home. Spiritually Boyle the artist and activist stands much closer to Lawrence than to either Joyce or Conrad.[6] The following lines from one of her poems could have been written by or about Lawrence:

> Poets, minor or major, should
> arrange to remain slender,
> Cling to their skeletons, not batten
> On provender, not fatten the lean spirit
> In its isolated cell, its solitary chains . . .

7
Sylvia Plath: The Lost Girl

In the journal of her formative years, Sylvia Plath reveals how powerfully and irresistably she felt herself drawn to two English novelists utterly unalike in temperament and style, D. H. Lawrence and Virginia Woolf. During Plath's career as a poet, they were to be emblematic of the opposing forces, Eros and Thanatos, which struggled for dominance in her psyche.

Although Woolf apparently was one of her favorite authors, Plath has little to record about the older writer's influence upon her writing (Axelrod 1984, 66).[1] On the other hand, her journals, letters, poems, and fiction reveal how closely she identified with characters in the work of the English novelist and poet who had died only two years before she was born.[2] It may seem silly to talk about influences when dealing with a young poet of Plath's honesty and originality, but in tracing these influences we may be able to locate the impulses that helped Plath find her own distinctive voice (Newman 1970 213). The influence of Lawrence early in her career seems to have been positive insofar as it encouraged her to break away from the more conventional models of creativity available to her while she was still immersed in a rather conservative literary and cultural environment.[3]

· Tall, blond, athletic, clothes-conscious, brimming with vigor, and very American in appearance and attitude, at first glance this youthful daughter of a college professor would seem to have had little in common with the consumptive son of an English coal miner or his working-class roots. However, when she was introduced to his writing in high school by Wilbury Crockett, her English teacher for three years (Wagner-Martin 1989, 43), she found herself fascinated by Lawrence. As an undergraduate at Smith College, she studied both his poetry and prose intensely (by coincidence she had lived in Lawrence House). Did they know, she once asked her classmates at a bull session, that among the "monumental topics of interest" were sex and Lawrence's

Sylvia Plath. Photograph reproduced courtesy of the Lilly Library, Indiana University, Bloomington, Indiana.

poem "Tortoise Shout"? In her junior year, she discovered *Women in Love* with a certain tingle of recognition (79, 88). It remained her favorite Lawrence and it seems likely that she may have identified at first with Gudrun, the more sexually focused of the Brangwen sisters, then with Ursula, and apparently attempted to become something like a Lawrencian woman. In 1953, while living in New York, she quotes Lawrence to describe the people of that city: "dead brilliant galls on the tree of life" (Plath AS 1995, 120).

While studying at Cambridge University, Plath veered away from Virginia Woolf, her early favorite, and turned toward the work of Lawrence, who was opening up for her poetry the possibilities of fusing her own experience with archetypal myths that "explained" her experience. She read most of his other novels and memorized passages on moral theory in preparation for her exam, "only to be *forbidden* to speak of his novels and requested to analyze his life *development* from either his short stories or non-fiction and verse." She was so infuriated by this limitation that she "got back" at the examiners by writing on "The Man Who Died," under the question on "fable and moral" (Plath AS 1975, 315). Lawrence's radical version of the Christ story fascinated her. Her teacher and Lawrence scholar Dr. Dorothea Krook (who was "more than a miracle"—243) read sections from this "incredible fable" of sexual awakening in a way that stirred her to the core. In a journal entry (128), she records her visceral response to Krook's reading:

> [I] felt chilled, as in the last paragraph of "The Dead," as if an angel had hauled me by the hair in a shiver of gooseflesh: about the temple of Isis bereaved, Isis in search. Lawrence died in Vence, where I had my mystic vision with Sassoon [Richard Sassoon, a history major at Yale who became Plath's lover]; I was the woman who died, and I came in touch through Sassoon that spring [with] that flaming of life, that resolute fury of existence. All seemed shudderingly relevant.

And she adds: "I have lived much of this. It matters."[4] Perhaps nowhere in literature is the influence of one writer upon another admitted and described more unreservedly. By paradoxically imagining herself as both of the actors in *The Man Who Died*— as a woman/priestess who must withdraw from the phenomenal world and as the crucified Christ who is resurrected through the power of sexual love (Stevenson 1989 107)—she would fuse Lawrence's counterpuntal themes into some of her finest imagery and most fascinating flights of her imagination—schizophrenic imagination, we are now told by some critics. In her poetic visions, she became a high priestess destined to perish and be reborn only to perish again.

During her brief and apparently brilliant stint of teaching at Smith College (1957–58), she read the work of Lawrence again and again, banking his images and themes for future use. Her immersion in the imaginary lives of Lawrence's rebellious women may have contributed to the tension that surfaced between Plath and "her much-loved yet ultimately resented mother" (Stevenson 1989 107). Lawrence's "little book" on American literature gave her added (Freudian) insight into a subject which she had already mastered. Even though she assigned several of his novels for one of her classes, she had no wish to share him with her students. "I don't like talking about D. H. Lawrence and about critics' views of him," she wrote to her brother Warren in 1957. "I like reading him selfishly for an influence on my own life and my own writing" (Plath AS 1975, 330). She admired in particular the Lawrence novel in which "a black, father-haunted, sexy troglodyte strives to break through the encrustations of white, supercivilized consciousness, which he associated with his mother" (quoted in Stade 1973, 17)—presumably this is a description of George Saxton in *The White Peacock*. For Plath at an impressionable age, reading about the death of Lettie's father, "a tall, handsome, dark man with pale grey eyes," in chapter 4 no doubt must have brought back unnerving memories of her own loss, and George's aphorism that "marriage is more of a duel than a duet" probably intensified her infatuation with the cruel but verifiable insights that Lawrence put in the mouth of his character. But there is almost no suggestion at this time of the subterranean malaise which would lead her to follow the course of Virginia Woolf.

Lawrence's influence diminished as she matured—other writers like H. D., Katherine Mansfield, Rebecca West, Doris Lessing, Kay Boyle, Carson McCullers, Meridel LeSeuer, and Margaret Drabble also embraced him early only to shed his influence as their own distinctive voices and visions developed. (Loyal Lawrencian to the end, Anaïs Nin may be an exception.) However, Plath continued to accumulate a small library of his work (Axelrod 1984, 76) and at least one notation in her *Journals* (196) suggests just how emotionally entangled she was at this stage of her life with his attempt to depict a woman's sexual satisfaction and her equal need for sexual fulfillment which only prostitutes and kept women were supposed to enjoy in the nineteenth century by Victorian fiat:

> Today from coffee till teatime at six, I read in *Lady Chatterley's Lover*, drawn back again with the joy of a woman living with her own gamekeeper.

In the same rapturous vein she takes up his other work that moved her:

> And *Women in Love* and *Sons and Lovers*. Love, love: Why do I feel I would have known and loved Lawrence. How many women must feel this and be wrong! I opened *The Rainbow*, which I have never read, and was sucked into the concluding Ursula and Skrebensky episode and sank back, breath knocked out of me, as I read of their London hotel, their Paris trip, their riverside loving while Ursula studied at college... This is the stuff of my life—my life, different, but no less brilliant and splendid—and the flow of my story will take me beyond this in my way—arrogant? I feel mystically that if I read Woolf, read Lawrence (these two, why? their vision, so different, is like mine), I can be inched and kindled to a great work. (196)

Much later, while returning to America with Ted Hughes on the *Queen Elizabeth*, she became involved in a rather embarrassing episode with New York customs over Lawrence's then banned novel: a "sweating and suspicious" official made them open their luggage, and "pawing over Sylvia's D. H. Lawrence, he pulled out *Lady Chatterley's Lover* and waved it in her face"— Stevenson 111.)

Plath continued her avid reading of Lawrence's short fiction (Wagner-Martin 1987, 156) while writing "Johnny Panic and the Bible of Dreams," a prose fantasy about a dreamy, woman working in a mental hospital who is annointed and then submitted to a sacrificial rite supervised by knife-wielding "high priests" of medicine. The story ends with "the knife in her heart." In its broad outline, the story may be interpreted as a wierdly imaginative and domesticated version of Lawrence's fantasy, "The Woman Who Rode Away," wherein an unhappy American woman who cannot stand her life permits herself to be ritually sacrificed by the stone knives of Indian medicine men. In his story, Lawrence wanted the voluntary submission to blood sacrifice to carry a mystical, preconscious meaning beyond intellectual comprehension, perhaps a sort of weariness-to-death with failed Western civilization (though many readers, like Joyce

Carol Oates, think the woman rides away to an even more insidious form of imprisonment—Oates 1985, 56). In Plath the self-immolating ritual expresses an unconscious suicide fantasy, coupled with a searing insight: in her final moment, the victim recognizes the self-destructive submissiveness that women are conditioned to accept by the powerful patriarchal structures of our society. The ritual of the sacrifice, given a social dimension lacking in the Lawrence story, carried "Johnny Panic" beyond the condition of personal dissatisfaction.

Returning to the ritual imagery of the "The Woman Who Rode Away," a more divided Plath transformed Lawrence's chilling fantasy of self-immolation into a metaphorical acceptance of fleshly existence in the curiously divided poem, "Two Sisters of Persephone."[5] In contrast to the one sister who lives the arid life of the mind, the other sister "burns open to sun's blade / On that green altar / Freely become sun's bride." Clearly the surrender, "freely" made or not, is accompanied by pain (Lawrence's blood ceremony to please the sun ends on the same note: "As they [the sun's rays] grew ruddier, they penetrated farther"). Later, this erotic intimacy with the sun will prove perilous for Plath's speaker.

In 1960, When Plath signed a contract to publish *The Colossus and Other Poems*, her husband Ted Hughes (the British poet most obviously influenced by Lawrence) bought her the recently published two-volume set of Lawrence's *Collected Poems* because he knew how much she loved his poetry. (Wagner-Martin 1987, 170). Previously she had read and been touched by Lawrence's "Love on the Farm." In this strange poem, Lawrence speaks with the voice of a woman who likens sexual pursuit to a hunt. She is overpowered and pleasured by a presence which, "like a stoat ... sniffs with joy before he drinks the blood." Plath's poem called "Pursuit" seems to be about a woman pursued by a blood-thirsty creature ("The panther's tread is upon the stairs"), perhaps an aspect of herself ("To quench his thirst I squander blood"). Starting with Lawrence's image of a phallic hunting-out, this poem advances in complexity to an allegory of creative cannibalism, "the central dilemma of Sylvia's concept of herself," the artist living off the woman (Butscher 1976, 192).

Other poems of Lawrence spoke to her and soon she had annotated most of them heavily, especially "The Mess of Love" ("It's not love any more, it's just a mess"). Through reading Lawrence, Graves, and Jung closely, she discovered that the objects and events of her daily life were the subjects she wanted to write about most, no matter how prosaic, painful, or frustrating. Among those subjects was the world of flora and fauna not unlike Lawrence's. For instance, in "Medallion" she describes an encounter with one of nature's creatures. From its opening image of "the bronze snake lay in the sun" to its closing image of a flung brick (instead of Lawrence's flung stick), she more or less follows the parabola of Lawrence's great poem "Snake." She seems to long for communication with the powers of nature as a means of release from the confinements of ordinary mundane routine. Plath's poem has sexual implications that Lawrence's poem does not invite.

In preparation for a thesis on the novels of Lawrence, she was reading *The Rainbow* for the first time (*Journals* 1972, 196). About this time, she had completed a "long 35-page chapter" of a novel which was going nowhere (*Journals* 199), partly because it lacked what she so strongly felt and envied in *The Rainbow*— "the rich physical passion—fields of forces—and the real presence of leaves and earth and beasts and weathers, sap-rich." This "rich physical passion" is also absent from her only published novel, *The Bell Jar*, but through the medium of Esther Greenwood's reflections about men, marriage, and children,[6] Plath manages to suggest how deeply dissatisfied Esther is not only with herself and the prospect of a civilized future, but also with the overrated promise of physical love (Esther remarks disparagingly that a man's testicles look like a toad). In this winter of her discontent, Plath may have sympathized with Ursula Brangwen's antiphallic phase at the conclusion of *The Rainbow.*

Indeed, the energy and imagery of these final scenes of *The Rainbow* seem to infuse the poem "The Eye-Mote" with the "rich physical passion" missing in Plath's prose. Ill and exhausted near the end of the novel, Ursula survives an encounter with a herd of horses while crossing Willey Green in a rainstorm. These horses are not intended to be hallucination, reality, or symbol. They provide a means for Lawrence to develop Ursula's character, connecting her consciousness with her unconsciousness. She must face the powers underlying reality. The horses are part of her real world and part of her psyche—the inconceivable part of the unconscious mind that Lawrence describes in *Psychoanalysis and the Unconscious* as being knowable only by direct experience. Plath's poem may take its cue from Lawrence.

It begins, "Blameless as daylight I stood looking / At a field of horses, necks bent, manes blown, / Tails streaming against the green" and continues, "Then I was seeing / A melding of shapes in a hot rain: horse warped on the altering green" (the "green altar" of "Two Sisters" becomes "the altering green"). Here, too, the horses seem to be equated with an uninhibited force of nature, a form of free energy. The wild energy of the horses implies freedom and danger, just as the tame dray horses in Lawrence's "The Horse-Dealer's Daughter" suggest precisely the opposite. Ursula is frightened by this demonic power but knows she must break down the invisible fences that confine her life; in "The Eye-Mote" the speaker yearns to capture the unleashed physical power of the beasts before she too is "warped on the altering green." Like Lawrence, she ranges beyond what one critic calls "the mere physicality and discrete epiphanies of traditional imagism" (McClatchy 1989, 201).

Another poem, called "Elm," should also be read in light of the conclusion to *The Rainbow*, which had by now fully infiltrated her imagination. The speaker, an American poet living in England, pregnant and lonely, announces, "I know the bottom" [of despair]. She says that she is "inhabited by a cry," possessed by "bad dreams" because the love she has sought "has gone off, like a horse," the sound of his hoofbeats receding under the merciless moon whose "radiance scathes her." She asks, "Are those the faces of love, those pale irretrievables? / Is it for such I agitate my heart?" Love for her has become ephemeral, deceptive, and destructive. In the final chapters of *The Rainbow*, Ursula is confronted by "the high blast of moonlight" that begins her downward path to wisdom, through the state of delirium which makes her think that she too has "plumbed the bottom." The departing horses are linked to the moment when Ursula realizes that she must abandon her relationship with Anton, which is turning her into a ravening bird of prey. She yearns for something more satisfying than the pure physicality of their love. In "Elm," Plath too appears to be lamenting the loss of that very kind of love— or is it mere appetite?—even as she recognizes its power in *Wreath for a Bridal*—"This pair seeks single state from this dual battle."

The title poem of *Ariel* (1966), one of her great achievements, transmutes a ride on her favorite horse, Ariel, into an experience of dissolution on the road to suicide. The central imagery of this remarkable poem may have been inspired by the dominant figure of "St. Mawr," Lawrence's novella about a young woman who possesses and is possessed by a powerful, barely tamed stallion "looming like some god out of the darkness." Plath must have remembered lines from Lawrence: that is, "St. Mawr could go like the wind, but with the luxurious heavy ripple of life which, like nothing else on earth, seemed to carry one at once into another world." At the end of the novella, Lou Witt, surrounded by a "turquoise ridge of mountains," tells her mother that she is moved by her memory of St. Mawr "to keep herself for the spirit that is wild."

In "Ariel," Plath expresses the exhilaration of swift movement on horseback and suggests that it is a metaphor for shifting identity, for every kind of ecstatic movement and life-awareness. The horse races out of "stasis in darkness" toward the sun rising over the "blue pour of tor," then becomes transformed into a deity, "God's lioness," with whom the rider unites. (Lawrence's poem, "St. Mark," develops an image of a winged lion "of the spirit" who goes "ramping up through the air" in the service of sexuality.) Mane flying in the wind, "God's lioness" is transported into another world where she becomes, for an ecstatic moment, a reincarnation of a long-tressed naked rider, Lady Godiva, unpeeling (for what? The Lawrence-like image of foaming wheat suggests the onset of orgasm). But the moment does not last. In the final stanza, the rider changes identity again and now becomes one with "the arrow, the dew that flies / suicidal . . . Into the red / Eye, the cauldron of morning." The sun, which represented the possibility of life and resurrection in "Two Sisters," has become a boiling destructive force. Plath seems to be deliberately answering Lawrence's message of hope with a message of her own: whereas Lou Witt is mesmerized by St. Mawr's life force, Plath's rider permits Thanatos to take the reins.[7]

Plath rides the poem as she rides the horse, "away from the cruel particularites of phenomenal life towards a world of pure undifferentiated force" (Gray 1990, 263). Plath works her way "inside" her flying subject, becomes the subject itself as it were in an act of unreserved empathy, and pulls the reader into the poem after her so that the experience is felt without the wall that usually separates the reader from the subject. Lawrence may have showed her how to collapse the distance between the observer and the observed, especially in the tree and tortoise poems of *Birds, Beasts and Flowers*, where Lawrence seems to occupy the objects he is describing.

Although Lawrence rarely tried the deep surreal imagery that became the hallmark of Plath's late poetry, he always welcomed the shock created by the frank expression of honest feeling. As Alvarez points out in responding to Eliot's criticism that Lawrence only wrote sketches for poems, with nothing ever quite finished," the whole of Lawrence's power and originality as a poet depends on the way he keeps close to his feelings" (Alvarez 1959, 357). The span of the lines is not the talking voice, which often masks feelings: it is direct and without self-consciousness. Because the form is dependent on the content ("my rhythms fit my mood," he wrote to Edward Marsh in 1913), he rid himself of conventional structures (and thus anticipated the theories of Olson and Creeley, who would argue that form is a matter of morality).

This aspect of Lawrence worked like a stimulant on Plath. The journal entry already cited makes it amply clear what in his writing she sought to emulate: "the real physical passion—fields of force—and the real presence of leaves and earth and beasts and weathers, sap-rich." By the time she was writing the Ariel poems, she had learned to heed that inner voice, more volatile but less voluble than Lawrence's, that urged her to follow the path of her passions. That course led her to express candidly and openly not only the pleasures of the senses but also the private agonies of a woman who felt that she was being crucified by life (this quasi-confessional bent in her work emulates a similar strain in Lawrence; it must be remembered that the autobiographical vogue was in its infancy when Plath broke free from the restraints of traditional poetry). Her reading of Lawrence encouraged her to express what she felt, not what she thought she should feel. That her poetry should have been influenced by his fiction is not incredible: she was, in effect, responding to the innovative magic of what David Daiches describes as Lawrence's "episodic intensification," or the novel structured as a "series of brilliantly rendered scenes or moments with flat or over-rhetorical passages in between" (Daiches 1976, 475).

From this open stance, Plath developed flexible verse forms which permitted her to catch the flow of her feelings in all their immediacy. Like Lawrence, she presented them without formulae and without avoidance, in all their newness, disturbance, and ugliness. The "precision and concentration with which she handled language, the unemphatic range of vocabulary, her ear for subtle rhythm and her assurance in handling and subduing rhymes and half-rhymes" (Alvarez 1971, 12) further suggest that despite the echoes of Roethke and the advice of Anne Sexton, it was the tutelage of Lawrence that was most useful to the development of her sensibility. After assimilating and then discarding many of his attitudes and prejudices (including some which are seen today as antifeminist), she began to fill her poems, especially those written in Devon after 1961, with her unique imagery. Of Plath's poems written after she moved to Devon with Ted Hughes in 1961, Stevenson says (229): "She was closing in on her mind's light as she had not before, and her grasp of this unearthly illumination was by now masterly, her armory of poetic techniques impressive." It was from Lawrence that she derived two essential lessons: that passion rather than intellect was the energy that drove poetry; and that in order to tap into that source of energy, she had to merge with her demon. Once she liquidated the influence of other writers including Lawrence (a late notation in her journal cryptically signals the shedding: "Lawrence, except in *Women in Love*, is too bare"), she learned to speak in her own voice, a voice often agitated and abstruse but always single and distinctive.

Joyce Carol Oates has pointed out (1984, 135) that "when the epic promise of 'One's-self I sing' is mistaken as the singing of the separate self, and not the Universal self [which Lawrence always sought], the results can only be tragic." Why Plath chose to occupy a private universe of the self which isolated her from common human discourse will remain, in all likelihood, unknown. We know, from both her poetry and her journals, that she suffered from terrifying moments of despair and loneliness, which Virginia Woolf speaking of herself said made her feel like "a painted fly in a glass cage"(quoted in Butscher 1986, 186, who notes the resemblance of this image to a bell-jar).

One explanation of this crisis, Oates suggests (1984, 115), may be found in Lawrence, who wrote that when he heard people complain of being lonely, he knew what afflicted them: "they have lost the Cosmos . . . the sun in us, the moon in us" (1966, 47). This is close to how Ursula Brangwen feels at the end of *The Rainbow* when she breaks off her relationship with Anton. But Ursula rediscovers the sun and the moon in Birkin. Even if we agree with Oates that it is easier to agree with Lawrence than to understand fully what he means, we nonetheless recognize in Plath's writing an overwhelming sense of love found and lost, of resurrection followed by death, of swimming frantically in empty space stripped of belief. We know that her ability to cope with almost anything deserted her in her time of need. In those last desperate poems, the energy is overwhelming and her attachment to life-affirmation seems stronger than her attraction to self-destruction. Recent biographers, especially Hayman and Alexander, have grappled with the secret of her suicide, but no adequate answer can be expected until the Plath estate ceases to exact editorial compliance as the price of full cooperation.

Margaret Drabble. Photograph reproduced courtesy of Mark Gerson.

8
Margaret Drabble: Cassandra in the Kitchen

Describing the development of feminist criticism, Elaine Showalter theorizes that the fiction of Dorothy Richardson, Katherine Mansfield, and Virginia Woolf "created a deliberate female aesthetic, which transformed the feminine code of self-sacrifice into an annihilation of the narrative self." For these women "the female sensibility took on a sacred quality," and the exercise of it became "a holy, exhausting, and ultimately self-destructive rite" (1977, 33–34). In the end, says Showalter, strive as they did, these women were unable to unify the fragments of female experience through artistic vision" (35).

The challenge to unify this experience acted as a catalyst in the fiction of a young English writer of the following generation, Margaret Drabble. Reviewing *The Needle's Eye* on the front page of the *New York Times Book Review* (1972), Joyce Carol Oates praised the novel as an "extraordinary accomplishment" in which the English novelist had "taken upon herself the task, largely ignored today, of attempting the active, vital, energetic, mysterious re-creation of a set of values by which human beings can live." Since many other readers also believe that Drabble has succeeded where her predecessors had failed, it would hardly detract from her achievement (she has been translated into sixteen languages and is the subject of innumerable doctoral theses and critical studies)[1] to suggest that this "vital, energetic, mysterious" act of re-creating a value system must inevitably call up the figure of Lawrence, a writer who had committed himself to a similarly ambitious quest.

In Drabble's domestic dramas, her chief characters are forced to struggle with the iron demands of their inherited Puritan conscience. If on one hand the Puritan ethic created the belief in the sacredness of work (and hence the self-discipline necessary for art), on the other it enforced emotional and sexual inhibitions that took a toll in anger and even illness. Drabble feels that the moralistic conscience should and can be transcended by love (which sometimes seems to mean "charity"). The typical heroine of her novels, usually from a comfortable middle-class background like her own, charts a course toward love in a sometimes unexpectedly alien world. She is torn between her lively if restrained sexual instincts and the moral code of propriety that her parents had more or less have imposed upon her. Just as Lawrence (and of course Freud) sought to articulate and clarify the conditions of this perennial conflict for his generation, Drabble attempts to do the same for her own, especially as it afflicts the lives of women who think of themselves as independent and sophisticated, like writers and professionals.[2] In wrestling with their sexuality, they invoke Lawrence.

In her early fiction, Drabble seemed unable to resolve this crisis of duty versus pleasure. The apprentice novels, as Kenyon notes, are underpinned by expansive use of Biblical words: vice, sin, salvation, soul, suffering, sacrifice, martyrdom; this language lends symbolic weight to the recognition that there is no solution to the eternal tug-of-war between instinct and morality (1988, 91). However, Drabble herself believes that such contradictions are not in opposition so much as they are part of a whole and she offered this explanation of them to Diana Cooper-Clark: "Life is a constant shifting from one extreme to another. This is the dynamic movement of D. H. Lawrence; the fact that everything turns into its opposite or is both at once" (71).[3] Much of the sense of surprise that Drabble achieves in her fiction derives from her Lawrence-like ability to manipulate that dynamic flux.

While Drabble hardly subscribes to the primitivist Lawrence, neither is she a rationalist. In *A Writer's Britain*,[4] Drabble is aware of the human connection with the physical world:

> The child and the peasant see inanimate objects and natural forces as possessed of a life of their own. Wordsworth was able, like Freud in later days, to restore an essential contact with the primitive, to divine its workings and to restore an earlier vision. (161)

In this passage, useful for understanding what motivates her characters, Drabble is proposing a version of Lawrence's doctrine of hylozoism: the human condition is part of a natural and geological continuum, and biology can be the source of psychic health and moral authority. Scrutinizing the domestic life of the English bourgeoisie, she implies that modern people are losing sight of their essential connections with their biological and physical natures and that they must regain a sense of this bond in order to survive whole. As Mary Moran say, "[She] believes that occasional recognition of the primitive, biological part of our identity is an antidote to the modern disease of alienation and extreme self-consciousness" (49).

Her gradual movement toward this view (and her subsequent skepticism about the sufficiency of the occasional) may be traced by a careful study of her progress.

Her first novel, *A Summer Bird-Cage* (1962), concerns the love life of two English sisters. Although much of the last chapter is devoted to accounts of domestic catastrophies (screaming babies, dirty nappies, and so on) that befall new mothers, the dialogue between Sarah and Louise on marriage and its shortcomings recalls in its candid, cynical, and advanced views those expressed in the opening scene of *Women in Love*. The conflict in women's lives is summed up by Sarah in language suggestive of Lawrence: "To live on the level of the heart rather than the level of the slipping petticoat, this is what we spend our life on and this is what wears us out" (215). Because Drabble's women, with their culturally eroded libidos, are so ill at ease with their bodies, the narrator avoids any descriptions of sex (Beards 1977, 23).

Her next novel, *The Millstone* (1965), follows the career of Rosamund Stacey, the clever daughter of wealthy socialist parents, who despite her intelligence and independence, is deeply dissatisfied with her life. Rosamund confesses, "I was guilty of a crime, all right, but it was a brand new, twentieth-century crime, not the good old traditional one of lust and greed. My crime was my suspicion, my fear, my apprehensive terror of the very idea of sex" (20). That fear seems to persist to the very end, when she rejects her former lover George (and the father of her child), and decides to commit herself fully to the rewards and tribulations of motherhood. But her "crime," as she calls it, is a common English disease, familiar to the reader of Lawrence. In Lawrence's novella "The Fox," March also carries the burden of a puritanical conscience which has all but suppressed her sexual passion and which has led her to seek satisfaction in what Lawrence wants us to see as a sterile relationship with Banford. March may find release in Henry; Rosamund seems fated by her background to a life of abstinance, a prospect which doesn't seem to bother her too much.

In *The Garrick Year* (1965), Emma Lawrence is an aspiring writer and disappointed actress (like Drabble herself), who contrary to the suggestion of her maiden name, has always distrusted passion as well as nature. Impulsively, she marries David Evans, an actor, partly because she falls in love with him but chiefly because she "wanted this feeling with which he inspired" her—something akin to fear and terror. She rather dislikes the personal attributes that she is able to discover in him. As a basis for entering matrimony, her attitude seems bizarre, to say the least, until we remember March's feelings for Henry in "The Fox" and Gudrun's feelings—something between sexual fascination and loathing—toward Gerald Crich as she submits to his lovemaking. In several scenes Emma recognizes the force of nature but she has not yet acknowledged its power over herself. When Emma, like Gudrun, finally accepts the validity of her innermost instincts and confronts David with the truth about her feelings, she achieves a personal freedom of action.

Of all her novels, probably *The Waterfall* (1969) most fully reminds us of Lawrence by virtue of the close-up analysis that Drabble accords the erotic sensibility of her heroine, Jane Grey. This analysis continually hints at irrational depths seething below the very proper surface. In her unawakened passional life, in her innocent gaucherie and awkwardness, Jane Grey at first may remind us of Lawrence's emotionally arrested or timid women like Miriam in *Sons and Lovers*, March in "The Fox", and Yvette Saywell in *The Virgin and the Gypsy* who are strangers to the sensual life and who like Constance Chatterley are bored to death while unconsciously waiting to be awakened by passion (see the discussion of the Sleeping Beauty theme in the Anaïs Nin chapter). Drabble told an interviewer that while composing *The Waterfall* she too had "to face the pathological state of inactivity" (Meyer 1974, 23). In this state, Jane becomes enthralled by her cousin's husband, James. Behind his calm exterior, he is a sexually demonic figure who sweeps her off her feet. A freak automobile accident shatters their lives, leaving James a physical shell of his former self. The chain of events leading up to the crash is narrated with great sensitivity to the irrational passions that can, as Lawrence intuited, possess even the most seemingly domesticated of women.

Yet some readers have been troubled by the conclusion to *The Waterfall*, finding it oddly unsatisfactory and wimpy. They feel that Drabble does not succeed in clarifying the import of her heroine's tragic experience ("I had difficulty not slamming *The Waterfall* on the floor. I do not want women to be turn-her-face-to-the-wall Jane" (Sadler 1986, preface). Are we to assume that as Jane and James climb their way up to the celebrated waterfall of the River Air in the concluding scene, they are embracing a wildness contained in an ostensibly orderly movement? Are we expected to view this cascading waterfall as the "watery equivalent of a Laurentian 'baptism of fire in passion' [*Sons and Lovers* 318], an initiation into "adult sexuality and achieved selfhood" (Creighton "Reading Margaret Drabble," 114)? Or will Jane eventually face the fate that confronted Constance Chatterley before her release from Clifford, leaving the reader to infer that she is being punished for her adultery? By contrast, Ursula, at the end of *The Rainbow*, emerges from her encounter with Skrebensky having earned the knowledge of her own needs. She chooses to risk being alone and possibly lonely rather than to accept a cramped, conventional sexual allegiance—for her a death worse than fate. Jane, too, has left a relationship (with her estranged husband) that could never touch the deepest, most passional core of her being, as her relationship with James apparently does. The fireworks may be over, but Jane clearly loves him and is willing to sacrifice for that love.

In the eyes of other critics, Drabble's heroines more often than not submit to self-denying compromise (their decisions are usually mitigated by the presence of children). With James incapacitated and dependent upon social services, Jane unquestionably must return to reality. Does this imply that Jane must accept the priorities of a world bounded by dirty nappies, children's needs, and sheer inertia? I am inclined to agree with Hanny's view that *The Waterfall* centers on "the search for existential honesty and the language of self solely in terms of romance, rejecting the claims of children" (Hannay 1986, 11). The subject of this densely textured novel, as in Lawrence, is sexual passion and hardly anything more. But hovering over its final pages is the question of whether sexual love with its power of mental healing justifies the sacrifice of conventional morality by which one has lived. In the end, Jane is not convinced intellectually that the sacrifice is really "worth" the suffering. She only knows that love must be paid for in suffering (Meyer 1974, 24). That seems to be her final position. At the end, the faint whiff of martyrdom suggested by her name becomes stronger, curiously at odds with the symbolic implications of the flowing waterfall.[5] Drabble seems to be struggling with an old dilemma: how to domesticate the passions which in Lawrence smash all order.

In *The Needle's Eye* (1972), Rose Vassiliou has fallen in love with a barrister named Simon Camish. In his own inhibited way, Simon adores her, but she appears to be bent on another form of martyrdom: she decides to resume her marriage with Christopher, her domineering Greek husband whom she really despises as a social climber and wife abuser. She returns to him partly for the sake of her children (not for financial reasons, since Rose has inherited wealth) and in part because, perversely, she simply wants to. We're never told why, but it is reasonable to infer that a strong prompting factor is sex—if not fulfilling at least lively. Hannay, probing the text more thoroughly, suggests that Christopher Vassiliou, a Mediterranean counterpart of Lawrence's peppy Italians, "shared Rose's irrationality far more than Simon could" (1986, 64).

For some critics, Drabble fails to embody the concept of an independent woman who values her sexuality. Like so many of Drabble' heroines, Showalter alleges, Rose finds "a kind of peace with the acknowledgement of, and submission to, female limitation" when she returns to her husband (1977, 305). This decision, according to Showalter, is both anti-Lawrencian and ultimately suicidal, prompted by duty alone. But Drabble herself wants the ending to be interpreted as optimistic because Rose and Christopher are willing to make the best of an almost impossible situation (Cooper-Clark 1980, 70) instead of retreating from it. Rose discovers that leaving Christopher is a bad solution for her, a view that suggests to some readers that Drabble had not quite shed her puritan background.

For other readers, Drabble seems to be striving to portray a woman of independent mind who defies both tradition and feminist entreaty without rejecting her sexuality. How should an intelligent woman caught in a tumultuous marriage behave? It may illuminate the way Drabble works to note that in her review of the Lucas biography of Frieda Lawrence, she lauds Frieda as a woman who "went her own way according to her own laws, radiating warmth and well-being." She refused to let Lawrence dominate her (Drabble 1973, 79), and she refused to leave him. Drabble may have intended to create a Frieda-like figure in Rose Vassiliou,[6] valorizing the woman who played by her own code of conduct, not by the masculine rule of either/or.

In her study of Arnold Bennett (1974), Drabble lauds the Edwardian novelist, who, she contends, "was hustled into his grave by Virginia Woolf" for his realism (Drabble 1991, 36). She accuses Lawrence, in his criticism of Bennett, of being even more unfair, cloudy of judgment, rude, and full of petty spite. Comparing the heroine of Lawrence's *The Lost Girl*, Alvina Houghton, who flees from a drab, ruined world of the Midlands into the mountains of Abruzzi, to the two Midland sisters in Bennett's *The Old Wives' Tale*, Drabble writes: "Sophia endures and Anna endures, whereas Lawrence's heroine escapes" (1974, 253). Lawrence, of course, thought that tragedy ought to be a great kick at misery and hated the idea of self-sacrifice, with the suffering that usually accompanied it. Hence he despised what he took to be Bennett's resignation to "fate." But Drabble told Monica Mannheimer that she preferred to accept the great lesson implicit in Bennett's best novels: That is, "We are not free from our past, we are never free of the claims of others, and we ought to not wish to be" (Rose 1980, 41). Her poem about Lawrence in *The New York Review of Books* (1980) begins: "David Herbert Lawrence was born a perfect Oedipus," implying that he too was tied, if unconsciously, to the past despite his declarations of independence (she would return to the theme of responsibility in her novel of the eighties, *A Natural Curiosity*).

What constitutes "the claims of others" and how those claims are legitimatized, of course, is the issue in the opposing outlooks of Drabble and Lawrence. Drabble thinks that "running off to Italy with an Italian actor" is not likely to result in "sexual emancipation for a draper's daughter." (1974) Alvina, says Drabble, has exchanged the Midlands for a subjugation that many women would consider to be a form of indentured slavery. Unrealistically and typically Lawrence "would not accept what Bennett had to accept" (1974, 107).

There is a serious ambiguity implicit in Drabble's comments. Is she saying that it is irresponsible for a woman to escape a dead-end existence? Is there something admirable about a life of desperation suffered stoically? She seems to be torn in two directions. We are conditioned to expect a "yes" or "no" answer to these questions, but as Jane Campbell shrewdly points out, these questions do not require a resolution. A kind of indeterminacy is woven into her novelist's Weltanshauung. Her refusal to close with a proper Kermodean "sense of ending" suggests an awareness of life's complexities that cannot be conveyed by the conventional novelistic tactic of closure (Campbell 1983, 25–44). Behind her philosophy of composition, says Joanne Creighton (*Reading Margaret Drabble*, 105), lies a repudiation of the artist who imposes an imperishable form on her work. Drabble has termed this the strategy of "shapeless diversity." Her heroines, accepting flux and contingency as necessary if not a finale to the human condition, opt for a signature consistent with their unsettled time. In *The Middle Ground*, Drabble says of her heroine Kate, "Let us leave her there, in an attitude of indecision confronted by choice. Anything is possible, it is all undecided" (1980, 276–77). Lawrence deployed a similar strategy in much of his fiction—for instance, Ursula in *The Rainbow*, March in "The Fox", and Kate in *The Plumed Serpent* are also waiting for a sign at the end.

Heretofore, the Drabble heroines resisted sexuality except as a suffering passion (the ambivalent wanting, not wanting, may be a clue to their indecisiveness). More recently, she seems to be moving in another direction. Her heroines begin to enjoy a new freedom of movement and being pleasured by male lovers. For instance, in *The Radiant Way* (1987), Esther Breuer, an art historian, decides to leave her roots and to live for a while in Italy. Traveling by train to Florence (as Lawrence once did), she sees a woman lean out from an upper window and calls, "'Mario! Mario! Ho buttato gui la pasta! Mario!'," she knows, like Aaron Sisson in *Aaron's Rod* and perhaps Alvina in *The Lost Girl*, "that she was listening to the tongue of angels" (189). She apparently visits the Etruscan tombs during her stay (194) and will in the sequel decide to live in Bologna for as long as it suits her fancy. All this impulsive freedom would have seemed frivolous to an earlier Drabble heroine. It may be significant that her close friend Alix Bowen, an English teacher, has read Lawrence responsively, and that her husband, Brian, who works at the College of Adult Education and who emerges as one of the few agreeable males in the novel, "likes to teach D. H. Lawrence" (186).

A Natural Curiosity (1989) is a sequel to *The Radiant Way*. In an author's note, Drabble states that she had not intended to write a sequel but felt that the earlier novel was "in some way unfinished, that it asked questions it had not answered, and introduced people [like Shirley Harper] who were hardly allowed to speak." More complex than its predecessors, the novel follows the lives of some of the characters whom we meet in *The Radiant Way* while adding others, such as Robert Holland, the likeable language teacher and Paul Whitmore, the imprisoned young murderer who becomes Alix Bowen's charge.

Now a volunteer social worker, Alix discovers that she needs more information about Paul's background in order to understand his homicidal behavior. She decides to query his parents and drives through "that no-man's land which he thinks of as Lawrence landscape." (130). The choice of name [Morel/Whitmore] and the setting itself, hardly accidental, create a contrapuntal relationship to *Sons and Lovers*, as if Drabble were suggesting that a new, far more ominous reality has replaced Paul Morel's: had Paul grown up in a Midlands village of 1989, he, too, might have suffered abuse and may have turned toward violence as Paul Whitmore does, bereft as he is of contact with a world more generous than his own. Later, Drabble steps outside the narrative and stamps her authorial voice on it, much as the pedagogue in Lawrence was prone to do.

Apparently Drabble wanted this novel to continue her discourse about a crucial issue that she raises in her Arnold Bennett essay on the subject of "escape" from responsibility:

> The contrasting fates of those two sisters in Arnold Bennett's *Old Wives' Tale* has long exercised me ... Frank Harris complained that Bennett had given Sophia a muck-rake instead of a soul. She had run off to Paris but had remained a housekeeper at heart.

Sophia, Drabble says, had "wasted her mad escape" and had returned home to the Five Towns, "a failed experiment." She continues:

> D. H. Lawrence had disliked Bennett's impassive narration and wrote his own riposte in the form of *The Lost Girl*, a novel about a provincial draper's daughter who runs off to Italy with a travelling Italian entertainer and discovers sex, intensity, passion, landscape, and what you will, in the freedom of the Apennines (252).

Lying in her bath while speculating about her future (*A Natural Curiosity*), Shirley Harper may be preparing to follow the course of Bennett's Sophia rather than that of Lawrence's Alvina Houghton. She appears to be resigning herself "to the reality of the suburban world." Even if this means that she is choosing a form of "non-existence," what other real choice, Drabble asks the reader, does poor Shirley have, given the uncertainty of her finances, her muddles over her dead husband's defunct business, and the mortgaged house? Life with Robert Holland in Paris has possibilities, but "like the Ciccio of D. H. Lawrence's [*The Lost Girl*]," the footloose, probably philandering Robert "is not a very likely prospect either" (253). Whereas in her study of Bennett, Drabble seemed to think that his Sophia had realistically assessed her options and had wisely chosen to spend her old age in the familiar surroundings of the Midlands, the passage of fifteen years seems to have planted doubts in Drabble's mind about that decision. Drabble jokes about Alvina's flight to Italy, yet clearly it is a first step in Alvina's self-emancipation. Like good Italian wine, that choice appears to have improved with time.

Lawrence may have occasionally regretted his determination to live his life abroad, but the closing pages of *Lady Chatterley's Lover* confirm the fear he had expressed much earlier in *Twilight in Italy*: that industrial societies like his England were slowly reducing our once-passional life to a deadly set of automated responses. When Alix Bowen (who comes the closest to being Drabble's spokeswoman) describes Margaret Thatcher's England as "not a bad country . . . just a mean, cold, ugly, divided, tired, clapped-out post-imperial post-industrial slag-heap covered in polystyrene hamburger cartons" (308), she seems to share Lawrence's impatience with the direction that English industrial capitalism has taken in modern times. In the third and final volume of her trilogy, *The Gates of Ivory* (1992) (in which Rose Vassiliou's son Konstantin plays a major role as a war photographer), Drabble's authorial intervention is a postmodern link with the tradition of George Eliot and D. H. Lawrence. But the large Lawrencian themes—the discontents of modern love, the forebodings of marital crisis, and the conviction that through "tenderness" the barriers to an enduring relationship may be overcome—seem to have lost interest for Drabble.

Recently Drabble has wondered aloud whether the novel is the right form for what she is attempting to do and she has written, "My novels are half way between fiction and sociology." The novelist Margaret Foster is inclined to agree with her, describing *The Middle Ground* (1980) not as a novel but a sociological tract. It does appear that Drabble has tipped the balance toward ideas and partisan arguments. The Thatcherian world which her characters inhabit presses on them and depresses them. They are afflicted by the spectres of a collapsing welfare state, of middle-age, and now of the possibility of AIDS. In her last three novels, rather than creating plausible people who are shaken and sundered by their passions and complicated inner mechanisms, Drabble has given us characters who behave more like dolls manipulated by a puppet-master. The Lawrence-like inconsistency and unpredictability of behavior that made her characters appear so real seems less visible in the trilogy. Unlike Lawrence, who never lost his faith in the necessary primacy of personal freedom, Drabble apparently wants us to believe that the social milieu has severely restricted the options open to her generation.[7]

9
Joyce Carol Oates: The Playing Fields of the Id

In novelist John Gardner's opinion, Joyce Carol Oates is "one of the great writers of our time" (quoted in Bloom 1987, 99). Whether or not one agrees with that judgment, her shattering vision of America "as a delusive wonderland of colliding forces, where love as often as hate leads to violence" (Clemons 1972, 72), has made her one of the most provocative figures of contemporary literature. The body of her work unfolds the raw emotional dramas underlying everyday life of what she calls "the exploited, the underclass of imperialist America" (1991a, 106). As an epigraph, these words of another chronicler of the passions might do: "Modern, unissued, uncanny America, / Your nascent demon people, / Lurking among the deeps of your industrial thicket / Allure me till I am beside myself."[1]

When asked to identify the specific writers who have been influential in the shaping of her vision, she has generally brushed aside such questions with a standard response: "I've been influenced many ways by nearly everyone I've read, and I've read nearly everyone." She reiterated this position to critic Walter Clemons (1972, 73): "My debt to other writers is very obvious. I couldn't exist without them."[2] However, she is less evasive in her essay discussing the craft of the novel (*New Heaven, New Earth* 37)[3] where she makes it clear that a writer to whom she has owed the most is D. H. Lawrence. Later, answering a query about the psychological influences on her work, she told an interviewer that Lawrence had been more useful to her than Freud (Phillips 1978, 221). As late as 1988 she was willing to say that in his poetry no less than in his prose, Lawrence remains one of "the voices of strangers closer to us than the voices of friends, more intimate, in some instance than our own" (1988a, 63), even though in some respects he has become like Freud a pre-atomic age man, as remote from her as the anony-

Joyce Carol Oates. Photograph reproduced courtesy of Layle Silbert.

mous cave artists of Altamira and Lascaux. She preferred not to disclose the specific ways in which she felt indebted to Lawrence, leaving it to her readers and critics to discern these connections.

She began to take Lawrence's novels seriously when she first realized how effectively and persuasively he had been able to describe the emotions of women as well those of men (Kazin 1971, 79).[4] Through his unique understanding of their psychology (Milozzo 198, 8),[5] he had successfully met the most difficult challenge facing a writer: to depict, with insight and sympathy, and inner lives of his characters, especially those very "demon people lurking among the deeps."[6] He had dismissed "the old stable ego of the character," the "moral scheme" of Tolstoy and Dostoyevsky as "dull, old, dead" (Lawrence 1982, 183) and in its place set out to discover not so much what a woman presumably *feels* according to the human conception, but what she *is* in her "allotropic state."[7]

In her study of Lawrence's poetry, *The Hostile Sun*, Oates clarifies the nature of her alliance with Lawrence—and what he may have meant by the term "allotropic." Lawrence, she observes, "strikes us as very contemporary—moody and unpredictable and unreliable, a brilliant performer when he cares to be, but quite maliciously willing to inform us of the dead spaces, the blanks in his imagination." He seems to be "writing, always writing, out of the abrupt, ungovernable impulses of his soul, which he refuses to shape into an art as perfected as Yeats's." When in this same passage Oates attributes to Lawrence a fascination with "the protean nature of reality and the various possibilities of the ego" (1973, 10–11), she seems to be identifying her own commitment to the concept of the allotropic ego.

Some five years later, G. F. Waller, following Oates's cue, asserted that "[her] fiction can be tellingly approached through a Lawrentian perspective" (*Dreaming America*, 163). But it was left for Mary Grant and Joanne Creighton to comment more fully on the nature of that perspective. The disorientating, frightening, sometimes ennobling, sometimes debasing power of love and sex are produced, Creighton contends, by the explosive forces of "blood bondage" (instinctive drives) rather than by social injustice, and it is these forces which flow through the center of Oates's fiction—as they do through Lawrence's. Grant holds that Oates's affinity with Lawrence was not so much with his advocacy of phallicism and blood-knowledge [in fact, this aspect of Lawrence made her uncomfortable] as it was with his "perpetual fights against the dehumanization and loss of self brought on with the encroaching industrial society, the Lawrence of Blutbruderschaft and of community" (Grant 1978, 13). Oates herself has written, "We seem to have inherited . . . the assumption that the grounds for discontent, anger, rage, despair—'unhappiness' in general—reside within the sufferer rather than outside of him" (1981). Like Lawrence, she felt that the idea of "sin" obfuscated the hard realities.

Her first novel, *With Shuddering Fall* (1964), seems to validate Creighton's interpretation. It takes up the struggle for self-discovery and self-definition that so absorbed Lawrence's characters during his middle period, focusing on "the numinous aura of sexuality, on how sexuality contributes to and so often mocks" attempts to order life (*Dreaming America* 1979, 17). It is set in Eden County, though its central characters, Shar and Karen, leave this world of their childhood for the transient deeps of the racetrack circuit. After the two become lovers, they engage in a typically Lawrencian love-and-death struggle for mastery and control, a battle which Karen wins because her nullity gives her greater strength than Shar's passion. Before meeting Karen, Shar had lived with a machine-like precision of control: the "oiled and clicking parts of his being . . . had run him for years, had initiated him to a pattern of reacting and understanding that was now being violated." He is confused and frightened by his lack of control in the "game" that Karen seems to be playing. Karen is in better command of their relationship because she "has not abandoned anything of herself and so was in a way protected" (Oates 1964, 116).

Thus we see that Shar is cut from the same cloth as the coldly efficient manager of the coal mines in *Women in Love*. Like Gerald, he courageously tries to open himself up to the loss of that controlling self that must supercede the birth of a new self. He undergoes a "baptism of fire in passion." Reminiscent of the way Gudrun abandons Gerald, Karen's soul contracts and refuses to participate in this potential communion. Although she can acknowledge the reality of Shar's passion, it only makes her despise him more completely. Frustrated by her withholding, Shar yearns to destroy her out of murderous spite. She tells him, "You make me sick," thereby pronouncing a death sentence on him. Shar's death releases him from his pain while Karen suffers a mental breakdown. Is Oates slyly suggesting that a similar fate would have befallen Gudrun had Lawrence continued for another chapter?

In passages that provide a contemporary parallel to the Brangwens' battles in *The Rainbow* and the demonic duel of wills between Gudrun and Gerald in *Women in Love*, Oates describes the infatuation and repulsion, the struggle for power, and the maneuvering for control that so often underlie sexual relationships. Reflecting Lawrence's view of the conflicted human psyche, Oates insists that the libidinal drive is dominant for all human beings, no matter how much they may seek to suppress it. Fulfillment comes only when man and woman throw aside reserve and open themselves to the elemental drives within. Until they are willing to risk loss of control, loss of the conscious self, they have little chance of liberating the authentic self within. In this novel as in her others, the characters act out their inchoate emotional impulses and thereby redefine themselves.

Are these often self-destructive characters merely everyday perverse/normal or are they pathological? No more pathological than the people in Lawrence's fiction, Oates asserts in *New Heaven, New Earth*, perhaps the best short analysis of his poetry available. Sympathetic to his detestation of psychoanalytic goals, she writes:

> The Aristotelean-Freudian-"classicist" model of psychological health—that emotions be purged, refined, made totally conscious and therefore discharged of their power—is certainly a dubious one ... Such a model assumes the malevolent nature of the "id"; from this is a simple step to the assumption that the "id" is the natural enemy of civilization ... Why must so much of human behavior be classified as "neurotic" when in fact it is simply natural ... given certain personalities and certain environments? (72)

In another place (*Woman Writer* 195), Oates writes: "Passion is weakness in the Christian romance, just as it is redemptive in the romances of D. H. Lawrence." Some readers would take this statement along with the passage quoted above as a clue to decoding the pattern of behavior in Oates's characters: if denial of passion is strength (195), passion itself is redemptive. But other readers may have justifiable difficulty in knowing how to take Oates' portrayal of compulsive sexual attraction and submission. In what sense is it "natural"? or redemptive? Is it the restrictive environment that makes it seem neurotic? Indeed, perhaps because her profusive writing sometimes smothers rather than evokes the intended emotional effect, her characters often seem to be mentally ill, stalled in their temperaments, incapable of moving to a level of behavior that would allow them the unpredictability we associate with life and fiction. Few writers, as Joanne Creighton says, have been "so obsessed with the pain and risk of love, the torture and unhappiness that are sometimes concommitant with sexual relationships." But in "Letter to Dale Boesky," Oates denies that her characters are "love-junkies," maintaining that they generally fall in love with people who unlock "a higher self" in them. Her characters, like Lawrence's, strain against the "too-close confines of a personality now outgrown, or a social 'role' too restrictive." Therefore, in her fiction, she claims, the troubled people are precisely those in whom the life-form itself is stirring. In *Wonderland*, Jesse contemplating union with Reva feels "as if the hot, hollow radiant core of his being, the elusive Jesse itself, were very close to his grasp."

Ellen Friedman identifies a Lawrencian undercurrent in *them*, another early novel (1969). She thinks that the failure of love to transcend the ego suggests that Oates shares Lawrence's conviction that "in sensual love, it is the two blood-systems, the man's and the woman's which sweep up into pure contact and almost fuse. Almost mingle. Not quite. There is always the finest imaginable wall between the two blood-waves but the blood itself must never break, or it means bleeding" (1980, 66). Oates shares Lawrence's belief ("This glowing unison is only a temporary thing, because the first law of life is that each organism is isolate in itself"—67) about the deathly aspects of romantic love in which the goal is oneness. The failure of fusion is another failure of the romantic promise, pointing to limitation, even the limitation of love that Lawrence describes. In attempting to find this fusion, Nadine courts death. She wants Jules to kill her and when he refuses to do so, she tries to destroy him. Nadine cannot accept the ambivalence created by the clash of conventional morality and her helpless love. Her attempts to make herself and her lover the emblem of a romantic abstraction ends in disaster (Friedman 1980, 83). In *Do With Me What You Will*, Elena and Jack are caught in a compulsive, agonizing relationship; yet each yearns, like Oliver Mellors, to fuck a flame into being.

In the essay entitled "Lawrence's Gotterdammerung: The Apocalyptic Vision of *Women in Love*," Oates wonders whether the torturous erotic love in Lawrence is his way to salvation or whether it is his burden.

> Is it something to be gone through in order that one's deepest self may be stirred into life? Or is it a very simple, utterly natural emotion? . . . Regardless of his dogmatic remarks about "mind conscious-

ness" and "blood consciousness", Lawrence does not seem to know whether sexual love is a form of ecstasy or a delusion, a transcending experience or a delirium, a pathological condition that crazes the lover.

Oates sympathizes with Lawrence's belief that a person may be baptized in the fires of passion. In *Contraries* while discussing Oscar Wilde, Oates scrutinizes a passage from Lawrence's "Preface" to *Women in Love* that would seem to confirm this possibility: "Nothing that comes from the deep, passional soul is bad, or can be bad" (1981, 12). However, unlike Lawrence, Oates has difficulty articulating the significance that she attributes to sexuality nor has she ever made explicit the components of her vision. Consequently, the reader may not see these largely torturous relationships in her fiction as a means of potentially liberating selfhood, as perhaps Oates intends them to be.

In *Wonderland* (1971), Oates was able to depict the dilemma, but was unable to resolve the moral questions it raised. That failure, she told Walter Clemons (77), distressed her. In *Marriages and Infidelities* (1972), she moved toward a "more articulate moral position, not just dramatizing nightmarish problems." In part, this shift of mood was precipitated by something she realized about Lawrence as well as other writers. "Blake, Whitman, Lawrence have had a vision of transformation of the human spirit I agree with strongly myself," she told Clemons. "I believe we achieve our salvation, or our ruin, by the marriages we contract. I conceived of a book of marriages. I thought by putting together a sequence of marriages, one might see how this one succeeds and that one fails. And how this leads to some meaning beyond the self" (77). In *The Hostile Sun*, Oates identifies with the dreamer who dreams that under the right conditions we could "live our lives in love."

As Eileen Bender observes (1987, 78) in her excellent study, Oates was intrigued with Lawrence's double vision of human possibility: the belief that the self may be transformed by encounters with savage rituals as well as by erotic experience, both being forms of surrender to larger forces outside the self (see *The Hostile Sun*, 48ff). Oates develops the characters of her next novel, *Do With Me What You Will* (1973), along these lines. Driven by his passion for Elena Howe, another man's wife, the idealistic Jack Morrissey fantasizes about escaping from the urban wilderness of Detroit and becoming a sacrificial victim, like the youths in the ancient Aztec rites (and, or course, like "the woman who rode away" and who surrendered herself to Indian sacrifice): "[They] were evidently allowed to become gods for a short period . . . or maybe they were selected . . . on the understanding that they would eventually have their hearts cut out at the altar in some kind of religious ceremony. They agreed to be gods, and then they agreed to have their hearts cut out" (427). Instead, Jack becomes Elena's "erotic agent," liberating her from "her spiritual torpor" through orgasm. Like many Lawrence heroines who are awakened to life by erotic experience, the renewed Elena "takes up her own quest, flooded for the first time with desire" (Bender 1987, 78).

In these early novels, by emphasizing the way man and woman relate to one another, Oates reworks a major interest of Lawrence, whose *The Rainbow* and *Women in Love* explore courtship and marriage with unparalleled intensity, microscopically probing the mysteries of human relations largely within the confines of heterosexuality ("The great relationship, for humanity, will always be the relation between man and woman. The relation between man and man, woman and woman, parent and child, will always be subsidiary. And the relation between man and woman will change for ever" (Lawrence 1936, 531). In "A Propos of *Lady Chatterley's Lover*, he declares that Christianity's greatest contribution to Western civilization was the invention of matrimony. For him, only in marriage did the true meaning of love unfold in that state straining for tenderness and toward transcendence of naked sexuality.

In "Connection Between Men and Women" (Oates 1970, 428), one of the characters observes enviously, obsessively of another woman, "She is married permanently to that man. Married. Married permanently"; and the enormously successful writer in "The Dead," despite her emotional failures, clings to a similar view: "Marriage was the deepest, most mysterious, most profound exploration open to man: she had always believed that, and she believed it now . . . [It] was the closest one could come to a sacred adventure" (1972, 474). In *The Hostile Sun*, Oates modifies this "theology of love" (46), explaining herself while she invokes Lawrence's views on the subject: "as the permanently opposed entities of male and female join, they create an inhuman, more-than-human equilibrium, whether they want to or not. . . Therefore one marries only the person with whom he has experienced this 'inhuman' love, which is not romantic love or perhaps even love at all."

Another kind of sacred adventure is described in a story called

"The Wheel" which brings to mind "The Man Who Died." Like Lawrence's Christ leaving his tomb, the protagonist leaves a hospital bed in bandages and experiences a rejuvenating erotic encounter with a woman:

> She touched me, I touched her; and the violence of that touch ran through me like fire exploding everywhere in my veins. I dissolved. I went back into nothing. I lost even the words that had held me whole—.
> I was born. (1974b, 468)

In the 1980s, Oates's fiction expanded into new areas of storytelling. She completed a trio of Gothic novels and experimented with modern retelling of classic tales before returning to more realistic forms like *Solstice* (1985). This novel reads like a deliberate re-imagining of Lawrence's novella, "The Fox," with a horse instead of a fox playing an important role in defining the plot, as though Oates had playfully combined the story of March and Banford with "St. Mawr," Lawrence's enigmatic novella about a powerful half-tamed stallion.

The younger and more mannish of Lawrence's two women in "The Fox," March becomes modernized as Monica, a vaguely dissatisfied young woman teaching in a Bucks County academy for boys. Like March, at the age of thirty she has no children and her life outside of her work seems sterile, lacking a vital center. The more fragile Banford, who provides the money for the purchase of Bailey Farm, becomes Sheila Trask, an affluent artist who exerts increasing influence on Monica. Dazed and disorientated by the growing erotic intimacy of her relationship with Sheila, Monica submits to a Henry-like figure in a night of brutal passion that leaves her spirit sick and despairing (in fact, there are two men with names like Henry Grenfel's, Hen and Henri, who seem to be on the verge of breaking up the obsessive relationship between the two women). Oates is writing a corrective epilogue to Lawrence's inconclusive novella, leaving us to infer that the demonic does not always become the unconscious way to wisdom as in "The Fox." Contrary to Lawrence, she implies that woman-to-woman connections, in spite of the social barriers against them, are more satisfying and challenging than heterosexual relations that involve demon egotists, oafs, dullards, and louts.

Oates is reticent about spelling out what has drawn the two women together, but she suggests that the reader sympathetic to the feminine sensibility will recognize the force that attracts them to each other almost instinctively once the younger woman has liberated herself from the dictates of compulsory heterosexuality. In one respect, the absence of a powerful Henry figure weakens the Oates novel, stripping it of the kind of elemental three-cornered conflict that crackles beneath the surface of "The Fox." But the tracing and retracing of tensions, the sensitive, relentless charting of the fluctuations in the unstable, curiously exotic relationship, adds to the Oates narrative a delicate dimension that Lawrence subordinates to the charged melodrama of the triangle. If the impulsive behavior of the two women puzzles the reader, comparing it to the behavior of Anna in *The Rainbow* and Lou Witt in "St. Mawr" may make it seem less implausible and irrational incomprehensible. *Solstice* is another example of Oates's device of writing her own version of classic stories—by Joyce, Chekhov, and in this case, Lawrence.

A more recent novel, *American Appetites* (1989) suggests that Lawrence still lurks on the periphery of Oates's imagination, though there is almost no sign of his presence in *Because It is Bitter and Because It Is My Heart* (1990). The following passage from *American Appetites* (24), describing a crisis in the relationship between the young political scientist Ian McCullough and his wife Glynnis makes explicit what is implicit in a parallel scene between Will and Anna Brangwen:

> Their lives had been irrevocably altered before Bianca's birth. Glynnis' very pregnancy and her moods, that so excluded him, and that ... Glynnis willed might exclude him. For her exultating her supremacy, in pregnancy, childbirth, nursing, had cut him out: made him feel not only irrelevant but, so often, in the way; his wife looked at him and felt the obligation of love, for of course she did love him, while another kind of love, physical, instinctual, as intimate as her own flesh, pulled at her. As hot, heavy, urgent, he guessed, as the milk in her breast that gave pain if it was not released.

The "Anna Victrix" chapter is pivotal to *The Rainbow*, a watershed experience in the movement of the plot. It is a most crucial time in the life of the Brangwens and that time is given its space. Oates, on the other hand, does not need to prolong the action nor subject it to minute, detailed analysis as Lawrence does because other relationships overshadow this one and claim the reader's attention.

Another interesting aspect of Oates's work has surfaced recently. Accordingly to Oates herself, some of her writing is "an attempt to memorialize [her] parents' vanished world . . . sometimes directly, sometimes in metaphor" (Oates, 1989b, 84). The value of the landscape in this vanished world of Oates's parents depends largely on its accumulation of human associations. One of her recent novels, *Marya: A Life* (1986), combines the events and places of her mother's early life with some of Oates's own adolescent and young-adult experiences. Oates does not appear to be lamenting the loss of a wilderness in upstate New York, but reinventing a pastoral in a universe devoid of shepherds and gods, where the natural world is threatened by our inability to "see" it. Lawrence, too, had explored such possibilities especially in the early stories and novels, where he had sought to create a vision of nature compatible with a humanistic view of the world.

In her criticism, she has said more than once that Lawrence is one of the greatest poets in the English language and that if he hadn't written fiction, he would have been far more readily acclaimed as such (Milozzo 1989, 78). Her book *The Hostile Sun*[8] reveals as much about the author's own practices in poetry as it does about Lawrence's and hints at how pervasive his influence has been on her own approach to writing poetry. As Waller says, "It is in these critical ideas rather than in the novels that one will find guidance into the poetry":

> Lawrence's poems are blunt, exasperating, imposing upon us his strangely hectic, strangely delicate music, in fragments, in tantalizing broken-off parts of a whole too vast to be envisioned—and then withdrawing again. They are meant to be spontaneous works, spontaneously experienced; they are not meant to give us the sense of grandeur or permanence which other poems attempt, the fallacious sense of immortality that is an extension of the poet's ego.

The title poem of her first volume, called *Women in Love*, best illustrates what she means in this tribute to Lawrence. The striking metaphor of love running into the earth, "to mineral earth's bone," suggests that Oates, in her own fragmentary music, shares the concerns that Lawrence had felt over the exploitation of nature, which for her as for him, is a living organism. Even the ambiguity of the concluding lines, "Love never flows / to any form" is reminiscent of some of the unresolved issues of Lawrence's work.

Her next volume, *Angel Fire*, uses an epigraph from Lawrence as a point of departure:

> Ours is the universe of the unfolded rose
> The explicit
> The candid revelation

"Firing a Field," Oates's poem in memory of Flannery O'Connor, is charged with a sense of Lawrence's fervor and flavor that characterize his poem "A Young Wife," where a passional fire melts a young couple into "one radiance." The poems of *The Fabulous Beasts* (1975) carry Lawrence's animal themes of *Birds, Beasts and Flowers* into the realms of fantasy, but the apocalyptic hallucinations of *The Lamb of Abyssalia* (1979), beyond subject matter, seem to have less in common with Lawrence's *Apocalypse*.

The volume called *Invisible Woman* (1982) signals an end to Oates's "fallacious sense of immortality" (her words) and a new preoccupation with the meaning of invisibility. Whereas her gaze previously was fixed on the visible material world, Oates now is concerned with absences more than presences. For instance, in "The Wasp," she is fascinated by the stinging insect that attacks her flesh (c.f., Lawrence's "Mosquito"). As a surgeon's tweezer extracts its stinger, Oates is moved by the disappearance of the fragile body to wonder, "Why do we think we must live forever?" And just as Lawrence pursues that image in "The Mosquito Knows—", so does Oates in "A Miniature Passion": the stinging becomes a painful sexual necessity. For both Oates and Lawrence, animals become metaphors for probing human vagaries.[9]

The title *Invisible Woman* evokes the mood that envelopes Sisson (*Aaron's Rod*) as he wanders around in a northern Italian city full of strangers:

> That was how he strictly felt: invisible and undefined, rather like Wells' Invisible Man. He had no longer a mask to present to people: he was present and invisible.

Ultimately, by rejecting the values of those who have made him feel worthless, Sisson achieves a kind of perverse victory. Oates seems persuaded that Lawrence understood the particular kind of emptiness that she associates with the public discomfort of women whose inner self goes unseen. On the original book jacket of these poems, Oates comments:

> A woman often feels "invisible" in a public sense precisely because her physical being—her "visibility"—figures so prominently in her identity. She is judged as a body, she is "attractive" or "unattractive,"

while knowing that her deepest self is inward and secret: knowing, hoping that her spiritual essence is a great deal more complex than the casual eye of the observer will allow.

In *The Rise of Life on Earth*, a conviction of ominous invisibility overcomes Kathleen Hennessy. At the end, as she resolves to take vengeance for her condition, she realizes "the terrible secret strength of those whom the human world has made invisible." Irritating chauvinist that he could be, Lawrence nonetheless recognized that the true self is "inward and secret," invisible to most eyes. He recognized this truth in his soul: like Aaron, he knew it intuitively, unthinkingly, without being schooled in this wisdom, and this awareness was a powerful part of his appeal for Oates.

Lawrence's continuing influence shows up in some of the poems in *The Time Traveller*, such as "Peaches, Pineapples, Hazelnuts" ("I love best / this sweet heavy Persian melon with its / fleshy meat like the softened skin / of the inner thigh"). Such lines remind us that Oates has not totally forgotten Lawrence's sexualization of fruits in *Birds, Beasts and Flowers*, where ripe apricots are likened to the female sexual organ. Now and then in this volume Oates appears to be putting her poems alongside Lawrence's, with no signs of anxiety attending the implied comparison.[10]

It is hard to predict what is next for a writer who is still in mid-career. Just as Oates abandoned "the old stable ego of the character," Bender sees her leaving behind the familiar realism and entering "a world of vertigo and nightmare," toward the compelling terror of Kafka's unstable universe which she briefly visited in *Do With Me What You Will*. A very recent book, *The Rise of Life on Earth*, (1991a) a Gothic extension of Lawrence's story, "The Horse Dealer's Daughter," makes this prediction plausible. During the eighties, Oates developed an ambivalent attitude toward Lawrence, taking him severely to task in the essay, "At Least I Have Made a Woman of Her: Images of Women in Yeats, Lawrence, and Freud" (*The Profane Art* (56): "Like Freud, Lawrence is one of those 'liberators' of the twentieth century whose gospel, as applied to and experienced by women, may in fact constitute a more insidious—precisely *because* iconoclastic—imprisonment." In other places, she criticizes his attitude towards lesbians, and her sympathetic portrayal of the two women in *Solstice* might be read as a rejoinder to Lawrence's treatment of the two lesbians in "The Fox."

Epilogue

In *The Heritage of British Literature*, Elizabeth Bowen observes that "[Lawrence's] novels have had the effect of a depth charge" on English literature. The preceding chapters examine what I think the Lawrence "depth charge" brought up to the surface in the lives and works of nine women writers. Lawrence made a profound and often lasting impact on the sensibilities of these writers who helped to shape modern letters, even though they perceived many of his views as antifeminist.[1] When these women did not engage him in argument, they took him as their muse, often drawn to his work, in the words of one critic, "as if they sensed something quasi-feminist in it."[2]

Among Lawrence's English contemporaries whose fiction was significantly touched by his thinking were Rebecca West and Katherine Mansfield. Early in their careers, they valued his openness of mind as a model for their own intentions. West especially admired Lawrence's courage, spontaneity, and what she believed to be his intuitive respect for a woman's psyche. Mansfield, though she quarrelled violently with him, asserted that she loved him like "a brother," and for a time thought of him as something of a mentor. Mansfield's stories exerted an important influence on the writing of the following decade while West proved that independence of mind was no barrier to a successful career as a writer. Like many of Lawrence's sophisticated female readers, she must have realized that a number of his major literary models had been women.[3]

In the following generation, as Mark Spilka points out, Doris Lessing read Lawrence with great attention. *Lady Chatterley's Lover* in particular left a mark on her early writing, especially on *The Grass is Singing*. Among younger writers the fiction of Margaret Drabble has shown a substantial response to Lawrence's presence as she reprocessed into new dilemmas the Lawrencian conflict between the senses and the moral restraints upon them.

Our understanding of American writers such a H. D., Kay Boyle, Meridel LeSueur, Anaïs Nin, Sylvia Plath, Eudora Welty, and Joyce Carol Oates is enriched when we read them against the backdrop of Lawrence. In particular H. D. interacted with Lawrence on more than one level. Her relationship with Lawrence has raised questions of thralldom and dominance and of who influenced whom, adding a new dimension to the reading of her work as well as his. What often appears to be an arcane series of images in her poetry gains in narrative complexity and texture in light of her interaction with Lawrence.

Sylvia Plath, as an undergraduate blazing her own trail, was especially responsive to Lawrence's presence while she was forging her own unique vision of the world. She "appropriated" (a term given currency by Hèléne Cixous) the imagery and ideas of his poems, novels, and stories, and transformed them into the highly original fabric of her own creations.

It was with a kind of joy and exhilaration that Anaïs Nin admitted the influence of Lawrence into her fiction. Her sexual education in part evolved from her early and affectionate attachment to his novels and tracts. Her *D. H. Lawrence* is not only a fresh reading of Lawrence, but it is also a blueprint of how she intended to adapt him to her own personal pursuit of liberation and literary distinction. She used the grain and discarded the chaff. Her novels and diaries, infused with his spirit and stripped of puritan scruples, became important landmarks in the early feminist movement of the seventies.

In the next generation, Carson McCullers drew upon Lawrence's insights into sadism and sexuality while creating the strange, obsessive characters who enliven her fiction, especially the novella *Reflections in a Golden Eye*. Joyce Carol Oates hailed Lawrence as "one of our true prophets" in *The Hostile Sun*, her concise appreciation of his poetry. However, her fiction more than her critical essays suggest the extent to which she is indebted to Lawrence. In one instance, she appears to be deliberately rewriting a familiar Lawrence text—perhaps the ultimate form of flattery.

It should come as no surprise to any observer of the contemporary scene that these women are essentially Eurocentric in outlook, educated in the belief that England was the true fountain of American culture, and that it was the English writers who stood for the great tradition to which all aspiring writers had to apprentice themselves. Thus it is totally plausible that two women rooted in middle western America should have chosen an English writer as their role model. For Meridel LeSueur, born into Bible Belt morality, Lawrence was the ax that broke the frozen sea by opening her to a vision of what possibilities were inherent in the compassionate imagination, while Kay Boyle identified in the expatriate, footloose Lawrence a romantic model for her own aspirations. Both his life and work offered writers like Boyle and LeSueur (and perhaps Eudora Welty) a more complex system of alternatives than they could find near at hand. In Lawrence's novels they could recognize, like any of his intelligent readers, the first stirrings of twentieth-century woman—intellectually curious, eager to debate, firm in her feelings, warm and loving and a true friend.

Among the present generation of writers, Barbara Guest and Caroline Kizer have mentioned their great affection for Lawrence while Erika Jong and Gael Greene at one point immersed themselves in Lawrence.

When he enters their work, it is usually on the level of gentle satire or parody of his ideas or style. And it is true that as the distance in time between ourselves and Lawrence widens, his impact on future writers is likely to diminish. But he is, according to Michael Adam, "still very much alive in a sense, even more so for the new generations than he was for his own . . . one can find hints and instances [in his writing] of a way of living hale and whole in a world wherein we are not strangers, exiles, [or] pilgrims." If much of what Lawrence had to say has been assimilated into common discourse, some of the questions he raised in the area of human sexuality remain to be resolved (i.e., is it possible that a consentual "triangle" might yield greater fulfillment than either monogamy or promiscuity, as Birkin implies in the finale of *Women in Love*, and that a same sex relationship may be complementary to a passion for the other sex rather than an alternative to it?). These issues we are still struggling with, and future writers may be drawn to Lawrence as an artist attuned to the complex erotic lives of both sexes, concerned with the mystery of elemental identity beyond "the old stable ego."

Perhaps it is appropriate that the parting words to this study should be pronounced by another novelist who was his contemporary, Olive Moore. Claiming that Lawrence "had all the housewifely virtues" (1932, 28), she writes:

> When he has ceased to be a demi-god, D. H. Lawrence will take his place as one of the finest imaginative prose writers of English letters. Nor is there a poet of his generation to approach him in language and intensity (32).

Lawrence's "radical" ideas exercised many young writers, both men and women. But it was the Lawrence described by Olive

Moore to whom these still impressionable writers, acutely sensitive and receptive to rhythms, tones and melodies, including the rhythms and tones of language, responded. As Auden said of Freud, "he is no more a person / Now but a whole climate of opinion."

Notes

Introduction

1. Quoted in *Time*, 30 April 1990, 89.
2. The sense in which I mean the term "presence" has little to do, I think, with Jacques Derrida's "metaphysics of presence." According to Quentin Kraft, Derrida uses the term in *On Grammatology* to convey "the idea of an unpremeditated relationship between consciousness and an object, a relationship that is pure because it is prior to language, therefore uncontaminated by language." This statement appears to enforce the deconstructionist contention that literary history's talk of source and influence is always fraudulent or at least obfuscating. See Kraft, "Toward a Critical Re-renewal: At the Corner of Camus and Bloom Streets," *College English* 54 (January 1992): 46–62 and Donald Davie, *Studies in Ezra Pound* (Manchester, England: Carcanet Press, 1991), 365–67.
3. Other women writers influenced by Lawrence to a lesser extent include Elizabeth Bowen, Gael Greene, Erika Jong, Doris Lessing, Denise Levertov, Carson MacCullers, Olive Moore, and Diane Wakoski. A publisher's reader thought that the omission of Virginia Woolf from this study was a serious flaw. Indeed Woolf shared with Lawrence certain qualities of mind that Eudora Welty characterized as "passionate, independent, acute, proudly and incessantly nourished, eccentric for honorable reasons, sensitive for every reason" (*New York Times Book Review*, 21 September 1958, 8). And Woolf identified with Lawrence's status as an outsider (see her "Notes on D. H. Lawrence," in *The Moment And Other Essays* and "The Leaning Tower" in *Collected Essays*. At the 1987 meeting of the D. H. Lawrence Society in San Francisco, Earl Ingersoll in "Virginia Woolf and D. H. Lawrence: Exploring the Good Darkness," asserts that Woolf and Lawrence shared what Woolf called "the same pressure to be ourselves," a pressure leading both of them to recognize that the shape of modern fiction would have to change if it were "to accommodate itself to a radically modern notion of itself" (see *The D. H. Lawrence Society of North America Newsletter* 17 [Summer 1988]). Rachel Blau DuPlessis in "for the Etruscans" (*New Feminist Criticism*, ed. Elaine Showalter) links Lawrence to Woolf in their attacks on bourgeois culture. But significantly she places them in opposed modernist camps. Siegal spends ten pages on Woolf's reaction to Lawrence. However, Lyndall Gordon barely mentions Lawrence in her excellent study of Woolf, and Patricia Laurence, the author of *The Reading of Silence: Virginia Woolf in the English Tradition* (Stanford, Calif.: Stanford University Press, 1991), writes in a letter to me dated 11 February 1992: "Though the class issue throws the gender divisions aside, Lawrence's views, his expressions of sexuality, and his style are nothing like hers [Woolf's]."
4. Woolf, "Notes on D. H. Lawrence," *The Moment*. Woolf also says that the

best novelists like Hardy and Lawrence had androgynous minds, while the poor writers, like Kipling, Galsworthy, and Bennett had masculine mentalities. Margaret Drabble, who admires Bennett's empathy for the two sisters in *Old Wives' Tale*, would take issue with Woolf's assessment of him.

5. In discussions with Louie Burrows, Lawrence supported the movement for women's suffrage. But Ronald Draper, in a recent essay, argues that at least two of his tales are "about the defeat of women's independence" and "part of Lawrence's answer to the suffragettes" whom he "despised" (1988, 158). Draper adds that despite his antifeminist attitude, Lawrence possessed a markedly "feminine temperament" (159).

6. Among recent studies by women which analyze Lawrence's response to women and his portrayal of them are Carol Dix's *D. H. Lawrence and Women* (Totowa, N. J.: Rowman and Littlefield, 1980); Hilary Simpson's *D. H. Lawrence and Feminism* (DeKalb: Northern Illinois University Press, 1982), Judith Ruderman's *D. H. Lawrence and the Devouring Mother* (Durham, N. C.: Duke University Press, 1984), and several essays in *Lawrence and Women*, ed. Ann Smith (New York: Barnes & Noble, 1978). Also see Margaret Storch's post-Millett piece, "The Lacerated Male: Ambivalent Images of Women in *The White Peacock*," in *The D. H. Lawrence Review*, 21, no. 12 (Summer 1989): "Lawrence had an empathy with women's social experience unusual among his male contemporaries" (121); and Elaine Feinstein's *Lawrence and the Women: An Intimate Life of D. H. Lawrence* (New York: Harper Collins, 1993). Feinstein's is the first study to focus exclusively on Lawrence's relationships with the women who were important influences in his life, many of whom, have counterparts in his novels. Feinstein shows how his novels grew out of his passionate attachment to these women—his mother, his wife Frieda, Louisa Burrows, Jessie Chambers and Alice Dax, Helen Corke, Katherine Mansfield, Ottoline Morrell, Cynthia Asquith, Dorothy Brett, and Mabel Dodge Luhan—gleaning most of her evidence from volumes of memoirs, letters, biographies, critical work, and interviews with friends and families of the writer.

7. Anaïs Nin says that "very often he [Lawrence] wrote *as a woman* might write." Quoted in Gilbert 1991, 95.

Chapter 1. Katherine Mansfield: "We Are *Unthinkably Alike*"

1. Joyce Carol Oates (*The Profane Art*, 51) believes that Lawrence projected the negative aspects of his own nature onto the character of Gudrun, who, she says is a distorted version of Mansfield.

2. In this context, Mansfield seems to mean "love" in the platonic rather than the sexual sense. Lawrence appears to have been more ambivalent. "It seems fair to conclude that Lawrence, who never wished to shut the door on new possibilities in life, entertained the idea of new sexual relations," Daniel Schneider writes (106–7). "[But] while Lawrence dallied with the idea . . . his honesty would not permit him to resort to the subterfuge of an affair." That the possibility of an affair later on crossed both their minds seems to be suggested in Mansfield's story, "Psychology" (see discussion further on).

3. The letter containing the statement has never been found, but Mansfield quoted it in a letter of her own to Murry, part of which is quoted in *The Letters III* (470). Paul Delany treats the break with Lawrence extensively (1978,

229–34). John Middleton Murry, in "D. H. Lawrence, Katherine Mansfield, and *Women in Love*," tries to understand why Lawrence wrote this letter (quoted in Meyers, *The Spirit of Biography*). According to Alpers, Lawrence hated in Mansfield the mirrored fear of the respiratory disease already laying siege to his own health. Aldous Huxley says more or less the same thing in *A Conversation on D. H. Lawrence*. Lawrence was apparently wrong about the nature of Mansfield's disease. Her life style was liberated and as Claire Tomalin suggests in her biography, it caused her death from venereal disease—more specifically, gonorrhea. Mansfield got back at Lawrence by calling Frieda "a real filthy pig" (*Collected Letters* 1: 182).

4. Rhonda Nathan thinks Lawrence had no literary influence at all on Mansfield, that in fact she and Murry "as personalities had a striking impact on Lawrence" (1988, 140). Fullbrook agrees with her—"From this [Lawrence's] style and approach Katherine Mansfield held herself aloof ... The literary opposition between herself and Lawrence was thus fruitful for her" (1986, 44–46). Gilbert and Gubar believe that her relationship with Lawrence was significant, but that her friendship with Virginia Woolf was just as crucial. It well may have been, though the evidence suggests mutual respect for craft rather than a fruitful interaction. Nathan sees Mansfield's relationship with Woolf as professional rather than personal (141). On this question, Jeffrey Meyers writes, "Influenced perhaps by the extreme antagonism of Lawrence, Katherine was hostile to Bloomsbury's sneers and snobbery, and felt excluded from that charmed circle of friends" (*Katherine Mansfield*, 137), which of course included Woolf.

5. That fragment bearing the stamp of Lawrence was published in the *Turnbull Library Record* of May 1979 and appears in Ian Gordon.

6. Nathan thinks that through the agency of Birkin, Lawrence is charging Gudrun with doing small things marvelously well while fearing "to make the grand gesture ... implying ultimately an acquiescence to minor status" (1988, 3). As seen by Birkin, Gudrun is "incapable of consistency in anything ... she has a fear of both work and success, and the fault lies with her 'type'" (3). Thus Gudrun/Mansfield is guilty of "running away from life as from art." Nathan accuses Lawrence of "rehearsing most of the points that were to become mainstays of Katherine Mansfield criticism," (2) damaging her reputation until it was rehabilitated by recent feminist inquiry. The validity of this reading depends upon whether one takes Birkin to be Lawrence's spokesman at every crucial juncture in the novel. Fullbrook sides with Nathan: in effect there were two kinds of myth about Katherine Mansfield, the witch and the saint. To D. H. Lawrence especially she was a destructive, witch-like figure. "[She] was an independent and forceful woman, with a caustic wit well calculated to find out Lawrence's weaker points. So, in *Women in Love*, he counter-attacked in his presentation of the destructive personality and sexuality of Gudrun Brangwen. And in characterizing Gudrun's art as 'miniature' art, he not only makes slighting reference to Katherine Mansfield's chosen story form, but also hits back at what he insisted on seeing as the purely reductive quality of her mocking and sardonic wit" (1986, 2–3). Why Lawrence would want to demean a genre he practiced so prolifically himself (*The Rainbow* is really a series of linked short stories) remains a mystery, and why he would frown on a "mocking and sardonic wit" is not clear, since that kind of wit rather than a real sense of humor was one of his own hallmarks.

7. A detailed and insightful analysis of "Psychology" found in Kobler

(1990, 90–92), who writes, "What is so wonderful about Mansfield's performance here is that she makes them together question their ability to be together, while also suggesting that on those 'other occasions' they were not any more together than they are now, even though they may have thought they were." If the visiting novelist is indeed based on Lawrence, then this passage may be glossed as Mansfield's version of their relationship.

8. Mansfield could not have read either "The Flying Fish" or "Sun." The first was started in Oaxaca (1925) and the second at Spotorno (1926).

9. Yet it is the moon that dominates Constantia's youth. Mansfield writes, "She had crept out of her bed in her nightgown when the moon was full, and lain on the floor with her arms outstretched, as though she was crucified. Why? The big, pale moon had made her do it" (1956, 260–61). Her relationship to the moon is cosmic and mystical (like Bernard Coutts's vision of the moon as a sacrificial instrument in "The Witch a la Mode"); it reflects her "need for identification with moon and tide, with ebb and flow of regular forces in the cosmos" (Magalaner 96). This scene should be read against Birkin's stoning of the moon's reflection in *Women in Love*.

10. Carol Siegel, in "Virginia Woolf's and Katherine Mansfield's Responses to D. H. Lawrence's Fiction," says that Mansfield took an interest in Lawrence's work not because he was her opposite but because he was a participant in her traditions. She rose "braced and purified" from the contemplation of Lawrence's vision of female experience, Siegel concludes (1989, 310).

Chapter 2. H. D.: Bid Me to Love

Susan Stanford Friedman's "H. D. Chronology: Composition and Publication of Volumes" (*H. D. Newsletter*, 1, [Spring 1987]) and *Signets* provide useful bibliographies of H. D.'s works, both published and unpublished.

1. Although many readers revere H. D. for her protofeminist tendencies, several critics assert that she allowed herself to be dominated by masculine ideology. Rachel Blau DuPlessis in particular describes what she considers to be H. D.'s "romantic thralldom" to a series of male figures and ideals.

2. The University of California Press has recently published a complete version of his *H. D. Book*. Part 1, chapter 1 ("Beginnings"), which appeared in *Coyote's Journal* 5/6 (1966), 8–31, tells how Duncan's study of H. D. became the story of his conversion to poetry. He makes clear that he, too, like H.D., was nurtured by Lawrence, especially by a high school teacher's reading of "Heat" (Mackey 1991, 146). Susan Stanford Friedman, Rachel Blau DuPlessis, Barbara Guest, Deborah Kelly Klopfer, Adalaide Morris, and others have written studies that concentrate on H. D.'s post-Pound poetry. Studying her fiction, Fuchs points out (1990, 343), has been more difficult, since so much of it was not easily available. *Signets* contains several good essays on H. D.'s fiction in the "Palimpsests"' section.

3. H. D.'s accident was a stillbirth, not a miscarriage as Gelpi says in *Notes on Thought and Vision*. Although a stillbirth is a form of miscarriage technically, a miscarriage can happen early in pregnancy. However, H. D. had a nearly term baby born dead—a much more devastating experience for most women. She blamed the death on the fact that the news of the sinking of the *Lusitania* was broken to her "rather brutally." I owe thanks to Jane Augustine, an H. D. scholar, for this information, letter of 14 July 1990.

4. Lawrence may appear as Orpheus in H. D.'s "Eurydice" (*Collected*

Poems, 51–55). For a discussion of his influence on H. D.'s revision of this poem, see DeShazer, 79–80. DeShazer thinks this poem disavows Lawrence as mentor and muse by drawing parallels between Eurydice's rejection of all that Orpheus stands for and H. D.'s "rebellion against Lawrence's dicta."

5. This poem appears in *New Poems* as "On That Day."

6. Quoted in Meyers (1990, 206). Meyers thinks that Lawrence and H. D. did not sleep together. Friedman suspects that "her vitally important friendship [which she characterizes as "intensely cerebral" *Signets* 8] with Lawrence fell apart as the affair that Frieda fostered never materialized, and as H. D.'s relationship with Cecil Gray began in early 1918" (*Signets* 242).

7. Letter from Jane Augustine, dated 14 July 1990. Both H. D. and Perdita have denied this allegation repeatedly. Photographs show that Perdita bears a striking physical resemblance to Gray, who spent some time with the Lawrences in Cornwall and with whom H. D. lived from March to July of 1918, when the affair ended. For an account of that friendship, see C. J. Stevens. According to H. D., the father was definitely not Ezra Pound (1979, 30). On the basis of an interview with Barbara Weekley, Frieda's aging daughter, Meyers (1990, 93) asserts that Lawrence may have been rendered physically sterile by a mumps-like illness at the age of sixteen. Since testing for male sterility was still in a primitive stage during the twenties, the accuracy of such a diagnosis would be suspect. In fact, Alice Dax has claimed that her son was fathered by Lawrence. Doyle (1989, 335) takes a neutral position on the Perdita issue.

8. Jane Augustine has helpfully pointed out to me that the indisputable psychological intimacy between Lawrence and H. D. was alone quite enough to cause Aldington's jealousy, his destruction of letters, and his suspect version of events in his biography of Lawrence (later, Aldington would help Lawrence to distribute copies of *Lady Chatterley's Lover*). But Ms. Augustine feels that Robinson's case for an actual affair is weak. The reader should see chapter 8 of Paul Delany's *D. H. Lawrence's Nightmare* for a detailed account of the H. D.-Lawrence relationship during the war years. But whatever may have happened between Lawrence and H. D. should not obscure the fact that in 1918 Aldington loved H. D. very much and was convinced that her writing was art of the highest order.

9. This phrase, H. D.'s, is quoted by DuPlessis to emphasize the intensity of the relationship.

10. Not for everyone. One critic argues that Achilles is Lord Hugh Caswell Dowding, the British air marshal with whom H.D. was obsessed during WW II; another believes he is Aldington the soldier. Jane Augustine maintains that biographical interpretations of this mythic poem are unreliable. She believes that Achilles and Helen are Osiris and Isis and that the poem is thus linked to *The Man Who Died*. Letter, 14 July 1990.

11. Gary Barnett (*H. D. Newsletter*, 1, no. 1, 33) speculates that the "Sigil" part of *The Dead Priestess Speaks* constitutes H. D.'s response to such an identification, "shifting the emphasis from the dead man to a woman whose voice of prophecy comes back into life from beyond the grave." Barnett thinks that "Sigil" echoes *Women in Love* in many details.

12. Susan Schweik has a twelve-page section in *A Gulf So Deeply Cut* that traces and illuminates the relationship between Lawrence's war poetry and H. D.'s.

13. In *Tribute*, H. D. comments when Guest brings her the novella, "Law-

rence was imprisoned in his tomb; like the print hanging in the waiting room, he was 'Buried Alive'" (134). She adds, "Yes, I [too] was buried alive" (137).

14. In H. D. and Lawrence: Two More Allusions" (*H. D. Newsletter*, 1, no. 2, 47), David Roessel says that Lawrence's death caused H. D. to open a dialogue with him in her poem "The Poet," in which she addresses a figure "who may be identified as Lawrence." Moreover, "Priest" may also refer to Lawrence, although it has been linked to her obsession with Peter Van Eck.

15. So does Diane Chisholm in H. D.'s Freudian Poetics. Unhappy about being the mute object of men's sexual fantasies, H. D. entered analysis with Freud in 1933 hoping that it would help her to articulate her own desires, dreams, and aspirations. According to Chisholm, it did. Some critics (e.g, DuPlessis) feel that it put her into another kind of thralldom.

16. For example, Shari Benstock's study of H. D. in *Women of the Left Bank: Paris, 1900–1940*, ignores Lawrence's presence in H. D.'s life, and Alfred Kazin's review of Barbara Guest in *The New York Review of Books* (29 March 1984), does not mention him, even though his name occupies a major space in Guest's index. Rachel Blau DuPlessis mentions Lawrence briefly, and Cassandra Laity reverses the roles in the relationship by alluding to H. D.'s "confining role as muse to D. H. Lawrence" (1989, 472). Indeed, H. D. strove in her writing "to clear a space for the disclosure of a feminist vision of everyday life and literature" (Weinstein 1992, 15). Yet in her novels and some of her poetry, there is the presence of male lovers (Pound, Lawrence, Aldington) in roles of affectionate authority that borders on traditional rather than feminist feeling.

17. For an early but lively discussion of the H. D.-Lawrence relationship, see Maurice Beebe's skeptical "Lawrence as Fictional Character," in Salgado (1988, 295–310).

Chapter 3. Rebecca West: We Must Choose Life

1. This novel was made into a play by John Van Druten and later into a successful film.

2. It is this very scene that many readers of Lawrence find the most compelling in the book.

3. On this point she was ambivalent. In "Elegy" (*A Carnival* 394), she writes: "In the allegory of the death of the soul which ends with the death of Gerald among the mountains, he cannot tell his story save by the clumsy creation of images that do not give up their meaning till the book has been read many times."

4. In *The Court and the Castle* (1953), West says that Lawrence proposed a new sort of social contract in which the individual would not alienate his right to passionate being, but that he knew too little about the way the world worked (223).

Chapter 4. Meridel LeSueur: Passion on the Prairie

1. In the best-known version of the Persephone myth, when Persephone, the daughter of Zeus, picks a blood-red narcissus, the earth suddenly splits in two. From the abyss a mysterious figure appears and drags her into the crevice. The earth seals shut. Deep in the darkness of the underworld, Persephone learns that she has been abducted by Pluto, the king of hell, to become his

queen. Eventually Pluto is made to allow Persephone to return to earth for two-thirds of the year.

2. In the unpublished draft of "Hyde Park at Night," Lawrence wonders whether the goddess, were she to materialize, would flee from him as apparently his current lover has done.

3. In a later poem, "Purple Anemones" (*Birds, Beasts and Flowers*), Persephone is presented in another, seemingly contradictory guise, as a misguided feminist who is to be pitied ("Poor Persephone and her rights for women"). This may reflect a shift in Lawrence's attitude toward the feminine activists of the twenties.

4. It contains an indispensable introduction by Elaine Hedges (1–27) to whom this author is indebted for biographical details.

5. L. D. Clark's discussion of Lawrence's sources for the hymns and how they were composed is unsurpassed. See "Metal to Membrane," in *Dark Night of the Body*.

6. From the sometimes contradictory remarks on the subject scattered throughout his letters and prose, we can infer that Lawrence approved of certain aspects of communism but abhorred socialism. For a fuller discussion of Lawrence's politics, see Paul Delany, "Lawrence's Quarrel with Liberalism," in *D. H. Lawrence's Nightmare*; Peter Scheckner's *Class, Politics, and the Individual*; and Anne Fernihough, *D. H. Lawrence; Aesthetics and Ideology*.

Chapter 5. Anaïs Nin: A Spy in the House of Lawrence

1. For example, in *Anaïs Nin: An Introduction* and in "Anaïs Nin: Studies in the New Erotology" (*Mosaic*), Orville Clark emphasizes the magnetism of what he calls the androgynous realities in Lawrence: "his deep sympathy and even identity with the object or person toward which feeling is directed and second, the profound attachment to the body and the senses" (57). Also worth consulting is 'To Reach Out Further Mystically' by Bettina Knapp . . . "in *Anaïs, Art and Artist*, (edited by Sharon Spencer) who argues that Lawrence was instrumental in "linking her [Nin's] cosmic experience to the creative process" (66).

2. Spencer thinks that Proust was a greater influence than Lawrence (1977, 142). If evidence is drawn solely from the diaries, this is undeniable. But the diary depends heavily on memory compared to the actuality of a novel.

3. Franklin and Schneider point out that the conclusion to *The Novel of the Future* with its highly Lawrencian orientation not only terminates the text but also takes us back to many of the main themes of her book on Lawrence (1974, 275).

4. If deduced textual evidence is not enough, in this passage we have Nin's own word that Lawrence's novel made a lasting imprint on her sensibility. Robert Ferguson, in *Henry Miller*, thinks that Nin became a real-life version of Lady Chatterley—eager to escape her bourgeoise marriage and tantalized by the hectic vitality of her "lower class" lover. George Bernard Shaw apparently believed that the influence of *Lady Chatterley* was healthy. He said, "*Lady Chatterley* should be on the shelves of colleges for budding girls. They should be forced to read it on the pain of being refused a marriage license" (quoted from *Bernard Shaw* by Frank Harris in Bowlby, 131).

5. Nancy Scholar sees Lawrence's influence on Nin as largely negative, "encouraging her penchant for flat statement rather than dramatization" (1944, 7).

6. When Christopher Lehmann-Haupt wanted to rewrite the review because it was "feminine writing," she threatened to withdraw it. It was published as she wrote it. She said that the eight plays and two fragments collected in that volume illuminated Lawrence's "attempt to crack the surface of naturalism in his novels," but that "the dramatic form, with its severe limitations on lyric expression, would not seem suited to Lawrence's aims" (*In Favor of the Sensitive Man* 71). Although she concludes that "he makes no attempt to break with conventions of the theater, as he did with those of the novel," she loyally continued to insist that Lawrence had proved himself to be "a spelologist of the unconscious" who "penetrated realms people feared and did not acknowledge" (1976b, 74).

7. In an interview with Patricia English (Zeller 1974, 185–186), Nin said, "I don't understand the women who attack him so for I think he was trying to understand what women felt by going into the very difficult land of the intuition and emotion which was still not a very clearly formulated concept."

8. Interpreting Nin's cryptic phrase "one-called world" as synonymous with "integration," Paul Grimley Kuntz in "Anais Nin's 'Quest for Order'," *Mosaic* 11, no. 2, writes: "In her concept of the right ordering between the sexes, between opposite tendencies found in a culture, in her belief that these opposites are found together, belong together, and are meaningless apart, Nin allies herself with D. H. Lawrence" (206). Kuntz finds in Nin a concept akin to Lawrence's theory of polarities.

Chapter 6. Kay Boyle: Venus Agonistes

1. *Gentlemen, I Address You Privately* was her second novel written, her third published.

2. Fifty years later, in "Preface" to the Virago edition of *Plagued by the Nightingale*, Boyle described the novel as follows: "some victimizing American girl betrays her devoted husband, destroys her marriage, shatters the life of an eccentric middle-aged Scotch woman, all in the name of high virtue and glorified romance." In *Primer for Combat*, an American woman sacrifices her husband, her children, her home, but not her integrity for the sake of a ski instructor. Boyle left her second husband, Lawrence Vail, for Joseph Franckenstein who was in the ski troops during World War II.

3. The Crosbys published Lawrence in the Black Sun Press which Harry and Caresse ran in Paris. Both of them became friends of Lawrence.

4. By coincidence the surname Fontana matches the name of the dwelling the Lawrences occupied in Taormina for two years, the Fontana Vecchia.

5. She also regards Dostoyevsky as an important influence.

6. Ian MacNiven, Lawrence Durrell's biographer, supports this view in *Twentieth Century Literature* (371).

Chapter 7. Sylvia Plath: The Lost Girl

1. In *Letters Home*, she mentions reading three of Woolf's novels and finding them stimulants to her own work (324).

2. Judith Kroll's *Chapters in a Mythology* (1976) though it makes no men-

tion of Lawrence, is a useful study of Plath's imagery. In tracing it back to its sources, Kroll maintains that the facts of Plath's life were subordinated to and absorbed by archetypal patterns and strategies that inspired and shaped her poetry. Ann Sexton argues in "The Barfly Ought to Sing" that in her "openness to metaphor," Plath was more like Roethke than any other writer (Newman 1970, 178). Charles Newman suggests as influences John Keats, Emily Dickinson, and Ted Hughes.

3. Lawrence's historical role as a liberator of female sexuality has been challenged by Robert Scholes's essay on "Uncoding Mama" in his *Semiotic Interpretation*, where he lists Lawrence along with Freud and Cleland as male writers who disregard the centrality of the clitoris in orgasm. Anyone interested in the subject should consult Mark Spilka's answer to Scholes in "Lawrence and the Clitoris," in *The Challenge of D. H. Lawrence*.

4. The parallels to Lawrence's life lend some support to her statement: like Lawrence, Plath became alienated from her father and uncomfortably close to her mother; like Lawrence, she came to feel like a displaced person; and her romantic relationship to a spouse of a different culture disintegrated at the end.

5. For a discussion of Lawrence's use of the archetypal Persephone myth, see the chapter on Meridel LeSueur.

6. It is worth noting that Plath may have named her daughter Frieda out of admiration for Frieda Lawrence, the prototype of Ursula Brangwen. On the other hand, Plath may have named her after her own Aunt Frieda.

7. Edward Butscher reads the concluding lines in a slightly different way. "Ariel's death drive" have been seen in the context of the sperm cells' flight into the huge egg wall, hence as a true mystical-mythical symbolism, the death that is a rebirth." Letter to the author dated 16 June 1991.

Chapter 8. Margaret Drabble: Cassandra in the Kitchen

1. An excellent survey of Drabble's current literary reputation may be found in Sadler, *Margaret Drabble*, 130–33.

2. Drabble has said that none of her books are about feminism "because my belief in the necessity for justice for women is so basic that I never think of using it as a subject. It is part of a whole" (Gilbert and Gubar 1985, 2313).

3. It is interesting to note here that two years earlier, in an interview for *Paris Review* (Winter 1978) when Drabble was asked by Barbara Milton which writers she admired most she named Angus Wilson, Doris Lessing, Saul Bellow, and of course Arnold Bennett, but did not mention Lawrence, who was then taking a lot of heat from the feminist critics. When asked by Olga Kenyon (*Women Writers Talk*) which writers influenced her, she again failed to mention Lawrence, although in her entry for Lawrence in the *Abridged Oxford Companion to English Literature*, she calls him a writer of "permanent value."

4. *A Writer's Britain* is full of appreciative references to Lawrence, especially about his ability to recreate in words "the contours of the countries of the heart" (277). She observes that both Arnold Bennett and Lawrence turned their backs on the districts that nourished them, yet both commemorate them in novels inspired by a mingled love and hatred (212). Drabble's heroines often feel the same way about their environment.

5. For Virginia Beards, the waterfall image is merely a device to mask the

truth—that Jane is accepting "sexual bondage" in a relationship devoid of intellectual, social, and artistic compatibility (22).

6. The parallel to Frieda Lawrence as a discontented housewife longing for sexual fulfillment reminds us that Drabble reviewed Robert Lucas's *Frieda Lawrence* for the August 1973 issue of *Encounter*, commenting on Frieda's disasterous sexual relationship with Ernest Weekley, the difficulties of life with Lawrence, and Frieda's cheering account of her old age.

7. Gael Greene points out that, paradoxically, as Drabble's view of the world has darkened during the course of her career, her scope has expanded, moving from women's issues to analysis of England's condition to themes of global urgency (217).

Chapter 9. Joyce Carol Oates: The Playing Fields of the Id

1. D. H. Lawrence, "The Evening Land."

2. These straight-faced statements may be made with tongue in cheek. In "The Dead" (*Marriages and Infidelities* 1972, 479), Ilena Donohue, whose overnight success as a writer is obviously modeled after Oates's, puts on her audience of admirers by saying, "I don't exist as an individual but only as a completion of a tradition . . . I want to honor the dead by reimagining their works." Ilena wants to do no such thing.

3. Significantly, the title *New Heaven, New Earth* is borrowed from a poem by Lawrence, suggesting that human beings are capable of surviving terrible events and moving on with their lives. This theme runs through much of Oates's fiction. One of the two epigraphs as well as the title for this volume comes from Lawrence's poem, "New Heaven and Earth."

4. Immediately following the interview with Kazin in *Harper's*, there is a story by Oates called "Bloodstains." The protagonist is named Laurence and his friend's wife is named Connie.

5. Asked in an interview which writers were especially effective in portraying women, she replied that Shakespeare, Tolstoy Flaubert, and Lawrence were the most successful (Milozzo 1989, 8).

6. In the same interview, Oates maintains that English novelists prefer to observe society rather than to explore inward states. There hasn't been among English novelists, she believes, "an intense interest in subjectivity, in the psychology of living, breathing, human beings." The one exception, in her estimation, is Lawrence (Milozzo 1989, 68).

7. This passage was substantially rewritten when Oates reprinted her original essay in *The Hostile Sun*.

8. "Allotropic state" is the term Lawrence chose to express his sense of "another ego," a second and subconscious ego, deeper and less orderly than what he called "the old stable ego." Mark Spilka pointed this out to me.

9. According to Oates, who seems to ignore the sense of his "November by the Sea" ("my sun, and the great gold sun"), Lawrence worships the sun because it is hostile; he accepts the "otherness" of nature, but since he does not seek oneness with it, he is not, as so many readers think, a romantic. For a somewhat different view, see the two indispensable full-length studies of Lawrence's poetry, Sandra Gilbert, *Acts of Attention* (2d ed.) and Holly Laird, *Self and Sequence*.

10. Greg Johnson points out that Oates favors a creative strategy similar to Lawrence's: her poems, like those of Lawrence, "often isolate singular perceptions or thematic obsession" that get dramatized in the fiction (203).

Epilogue

1. When Kate Millett attacked Lawrence as a "male chauvinist," she set off a minor movement. Among the many critics who remain skeptical about his attitude toward women, Cornelia Nixon accuses him of being antifeminist and protofascist. David Holbrook maintains that Lawrence was guilty of immense falsification of sexual truth and would have denied women's fulfillment altogether in total submission to man. But the tide may be turning. Sandra Gilbert has pointed out recently that it is unfair to judge a writer of Lawrence's magnitude solely by applying questions of political correctness to his imagery of sex. In the spring 1992 issue of *Novel*, Mark Spilka tracks one of the currents trends in Lawrence studies, a gender approach that accommodates his use of women's voices in a kind of polyphonic play with the voices of the author and the male heroes. This approach counters Kate Millett's belief that Lawrence is treacherous because he uses women characters to buttress his misogynistic views and would seem to offer a kind of postfeminist return to the positive and creative possibilities in male writing. Fully cognizant of Lawrence's rhetorical excesses, Michael Bell has an instructive chapter on the way the polyphonic play of voices permits opposite readings of the same work (13–50).

2. Sandra Gilbert, "Feminism and D. H. Lawrence," *Anaïs: An International Journal* 9 (1991): 94. Gilbert says that she "found Lawrence's writing so compelling that, quite simply, I couldn't read enough of it." She adds, "Of course I struggled against his misogyny" (93).

3. See Carol Siegel's *Lawrence Among the Women*.

Works Cited

Aaron, Daniel. 1961. *Writers on the Left*. New York: Harcourt Brace.

Adam, Michael. 1975. *D. H. Lawrence and the Way of the Dandelion*, with recollections by Frieda Lawrence. Penzance, Cornwall: Ark Press.

Alexander, Paul, ed. 1985. *Ariel Ascending: Writings About Sylvia Plath*. New York: Harper & Row.

——— 1991. *Rough Magic*. New York: Viking Press.

Alpers, Anthony, 1980. *The Life of Katherine Mansfield*. New York: Viking Press.

——— 1984. *The Stories of Katherine Mansfield*. Oxford and Auckland: Oxford University Press.

Alvarez, A. 1959. "Lawrence: The Single State of Man," *A D. H. Lawrence Miscellany*, ed. Harry Moore. Carbondale, Illinois: Southern Illinois University Press.

——— 1971. "Sylvia Plath: A Memoir," *New American Review*, 12.

Augustine, Jane. 1990. Letter of July 14 to author.

Axelrod, Steven. 1984. "Plath's Literary Relations: An Essay and An Index to the *Journals* and *Letters Home*," *Resources for American Literary Study*, 14 (spring/autumn) Nos. 1 & 2.

——— *Sylvia Plath: The Wound and the Cure of Words*. Baltimore: John Hopkins Press, 1992.

[Baker, Ida]. 1972. *Katherine Mansfield: The Memories of L. M.* New York: Taplinger.

Balakian, Nona. 1991. *Critical Encounters*. New York: Ashod Press.

Balbert, Peter. 1989. *D. H. Lawrence and the Phallic Imagination*. New York: St. Martin's Press.

Barnett, Gary. 1987. "H. D. and Lawrence: Two Allusions," *H. D. Newsletter*, 1, no. 1 (Spring).

Beards, K. Virginia. 1977. "Margaret Drabble: Novels of a Cautious Feminist," *Contemporary Women Novelists*, edited by Patricia Meyer Spacks. Englewood Cliffs, New Jersey: Prentice Hall.

Bell, Elizabeth. 1992. *Kay Boyle: A Study of the Short Fiction*. Boston: Twayne.

Bell, Michael. 1992. *D. H. Lawrence: Language and Being*. Cambridge: Cambridge University Press.

Bender, Eileen Teper. 1987. *Joyce Carol Oates, Artist in Residence*. Bloomington: Indiana University Press.

Benstock, Shari. 1986. *Women of the Bank: Paris, 1900–1940*. Austin: University of Texas Press.

Berkman, Sylvia. 1951. *Katherine Mansfield*. New Haven: Yale University Press.

Bloom, Harold. 1973. *The Anxiety of Influence.* New York: Oxford University Press.

——— ed. 1987. *Joyce Carol Oates.* New York: Chelsea House.

Bowen, Elizabeth. 1982. *Afterthought.* London: Longmans, Green.

Bowen, Elizabeth. 1983. *The Heritage of English Literature.* London: Thames and Hudson.

Bowlby, Rachel. 1985. *Margaret Drabble.* London: Methuen.

——— 1992. "But She Would Learn Something from Lady Chatterley: The Obscene Side of the Canon," *Decolonizing Tradition* edited by Karen Lawrence. Urbana: The University of Illinois Press.

Boyle, Kay. 1930. *Wedding Day and Other Stories* New York: Jonathan Cape and Harrison Smith.

——— 1930. *Plagued by the Nightingale.* London. rpt. Virago Ltd. 1980.

——— 1932. *Year Before Last.* New York: Jonathan Cape and Harrison Smith, 1932; rpt. New York Penguin Books, 1986.

——— 1933. *The First Lover and Other Stories,* New York: Harrison Smith and Robert Haas.

——— 1934. *My Next Bride.* New York: Harcourt, Brace.

——— 1936. *The White Horses of Vienna and Other Stories.* New York: Harcourt, Brace.

——— 1936. *Death of a Man.* New York: Harcourt, Brace.

——— 1940. *The Crazy Hunter: Three Short Novels.* New York: Harcourt, Brace.

——— 1946. *Thirty Stories.* New York: Simon and Schuster.

——— and Robert McAlmon. 1968. *Being Geniuses Together 1920–1930.* rev. ed. Garden City: Doubleday.

Broyard, Anatole. 1987. "The Combustible Lawrence," *New York Times Book Review,* November 8.

Bundtzen, Lydia K. 1983. *Plath's Incarnations: Women and the Creative Process,* Ann Arbor: University of Michigan Press.

Buford, William. 1947. *The Art of Anaïs Nin.* Yonkers, New York: Outcast Chapbooks, no. 11.

Burgess, Anthony. 1990. *You've Had Your Time.* New York: Grove Weidenfeld.

Butscher, Edward. 1976. *Sylvia Plath [:] Method and Madness.* New York: Seabury Press.

——— ed. 1978. *Sylvia Plath: The Woman and the Work.* London: Peter Owen.

——— 1978. *Sylvia Plath: The Woman and the Work.* London: Peter Owen.

Campbell, Jane. 1983. "Becoming Terrestrial: The Stories of Margaret Drabble," *Criticism* 25.

Chisholm, Dianne. 1990. "H. D.'s Autoheterography," *Tulsa Studies in Women's Literature* 9, no. 1 Spring.

——— 1992. *H. D.'s Freudian Poetics.* Ithaca: Cornell University Press.

Cixous, Helene. "Castration or Decapitation?" Translated by Annette Kuhn. *Signs: Journal of Women in Culture and Society* 17, 1 (autumn).

Clark, L. D. 1964. *Dark Night of the Body.* Austin: University of Texas Press.

Clark, Orville. 1978 "Studies in New Erotology," *Mosaic,* 11, no. 2.

Clemons, Walter. 1972. "Joyce Carol Oates: Love and Violence," *Newsweek*, December 11.

Coetzee, J. M. 1993. "Homage [on influence]," *The Threepenny Review*, Spring 5–7.

Cooper-Clark, Diana. 1980 "Margaret Drabble: Cautious Feminist," *Atlantic Monthly*. 246, no. 5, Nov.

Cournos, John. 1926 *Miranda Masters*. New York: Alfred Knopf.

Creighton, Joanne. 1985. "Reading Margaret Drabble's *The Waterfall*," *Critical Essays on Margaret Drabble*, edited by Ellen Cronan Rose. Boston: G. K. Hall.

——— 1985. *Joyce Carol Oates*. New York: Methuen.

Cushman, Keith and Dennis Jackson, eds. 1991. *D. H. Lawrence's Literary Inheritors*. New York: St. Martin's Press.

Daiches, David. 1976, "Anti-Romanticism and Reactions," *The Modern World III Reaction*, edited by Eric Mottram, et. al. London: Aldus Books.

Davie, Donald. 1991. *Studies in Ezra Pound*. Manchester, England: Carcanet Press.

Deakin, Motley. 1980. *Rebecca West*. Boston: Twayne.

Delany, Paul. 1978. *D. H. Lawrence's Nightmare*. New York: Basic Books.

Delavenay, Emile. 1972. *D. H. Lawrence: The Man and His Work*. London: Heineman.

DeShazer, Mary K. 1986. *Inspiring Women*. New York: Pergamon Press.

Dix, Carol. 1980. *D. H. Lawrence and Women*. Totowa, N.J. Rowan and Littlefield.

Dobson, Sylvia. 1982, *Conjunctions* 2 (summer).

Doyle, Charles. 1989. *Richard Aldington: A Biography*. Carbondale: Southern Illinois University Press.

Drabble, Margaret. 1965. *The Garrick Year*. New York: William Morrow.

———. 1965. *The Millstone*. London: Weidenfelt and Nicholson.

———. 1969. *The Waterfall*. New York: Knopf.

———. 1969. *Wordsworth*. New York: Arco Press.

———. 1972. *The Needle's Eye*. New York: Knopf.

———. 1972. "Cassandra in a World Under Siege," *Ramparts*, 10.

———. 1973 "Lawrence's Aphrodite." (review of Robert Lucas's *Frieda Lawrence*) *Encounter*. 41, no. 2 August, 77–78.

———. 1974. *Arnold Bennett*. New York: Knopf.

———. 1975. *Realms of Gold*. New York: Knopf.

———. 1977. *The Ice Age*. New York: Knopf.

———. 1979. *A Writer's Britain: Landscape in Literature*. New York: Knopf.

———. 1980. *The Middle Ground*. New York: Knopf.

———. 1987. *The Radiant Way*. London: Weidenfeld and Nicholson.

———. 1989. *A Natural Curiosity*. New York: Viking Press.

———. 1991. "Fallen Woman," *New York Review of Books*, February 14.

———. 1992. *The Gates of Ivory*. New York: Viking Press.

Draper, R. P. 1969. *D. H. Lawrence*. New York: Humanities Press.

——— 1988. "The Defeat of Feminism: D. H. Lawrence's *The Fox* and 'The

Woman Who Rode Away'," *Critical Essays on D. H. Lawrence*, edited by Dennis Jackson and Fleda Brown Jackson. Boston: G. K. Hall.

Duncan, Erika. 1982. "Writing and Surviving: A Portrait of Meridel LeSueur," *Book Forum*, VI, no. 1.

——— 1960. "Beginnings; *Coyotes Journal* 5/6.

Duncan, Robert. 1979. "The H. D. Book, Part Two: Nights and Days, Chapter 9," *Chicago Review*, 30, no. 3, 37–85.

DuPlessis, Rachel Blau. 1986. *H. D.: The Career of That Struggle*. Bloomington: Indiana University Press.

Evans, Faith, ed. 1988. *Family Memories* [Rebecca West]. New York: Viking Penguin.

Evans, Oliver. 1968. *Anaïs Nin*. Carbondale: Southern Illinois University Press.

Feinstein, Elaine. 1993. *Lawrence and the Women: An Intimate Life of D. H. Lawrence*. New York: Harper Collins.

Ferguson, Robert. 1991. *Henry Miller*. New York: W. W. Norton.

Fernihough, Anne. 1993. *D. H. Lawrence: Aesthetics and Ideology*. New York: Oxford University Press.

Fiction!: Interviews with Northern California Novelists by Dan Tooker and Roger Hofheims, 1976.

Firchow, Peter. 1980. "Rico and Julia: The Hilda Doolittle-D. H. Lawrence Affair Reconsidered." *Journal of Modern Literature*, 7, no. 1 (51–76)

Fitch, Noel Riley. 1994. *Anaïs: The Erotic Life of Anaïs Nin*. New York: Little Brown.

Ford, Hugh. 1975. *Published in Paris*. New York: Macmillan.

Franklin, Benjamin and Duane Schneider. 1979. *Anaïs Nin: An Introduction*. Athens, Ohio: Ohio University Press.

Freeman, Barbara. 1972. "A Dialogue with Anaïs Nin," *Chicago Review*, 24, no. 2.

Friedman, Ellen. 1980. *Joyce Carol Oates*. New York: Frederick Ungar.

Friedman, Susan Stanford. 1981. *Psyche Reborn: The Emergence of H. D.* Bloomington: Indiana University Press.

——— "H. D. Chronology," *H. D. Newsletter*, In Spring, 1987.

——— and Rachel Blau DuPlessis, eds. 1990. *Signets: Reading H. D.* Madison: University of Wisconsin Press.

——— 1991. *Penelope's Web: Gender, Modernity, H. D.'s Fiction*. Cambridge: Cambridge University Press.

Fuchs, Miriam. 1990. "H. D.'s Self-Inscription: Between Time and 'Out-of-Time' in The Gift", *The Southern Review*, 26, no. 3 (Summer).

Fullbrook, Katherine. 1986. *Katherine Mansfield*. London: Harvester Press.

Gelfant, Blanche. 1984. *Women Writing in America*. Hanover, New Hampshire: University Press of New England.

Gelpi, Albert, 1982 "Introductions," *Notes on Thought and Vision*. San Francisco: City Lights Books.

Gilbert, Sandra and Susan Gubar. 1985. *The Norton Anthology of Literature by Women*. New York: W. W. Norton.

Gilbert, Sandra. 1990. "Preface to the Second Edition: Some Notes Toward a

Vindication of D. H. Lawrence," *Acts of Attention.* Carbondale; Southern Illinois University Press.

——— 1991. "Feminism and D. H.Lawrence," *Anaïs: An International Journal,* Vol. 9, 92–100.

Glendinning, Victoria. 1981. "Afterword," *Sunflower.* London: Virago.

——— 1986. "Afterword," *Cousin Rosamund.* New York: Viking.

——— 1987. *Rebecca West.* New York: Knopf.

Goldensohn, Barry. "Euridice Looks Back, *The American Poetry Review,* November/December 1994, 43–52.

Gordon, Ian. ed. 1974. *Undiscovered Country: The New Zealand Stories of Katherine Mansfield.* London: Longmans, Green.

Gordon, Lyndall. 1985. *Virginia Woolf.* New York: W. W. Norton.

Grant, Mary. 1978. *The Tragic Vision of Joyce Carol Oates.* Durham: Duke University Press.

Gray, Richard. 1990. *American Poetry of the Twentieth Century.* London and New York: Longmans, Green.

Green, Martin. 1974. *The Von Richthofen Sisters.* New York: Basic Books.

——— 1975. "D. H. Lawrence in Parts and Pieces," *New York Times Book Review,* September 21, 7–8.

Greene, Gayle. 1992. "The Horror," *The Nation* (August/September).

Gregory, Horace, 1961. "Introduction," *Helen in Egypt.* New York: New Directions.

Guest, Barbara. 1984. *Herself Defined.* Garden City: Doubleday.

Hahn, Emily. 1975. *Lorenzo.* Philadelphia and New York: J. B. Lippincott.

Hample, Patricia. 1975. "Meridel LeSueur—Voice of the Prairie," *Ms,* 4 (August).

Hankin, C. A. 1980. *Katherine Mansfield and Her Confessional Stories.* New York: St. Martin's Press.

Hanson, Clare and Andrew Gurr. 1981. *Katherine Mansfield.* London and Basingstoke: Macmillan Ltd.

Hannay, John. 1986. *The Intertextuality of Fate.* Columbia: University of Missouri Press.

Harris, Janice Hubbard. 1984. *The Short Fiction of D. H. Lawrence.* New Brunswick, N. J.: Rutgers University Press.

Hayman, Ronald. 1991. *The Death and Life of Sylvia Plath.* New York: Birch Lane Press.

H. D. (Hilda Doolittle) 1921. *Hymen.* London: Egoist Press.

——— 1924. *Heliodora and Other Poems.* Boston: Houghton Mifflin.

——— 1926. *Palimpsest.* Boston and New York: Houghton Mifflin; repr. Southern Illinois Press, 1968.

——— 1928. *Hedylus.* Oxford: Basil Blackwell.

——— 1931. *Red Roses for Bronze.* Boston and New York: Houghton Mifflin.

——— 1960. *Bid Me To Live.* New York: Grove Press. Reprint, London: Virago Press, 1984.

——— 1961, *Helen in Egypt.* New York: New Directions.

——— 1969. "Letters of H. D.," *Contemporary Literature* 10, no. 4 (autumn).

——— 1972. *Hermetic Definition*. New York: New Directions.

——— 1973. *Trilogy* (The Walls Do Not Fall; Tribute to the Angels; The Flowering of the Rod). New York: New Directions.

——— 1974. *Tribute to Freud*. Boston: David Godline.

——— 1979. *End to Torment*. New York: New Directions.

——— 1981. *HERmione. New York: New Directions. Also as her* by Virgo Press in 1984.

——— 1982. *The Gift*. Introduction by Perdita Schaffner. New York: New Directions.

——— 1982. *Notes on Thought and Vision & The Wise Sappho*. San Francisco; City Lights Books.

——— 1983. *Collected Poems 1912–1944* edited by Louis Martz. New York: New Directions.

——— 1985. *Nights*. New York: New Directions.

——— 1992. *Paint It Today*, edited by Cassandra Laity. New York: New York University Press.

——— 1992. *Asphodel*, edited by Robert Spoo. Durham, N.C.: Duke University Press.

H. D. "Eurydice," *The Egoist*, May 1917.

H. D. Newsletter, 1, no. 1 (spring 1987) and 2, no. 2 (winter 1987)

Hinz, Evelyn. 1971. *The Mirror and the Garden*. Columbus: Ohio State University Libraries.

——— 1978. "The World of Anaïs Nin" [critical essays]. *Mosaic*, 11, no. 1. Winnipeg: University of Manitoba Press.

Hogan, Linda. 1983. "A Voice for the Dispossessed: Meridel LeSueur and Political Renewal," *Bloomsbury Review* (September/October)

Holbrook, David. 1992. *Where D. H. Lawrence Was Wrong About Women*. Lewisburg: Bucknell University Press.

Humma, John B. 1983. "The Interpenetrating Metaphor: Nature and Myth in Lady Chatterley's Lover," *PMLA* (January), 77–86.

[Huxley, Aldous]. 1974, *A Conversation on D. H.Lawrence*. Los Angeles: Friends of the UCLA Library.

Jacobson, Dale. 1992. "Review," *North Dakota Quarterly* (fall), 205–210.

Jackson, Dennis and Fleda Brown. 1988. *Critical Essays on D. H. Lawrence*. Boston: G. K. Hall.

Jason, K. Philip, ed. 1973. *Anaïs Nin Reader*. New York: Avon Books.

Johnson, Diane. 1992. "Something for the Boys," *The New York Review of Books*, January 16.

Johnson, Greg. 1987. *Understanding Joyce Carol Oates*. Columbia: University of South Carolina Press.

Jong, Erika. 1984. *Parachutes and Kisses*. New York: New American Library.

Kalnins, Mara. ed. 1986. *D. H. Lawrence Centenary Essays*. Bristol, England: Classical Press.

Kazin, Alfred. 1971. "Oates." *Harper's*, 243, August.

———. 1984. *New York Review of Books*, March 29. "A Nymph of the New."

Kelly, Aileen. 1992. "Revealing Bakhtin," *New York Review of Books*, September 24.
Kenyon, Olga. 1988. *Women Novelists Today*. New York: St. Martin's Press.
——— 1990. "Margaret Drabble," *Woman Writers Talk*. New York: Carroll and Graf.
King, Michael. Ed. 1986. *H. D.: Woman and Poet*, Orono, Maine: National Poetry Foundation.
Kinkead-Weekes, Mark. 1986. "The Marriage of Opposites in *The Rainbow*," in Kalnins, Mara, ed. *D. H. Lawrence: Centenary Essays*. Bristol: Classical Press.
Kirsch, Robert. 1969. "Studying Diary Masterwork of Noted Writer Anaïs Nin" (Calendar, Sunday). *Los Angeles Times*, November 10.
Knapp, Bettina. 1978. *Anaïs Nin*. New York: Frederick Ungar.
——— "To Reach Out Further Mystically," in *Anaïs, Art and Artist*, edited by Sharon Spencer (1985), Greenwood, Fl., Pankvill.
Kobler, J. F. 1990. *Katherine Mansfield: A Study of the Short Fiction*. Boston: Twayne Publishers.
Konner, Melvin, M. D. 1990. "Women and Sensuality," *New York Times Magazine (Good Health)*, April 29.
Kraft, Quentin. 1992. "Toward a Critical Renewal," *College English*, 54 (January), 46–82.
Kristeva, Julie. 1991. *Strangers to Ourselves*. New York: Columbia University Press.
Kroll, Judith. 1976. *Chapters in a Mythology: The Poetry of Sylvia Plath*. New York: Harper & Row.
Kuntz, Paul Grimley. 1978. "Anaïs Nin's Quest for Order," *Mosaic*, 11, no. 2.
Laird, Holly. 1988. *Self and Sequence*. Charlottesville: University Press of Virginia.
Laity, Cassandra. 1989. "H. D. and A. C. Swinburne," *Feminist Studies*, 15, no. 5 (Fall), 461–484.
Lawrence, D. H. 1918. *New Poems*. London: Secker.
——— 1922. *Aaron's Rod*. London: Heinemann.
——— 1923. *Kangeroo*. London: Heinemann.
——— 1931. *The Man Who Died*. New York: 1931.
——— 1936. *Phoenix: The Posthumous Papers*. New York: Viking Press.
——— 1951. *Four Short Novels*. New York: Viking Press.
——— 1959. *The Plumed Serpent*. New York: Vintage Books.
——— 1961. *The Rainbow*. New York: Viking Press.
——— 1961. *Women in Love*. New York: Viking Press, 1961.
——— 1961. *Studies in Classic American Literature*. New York: Viking Press.
——— 1964. *The Complete Poems*. Vol. i, ed. Vivian de Solo Pinto and Warren Roberts. London: Heinemann.
——— 1965. *The Complete Plays*. London: Heinemann.
——— 1965. *Four Short Novels*, New York: Viking Compass.
——— 1966. *Apocalypse*. New York: Viking Press (Compass Editions).
——— 1979. *The Letters*, Vol 1. Cambridge, England: Cambridge University Press.

———— 1982. *The Letters*, Vol 2. Cambridge and New York: Cambridge University Press.

———— 1984. *The Letters*, Vol 3. Cambridge: Cambridge University Press.

———— 1987. *The Letters*, Vol 4. Cambridge: Cambridge University Press.

Laurence, Patricia. 1991. *The Reading of Silence*. Palo Alto: Stanford University Press.

LeSueur, Meridel. 1940. *Salute to Spring*. New York: International Publishers.

————. 1945. *North Star Country*. Lincoln: University of Nebraska Press. Preface by the author to the Bison Book Edition, 1984.

————. 1975. *The Rites of Ancient Ripening*. edited by Mary Ellen Shaw. Minneapolis: Vanilla Press.

————. 1978. *The Girl*. Minneapolis: West End Press. With an "Afterword" by the author, Albuquerque, N. M.: West End Press, 1990.

————. 1982. *Ripening: Selected Work, 1927–1980*. ed. Elaine Hedges. Old Westbury, New York: Feminist Press.

————. 1990. *Harvest Song: Collected Essays and Stories*. Albuquerque, N. M.: West End Press.

————. 1991. *River Road: A Story of Abraham Lincoln*. Duluth, Minn.: Holy Cow Press.

Locke, Raymond Friday. 1971. "Anais Nin and the Paintings of D. H. Lawrence," *Mankind: The Magazine of Popular History* (August)

Lodge, David. 1992. "Lawrence in Love," *The New York Review of Books*, February 13.

Mackey, Nathaniel. 1991. "From Glassire's Lute: Robert Duncan's Vietnam War Poems," *Talisman*, no. 6 (Spring), 141–164.

Maddox, Brenda. *D. H. Lawrence: The Story of a Marriage*. 1994. New York: Simon and Schuster.

Magalaner, Marvin. 1971. *The Fiction of Katherine Mansfield*. Carbondale: Southern Illinois University Press.

Malcolm, Janet. 1984. *The Silent Woman: Sylvia Plath and Ted Hughes* New York: Alfred Knopf.

Mansfield, Katherine. 1927. *The Journal of Katherine Mansfield*, edited by John Middleton Murry. London: Constable.

————. 1930. *Novels and Novelists*, edited by John Middleton Murry. London: Constable.

———— 1932. *The Letters of Katherine Mansfield*, edited by John Middleton Murry. New York: Alfred Knopf.

————. 1939. *The Scrapbooks of Katherine Mansfield*, edited by John Middleton Murry. London: Constable.

———— 1956. *Stories*. New York: Random House.

———— 1984. *The Collected Letters of Katherine Mansfield*, edited by Vincent Sullivan and Margaret Scott. 1 (1903–1917). Oxford: Clarendon Press.

———— 1987. *The Collected Letters of Katherine Mansfield*, edited by Vincent Sullivan and Margaret Scott, 2. (1918–1919). Oxford: Clarendon Press.

Mantel, Hilary. 1989. "England, Whose England?" *New York Review of Books*, November 23.

Marcus, Jane, ed. 1982. *The Young Rebecca: Writings of Rebecca West 1911–1917.* New York: Viking.

McClatchy, J. D. 1989. *White Paper on Contemporary American Poetry.* New York: Columbia University Press.

Melicia, Joseph. 1993. Akin to a Film," *American Book Review* (August/September), 17.

Mellen, Joan. 1994. *Kay Boyle: Author of Herself.* New York: Farrar, Straus & Giroux.

Meyer, Valerie Grosvenor. 1974. *Margaret Drabble: Puritanism and Permissiveness.* London: Vision Press.

——— 1991. *Margaret Drabble: A Reader's Guide.* New York: St. Martin's Press.

Meyers, Jeffrey. 1978. *Katherine Mansfield: A Biography.* New York: New Directions, 1978,

——— 1987. ed. *The Legacy of D. H. Lawrence.* New York: St. Martin's Press.

——— 1989. *The Spirit of Biography.* Ann Arbor: UMI Press.

——— 1990. *D. H. Lawrence.* New York: Alfred Knopf.

Millett, Kate. 1971. *Sexual Politics.* New York: Avon Books.

Milozzo, Lee, ed. 1989. *Conversations with Joyce Carol Oates.* Jackson: University of Mississippi Press.

Milton, Barbara. 1978. "Interview with Margaret Drabble," *Paris Review* 74 (winter).

Moi, Toril. 1987. *Sexual/Textual Politics: Feminist Literary Theory.* London and New York: Methuen.

Moore, Harry. 1974. *The Priest of Love.* New York: Farrar Straus and Giroux.

Moore, Olive 1932. *Further Reflections on the Death of a Porcupine.* London: Blue Moon Press.

Moran, Mary. 1983. *Margaret Drabble: Existing Within Structures.* Carbondale: Southern Illinois University Press.

Moss, Howard, 1986 *Minor Monuments.* New York: Ecco Press.

Napora, Joseph. 1982. "The Story and the Living: Meridel LeSeuer's *The Girl*" in *We Sing Our Struggle*, edited by Mary McAnally. Tulsa: Cardinal Press.

Nathan, Rhoda B. 1988. *Katherine Mansfield.* New York: Continuum Press.

Nekola, Charlotte and Paula Rabinowitz. 1987. *Writing Red: An Anthology of American Women Writers, 1930–1940.* New York: The Feminist Press.

Newman, Charles. 1970. *The Art of Sylvia Plath.* London: Faber and Faber.

Nin, Anais. 1930. "D. H. Lawrence Mystic of Sex." *The Canadian Forum: A Monthly Journal of Literature and Public Affairs* [Toronto], 11, no. 121 (October) 15–17.

——— 1932. *D. H. Lawrence: An Unprofessional Study.* reprinted, Chicago: Swallow Press, 1964.

——— 1944. *Under a Glass Bell*, New York: Gemor Press.

——— 1945. *This Hunger* (containing "Hedja," "Stella," and "Lillian and Djuna.") New York: Gemor Press.

——— 1947. *On Writing.* New York: Gemor Press.

——— 1948. *Winter of Artifice*, Chicago: Swallow Press.

——— 1950. *The Four-Chambered Heart.* New York: Duell, Sloane, and Pearce.

——— 1958. *Solar Barque.* Ann Arbor, Michigan: Edwards Brothers.
——— 1969. *Children of the Albatross.* Chicago: Swallow Press.
——— 1968. *A Spy in the House of Love.* New York: Bantam Books.
——— 1969. *The Diary: Volume Three 1939–1944.* New York: Harcourt Brace.
——— 1971. "A D. H. Lawrence Postscript" *Mankind: The Magazine of Popular History* [Los Angeles] 3, no. 2 (August), 21. Included in *The Diary: Volume Four 1944–1947.*
——— 1971. *The Diary: Volume Four 1944–1947.* New York: Harcourt Brace.
——— 1975. *A Woman Speaks.* Chicago: Swallow Press.
——— 1976. *The Diary: Volume Six 1955–1966.* New York: Harcourt Brace.
——— 1976. *In Favor of the Sensitive Man and Other Essays.* New York: Harcourt Brace.
——— 1977. *The Delta of Venus.* New York: Harcourt Brace.
——— 1977. *Little Birds.* New York: Harcourt Brace.
——— 1980. *The Diary: Volume Seven 1966–1974.* New York: Harcourt Brace.
Nixon, Cornelia. 1986. *Lawrence's Leadership Politics and the Turn Against Women.* Berkeley and San Francisco: University of California Press.
Oates, Joyce Carol. 1964. *With Shuddering Fall.* New York: Vanguard, 1964.
——— 1969. *Women in Love and Other Poems.* New York: Albondacani Press, 1969.
——— 1970. *The Wheel of Fire and Other Stories.* New York: Vanguard Press.
——— 1971. *Wonderland.* New York: Vanguard Press.
——— 1971. *Marriages and Infidelities.* New York: Vanguard Press.
——— 1972. *New York Times Book Review.* June 4, 1972.
——— 1973. *Do With Me What You Will.* New York: Vanguard, 1973.
——— 1973. *Angel Fire.* Baton Rouge: Louisiana State University Press.
——— 1974. *New Heaven, New Earth: The Visionary Experience in Literature.* New York: Vanguard Press.
——— 1974. "Bricks and Mortar," *Ms.* August.
——— 1974. *The Goddess and Other Women.* New York: Vanguard.
——— 1974. *The Hostile Sun.* Los Angeles: Black Sparrow Press.
——— 1975. "Afterword" to *The Poisoned Kiss* and in "Letter to Dale Boesky," *International Review of Psychoanalysis,* 2.
——— 1975. *The Fabulous Beasts.* Baton Rouge: Louisiana State University Press.
——— 1978. *Women Whose Lives Are Food, Men Whose Lives Are Money.* Baton Rouge: Louisiana State University Press.
——— 1979. *The Lamb of the Abyssalia.* [n.p.] Pomegranate Press.
——— [1981. "Lawrence's Götterdammerung: The Apocalyptic Vision of *Women in Love,*" *Contraries.* Oxford: Oxford University Press.
——— 1981. "Why Is Your Writing So Violent? *New York Times Book Review.* March 29, 15, 35.
——— 1981. *Angel of Light.* New York: E. P. Dutton.
——— 1982. *Invisible Woman.* Princeton: Ontario Review Press.
——— 1983. *The Profane Art.* New York: E. P. Dutton.

——— 1985. *Solstice.* New York: E. P. Dutton.
——— 1988. *Woman Writer.* New York: E. P. Dutton.
——— 1988. "D. H. Lawrence," in *Critical Essays on D. H. Lawrence,* edited by Dennis Jackson and Fleda Brown Jackson. Boston: G. K. Hall.
——— 1989. *American Appetites.* New York: E. P. Dutton.
——— 1989. *The Time Traveller.* New York: E. P. Dutton.
——— 1989. "My Father, My Fiction," *New York Times Magazine,* March 19.
——— 1991. *The Rise of Life on Earth.* New York: New Directions.
——— 1991. *Heat and Other Stories.* New York: Dutton.
——— 1991. "Sylvia Plath," *Times Literary Supplement* (June 21, 19–20.
Orel, Howard. 1986. *The Literary Achievement of Rebecca West.* London: Macmillan.
Patmore, Bridget. 1968. *My Friends When Young.* London: Heinemann.
Pearson, Gabriel. 1984. "Behind the Mask of the Pythoness," *Times Literary Supplement.* London, April 27.
Pennings, Rhonda. 1988. "Men and Women as Nurturers in the Work of Meridal LeSueur and Thomas McGrath," *North Dakota Quarterly* (fall), 153–164.
Phillips, Robert. 1978. "Joyce Carol Oates: The Art of Fiction," *The Paris Review,* 74 (fall-winter), 199–226.
Plath, Aurelia Schober, ed. 1975. *Letters Home.* New York: Harper & Row.
Plath, Sylvia. 1961. *The Colossus and Other Poems.* New York: Knopf.
——— 1971. *Ariel.* New York: Harper & Row.
——— 1971. *The Bell Jar.* New York: Harper & Row.
——— 1971. *Crossing the Water.* New York: Harper & Row.
——— 1972. *Winter Trees.* New York: Harper & Row, 1972.
——— 1979. *Johnny Panic and the Bible of Dreams.* New York: Harper & Row.
——— 1981. *Collected Poems,* edited by Ted Hughes. New York: Harper & Row.
——— 1982. *The Journals of Sylvia Plath,* edited by Frances McCullough. New York: Dial Press.
——— n.d. *Wreath for a Bridal.* Farnham, Surrey: Sceptre Press.
Preston, Peter and Peter Hoare. eds. 1989. *D. H. Lawrence in the Modern World.* Cambridge: Cambridge University Press.
Preussner, Dee. 1979–1980. "Talking with Margaret Drabble," *Modern Fiction Studies* 25.
Rasula, Jed. 1983. "A Renaissance of Women Writers," *Sulfur* 7, 160–172.
Ray, Gordon. 1974. *H. G. Wells & Rebecca West.* New Haven: Yale University Press.
Robinson, Janice. 1984. *H. D.: The Life and Work of an American Poet.* Boston: Houghton Mifflin.
Robinson, Roger, ed. 1994. *Katherine Mansfield: In from the Margin.* Baton Rouge: Louisiana State University Press.
Roessel, David. 1987. "H. D. and Lawrence: Two More Allusions," *H. D. Newsletter* (Winter) 1, no. 2.
Rose, Ellen Cronan. 1890. *The Novels of Margaret Drabble.* New York: Barnes and Noble.

———. ed. 1985. *Critical Essays on Margaret Drabble*. Boston: G. K. Hall.
Rose, Jacqueline. 1993. *The Haunting of Sylvia Plath*. Cambridge: Harvard University Press.
Rosenblatt, John. 1979. *Sylvia Plath: The Poetry of Initiation*. Chapel Hill: University of North Carolina Press.
———. ed. 1985. *Critical Essays on Margaret Drabble*. Boston: G. K. Hall.
Ruderman, Judith. 1984. *D. H. Lawrence and the Devouring Mother*. Durham, N. C.: Duke University Press.
Sadler, Lynn Veach. 1986. *Margaret Drabble*. Boston: Twayne.
Salgado, Gamini and G. K. Das, eds. 1988. *The Spirit of D. H. Lawrence*. Totowa, N. J.: Barnes and Noble.
Scheckner, Peter. 1985. *Class, Politics and the Individual*. Cranbuy, N. J.: Associated University Presses.
Schneider, Daniel. 1986. *The Consciousness of D. H. Lawrence*. Lawrence, Kansas: The University Press of Kansas.
Scholar, Nancy. 1944. *Anaïs Nin*. Boston: Twayne Publishers.
Scholes, Robert. 1991. *Semiotic Interpretation*. New Haven: Yale University Press.
Schweik, Susan. 1991. *A Gulf So Deeply Cut: American Women Poets and the Second World War*. Madison, Wisconsin: University of Wisconsin Press.
Scott, Bonnie Kim. 1990. *The Gender of Modernism*. Bloomington: Indiana University Press.
Showalter, Elaine. 1977. *A Literature of Their Own*. Princeton, New Jersey: Princeton University Press.
——— ed. 1985. *The New Feminist Criticism*. New York: Pantheon.
——— 1991. *Sister's Choice*. New York: Clarendon Press/Oxford University Press.
Siegel, Carol. 1989. "Virginia Woolf's and Katherine Mansfield's Responses to D. H. Lawrence's Fiction," *The D. H. Lawrence Review*. Vol. 21, No. 3, (Fall) 291–312.
——— 1991. *Lawrence Among the Women*. Charlottesville and London: The University Press of Virginia.
Simpson, Hilary. 1982. *D. H. Lawrence and Feminism*. DeKalb: Northern Illinois University Press.
Sklar, Sylvia. 1975. *The Plays of D. H. Lawrence*. London: Vision Press.
Smith, Ann, ed. 1978. *Lawrence and Women*, New York: Barnes and Noble.
Snyder, Robert. 1976 *Anaïs Nin Observed*. Chicago: Swallow Press.
Spaeth, Janet, 1989. "Review," *North Dakota Quarterly* (Winter).
Spanier, Sandra Whipple. 1986. *Kay Boyle [:] Artist and Activist*. Carbondale: Southern Illinois University Press.
Spencer, Sharon. 1977. *Collage of Dreams: The Writings of Anaïs Nin*. Chicago: Swallow Press.
——— 1986, ed. *Anaïs, Art and Artists* [a collection of essays]. Greenwood, Florida: Penkevill.
Spilka, Mark. 1955. *The Love Ethic of D. H. Lawrence*. Bloomington: Indiana University Press.

———. 1990. "Lawrence and the Clitoris", in *The Challenge of D. H. Lawrence*. ed, Michael Squires and Keith Cushman. Madison, Wisconsin: University of Wisconsin Press.

Stade, George. 1973. "Introduction," by Nancy Steiner, *A Closer Look at Ariel*. New York: Popular Library.

Stevens, C. J. *Lawrence at Tregerthen*. 1988. Troy, New York: Whitsen Publishing.

Stevenson, Anne. 1989. *Bitter Fame*. Boston: Houghton Mifflin.

Storch, Margaret. 1989. "The Lacerated Male: Ambivalent Images of Women in *The White Peacock*," *D. H. Lawrence Review*, 21, no. 12, Summer

Stovel, Nora Foster. 1989. *Margaret Drabble*. Mercer Island, Washington: Starmont House.

Todorov, Tzvetan. 1990. *Genres of Discourse*. New York: Columbia University Press.

Tomalin, Claire. 1988. *Katherine Mansfield: A Secret Life*. New York: Alfred Knopf.

Tooker, Dan and Roger Hofheins, 1976. *Fiction!: Interviews with Northern California Novelists*. New York and Los Altos: Harcourt Brace.

Torborg, Norman. 1984. *Isolation and Contact*. Göteborg, Sweden: Menab/Gotab.

Twentieth Century Literature. 1988, edited by Sandra Spanier. 34 (Fall) no. 3 [Kay Boyle].

Under the Sign of Pisces: Anaïs Nin and her Circle 1971. edited by Richard Centing (Fall).

Van Ghent, Dorothy. 1953. *The English Novel: Form and Function*. New York: Harper & Row.

Wagner-Martin, Linda. 1987. *Sylvia Plath: A Biography*. New York: Simon and Schuster.

Wakoski, Diane. 1979. "Conversation with Diane Wakoski," *Hawaii Review* (Fall).

Walker, Carolyn. 1974. "Fear, Love, and Art in Oates's 'Plot'," *Critique* 15, No. 1.

Waller, G. F. 1979. *Dreaming America*. Baton Rouge: Louisiana State University Press.

———. 1979. "Through Obsession to Transcendence: The Lawrentian Mode of Oates's Recent Fiction," *Critical Essays on Joyce Carol Oates*, edited by Linda Wagner. Boston: G. K. Hall.

Weinstein, Norman. 1992. "If You Can Find Her," *American Book Review*, XIII (December-January), 15.

Weldon, Fay. 1985. *Rebecca West*. Harmondsworth: Penguin.

Welty, Eudora. 1958. *New York Times Book Review* (September 21), 8.

West, Rebecca. 1918. *The Return of a Soldier*. New York: George Doran.

———. 1922. *The Judge*. New York: George Doran.

———. 1928. *The Strange Necessity*. Garden City, New York: Doubleday Doran.

———. 1929. *Harriet Hume*. New York: Doubleday Doran.

———. 1931. *Ending in Earnest: A Literary Log*. New York: Doubleday Doran.

———. 1931. *Arnold Bennett Himself*. New York: John Day.

——— 1936. *The Thinking Reed*. New York: Viking Press.

——— 1947. *The Meaning of Treason*. New York: Viking Press; 1949 London: Macmillan.

——— 1955. *A Train of Powder*. New York: Viking Press.

——— 1957. *The Court and the Castle*. New Haven: Yale University Press. With subtitle, *A Study of the Interaction of Political and Religious Ideas in Imaginative Literature*, London: Macmillan.

——— 1964. *The New Meaning of Treason*. New York: Viking Press.

——— 1977. *Rebecca West: A Carnival*. New York: Viking Press. The alternative title to this collection is *Rebecca West: A Celebration: Selections from Her Writings by the Publisher with Her Help*.

——— 1981. *Sunflower*. London: Virago.

——— 1984. "Interview," *Writers at Work*, 6th series, ed. George Plimpton. New York: Viking Press.

——— 1986. *Cousin Rosamund*. New York: Viking Press.

——— 1988. *Family Memories*, edited by Faith Evans. New York: Viking Penguin.

Wilson, Edmund. 1944. "Doubts and Dreams," *The New Yorker*, April 1, 78–82.

———. 1945. "Sherwood, Marquand, AN," *The New Yorker*, November 10, 101–102.

Wolfe, Peter. 1971. *Rebecca West; Artist and Thinker*. Carbondale: Southern Illinois University Press.

Woolf, Virginia. 1948. *The Moment and Other Essays*. New York: Harcourt Brace.

———. 1967. *Collected Essays*. New York: Harcourt Brace.

"The World of Anaïs Nin," *Mosaic* 11, no. 2 ed. Evelyn Hinz. Winnipeg: University of Manitoba Press 1978.

Worthen, John. 1992. *D. H. Lawrence: The Early Years, 1885–1912*. Cambridge: Cambridge University Press.

Zeller, Robert, ed. 1974. *A Casebook on Anaïs Nin*. New York and Scarborough, Ontario. New American Library. Contains a history of Nin's unorthodox publishing methods by Benjamin Franklin.

Zinnes, Harriet. 1963. "Anaïs Nin's Work Reissued" *Books Abroad*, 37 (Summer).

Zweig, Paul. 1983. "A Voice Speaking to No One," In *Praise of What Persists* edited by Stephen Berg. New York: Harper & Row.

Index

If a title is not accompanied by the author's name, it is a work of Lawrence.

Aaron's Rod, 10, 36, 42, 48, 52, 56, 66, 81, 84, 94–95, 130, 144–45
Achilles, 52–55, 58, 154
Adam, Michael, 148
Aldington, Richard, 15, 22, 47–48, 51, 52–54, 58, 62, 154–55
Alexander, Paul, 121
Allotropic ego, 134, 159
Amores, 37, 54
Alpers, Anthony, 14, 38, 39, 41, 43, 152
Alvarez, A., 119–20
American Bookman, The, 69
Andrews, Henry, 70
Apocalypse, 40, 144
"A Propos of *Lady Chatterley's Lover*," 140
Arlen, Michael, 37
Asquith, Lady Cynthia, 31, 97, 151
"At the Bay," (Mansfield), 41
"Attack, The," 59, 61
Auden, W.H., 148
Augustine, Jane, 153–54
"Autumn Sunshine," 76
Axelrod, Steven, 111

Baker, Ivy, 36
Bakhtin, Mikhail, 29
Balakian, Nona, 28
Bandol, 67
Barlow, Gerald (*Touch and Go*), 39
Barnes, Djuna, 86
Barnet, Gary, 154
Barthes, Roland, 21, 22
Basil (*Paint It Today*), 50
Bay, 57
Beards, K. Virginia, 125, 158
Beason, Thomas (*Salute to Spring*), 81
Beauchamp, Leslie, 37
Beauvoir, Simone de, 11, 21, 22

Beebe, Maurice, 155
Beerbohm, Max, 63
Bell, Michael, 160
Bellow, Saul, 158
Bender, Eileen, 139–40, 145
Bennett, Arnold, 72, 128–29, 131, 151, 158
Benstock, Shari, 155
Berkman, Sylvia, 43
Beye, Lillian (*Solar Barque*), 93
Bid Me to Live (H.D.), 48, 60
Birds, Beasts and Flowers, 49, 81, 119, 144–45, 156
Birkin, Rupert (*Women in Love*), 29, 35, 38, 97, 148, 152
Blake, William, 139
Blood consciousness (in LeSueur), 76; (in Boyle), 107
Bloom, Harold, 22
Bloom, Molly, 18
Bloomsbury, 152
Bowen, Alix (*The Radiant Way*), 130, 132, 150
Bowen, Elizabeth, 12, 13, 25, 42, 44, 146
Bowlby, Rachel, 156
Boy in the Bush, 31, 102
Boyle, Kay, 12, 13, 18; 100–110; *Being Geniuses Together*, 101; *Year Before Last*, 102; *Gentlemen, I Address You Privately*, 103, 157; "The White Horses of Vienna," 104; "Episode in the Life of an Ancestor," 104; *Wedding Day and Other Stories*, 104; "Summer," 105; *First Lover and Other Stories*, 105; "The Rest Cure," 105; *My Next Bride*, 106; *The White Horses of Vienna*, 107; "Maiden, Maiden," 107; *Life Being the Best and Other Stories*, 107; "Peter Fox,"

107; *Plagued by the Nightingale*, 108, 157; *Death of a Man*, 108; "The Meeting of the Stones," 108; *The Crazy Hunter*, 109; *Thirty Stories*, 109; 114, 136, 148; *Primer for Combat*, 157; photo, 100
Brangwen sisters, 80
Brangwen, Gudrun, 35, 41, 70, 92–93; 112–13; 126, 136–37; 151–52
Brangwen, Ursula, 9, 38, 39, 93, 96, 107, 112–13, 115, 117, 121, 158
Brangwen, Anna, 9, 37, 80, 142
Brangwen, Will, 142
Brett, Lady Dorothy, 31, 42, 151
Brontës, The, 65
Brontë, Charlotte, 9
Brontë, Emily, 9
Broyard, Anatole, 98
Bryher, 51, 62
Burford, William, 97
Burrows, Louie, 31, 151
Butscher, Edward, 116, 158

Cafe Royale (Pompadour), 37
Cambridge University, 113
Campbell, Jane, 129
Capri, 35, 43, 65
"Captain's Doll, The," 92, 94, 103
Carnavali, Emanuel, 102
Carswell, Catherine, 31
Cather, Willa, 69–70
Chambers, Jessie, 31, 151
Chatterley, Clifford, 20, 29, 127
Chatterley, Constance ("Connie"), 28, 84, 97, 107, 115, 126
Chekhov, Anton, 142
Chisholm, Dianne, 57, 155
Chopin, Kate, 75
Cipriano (*The Plumed Serpent*), 29, 40
Cixous, Helen, 147
Clarke, Susan, 104
Clarion, The, 63
Clark, L.D., 156
Clark, Orville, 156
Cleland, John, 16, 158
Clemons, Walter, 133, 139
Conjuctions, 62
Conrad, Joseph, 109
Cooper-Clark, Diana, 124, 128
Corfe Castle, 50, 54

Complete Plays of D.H. Lawrence, The, 99
Corke, Helen, 31, 151
Cornwall, 35, 38
Cournos, John, 61
Coutts, Bernard, 153
Creeley, Robert, 30, 120
Creighton, Joanne, 127, 129, 135
Crich, Winifred, 9, 39, 80, 103
Crich, Gerald, 20, 28, 38, 39, 67, 70, 92, 126, 136–37
Crockett, Wilbury, 111
Crosbys, Harry and/or Caresse, 103, 107, 109, 157
Cullingford, Elizabeth Butler, 22

Daiches, David, 120
"Daughters of the Late Colonel, The," (Mansfield), 41
"Daughters of the Vicar, The," 41
Davidson, Jo, 106
Davie, Donald, 150
Dax, Alice, 151, 154
Day, Gethin ("The Flying Fish"), 40
"Dead, The" (Joyce), 113
Deakin, Motley, 72
"Death of a Porcupine," 108
Delany, Paul, 150, 154, 156
Delavenay, Emile, 39
Derrida, Jacques, 150
DeShazer, Mary, 154
Devon, 121
Dialogic model(Bakhtin), 13, 29
Dickinson, Emily, 25, 107, 158
Dix, Carol, 151
Dobson, Sylvia, 62
D.H.Lawrence and the Devouring Mother, 10
D.H.Lawence and the Child, 9
D.H. Lawrence's Nightmare (Delany), 154
D.H. Lawrence Society of America, 10, 150
D. H. Lawrence Review, 151
"D.H.Lawrence's Sensibility" (Fergusson), 15
Doolittle, Hilda (see H.D.), 45
Dostoyesky, Feodor, 29, 86, 15
Douglas, Norman, 65–66
Dowding, Lord Hugh Caswell, 154
Doyle, Charles, 48–49, 50, 154
Drabble, Margaret, 12, 13, 28, 114;

122–32; *The Needle's Eye,* 123, 127–28; *A Summer Bird Cage,* 125; *The Millstone,* 125; *The Garrick Year,* 125; *The Waterfall,* 126; *The Middle Ground,* 129, 132; *A Natural Curiosity,* 129–30; *The Radiant Way,* 130; *The Gates of Ivory,* 132, 136, 151; *A Writer's Britain,* 158; photo, 122
Draper, Ronald, 151
Dukes, Tommy, 105
Duncan, Erika, 75, 83, 85
Duncan, Raymond (Sorrel), 107
Duncan, Robert, 47, 52, 55–56, 153 (*H.D.'s Book*)
DuPlessis, Rachel Blau, 62, 150, 153–55

Eliot, George, 9, 132
Eliot, T.S., 25, 26, 30, 91
Ellis, Havelock, 53
Eros and/or Thanatos (in Sylvia Plath), 111, 119
Escaped Cock, The, 103
Ethos of eroticism, 28
Etruscan Places, 67
Evans, Faith, 72
Evans, Oliver, 72, 98
"Evening Land, The," 159

Fairfield, Cicily Isabel (Rebecca West), 63
Fassendyll, Sybil, 71
Fear of Flying (Jong), 28
Feinstein, Elaine, 9, 22, 31, 151
Feminist Press, 82
Ferguson, Robert, 156
Fergusson, Francis, 15, 22
Ferlinghetti, Lawrence, 47
Fernihough, Anne, 156
Fiction!, 109
Fiesole, 49
Firchow, Peter, 61
"Flying Fish, The," 40, 153
Fontana Vecchia (Taormina), 157
Ford, Hugh, 89
Ford, Josephine (Dorothy Yorke), 48
Forster, E.M., 17, 41
Foster, Margaret, 132
"Fox, The," 78, 81–82; 96–97, 105, 125–26, 120, 130, 140, 145
Friedman, Susan, 45, 61–62

Franckenstein, Joseph, 157
Franklin, Benjamin, 96, 99 (and Duane Schneider), 156
Franz ("Persephone"), 78–79
Freda ("Persephone"), 78–79
Frederick (*Bid Me to Live*), 54
Freeman, Barbara, 88
Freewoman, The, 63
Freud, Sigmund, 52, 55, 58, 60, 97–98, 114, 123, 133, 137, 145, 148, 155, 158
Friedman, Ellen, 138
Friedman, Susan Stanford, 153
Fuchs, Miriam, 45, 153
Fullbrook, Katherine, 152

Gale, Zona, 83
Gelfant, Blanche, 83
Gelpi, Albert, 153
Gerson, Mark, 122
Gertler, Mark, 37
Gilbert, Sandra, 30–31, 47, 151–52, 159, 160
Gilbert and Gubar, 88, 158
Giradoux, Jean, 86
Glendinning, 66, 70
Golden Notebook, The (Lessing), 14–16
Goldensohn, Barry, 48
Gombarov, 61
Gordon, Ian, 39, 152
Gordon, Lyndall, 150
Gray, Cecil, 50–51, 154
Gray, Richard, 119
Green, Martin, 31
Grey, Jane (*The Waterfall*), 126
Grumbach, Doris, 102
Grant, Mary, 135–36
Greene, Gael, 148, 159
Gregory, Horace, 58
Gubar, Susan, 47, 152
Guest, Barbara, 50, 148, 153, 154–55
Gurdjieff, George, 43

H.D., 9, 11, 30, 46–62; "'Eurydice,' 47, 49–50, 153; *Collected Poems,* 45; Trilogy," 55–56; *Helen in Egypt,* 45, 52, 55, 58–59; *Hermetic Definition,* 58; *End to Torment,* 45; *The Gift,* 45, 56; *Hermione,* 45; *Palimpsest,* 53; *Tribute to Freud,* 47, 60, 154; *Bid Me to Live,* 48–52, 54; *Paint It*

Today, 50, 52; "*The Flowering of the Rod,*" 52, 56; "Poem 6," 53; *Pilate's Wife*, 52, 56; *Hipparchia*, 53; *Hedylus*, 53; *Red Roses for Bronze*, 54; "Toward the Piraeus," 55; "The Walls Do Not Fall," 56; "Tribute to the Angels," 57; "Winter Love," 58; *Notes on Thought and Vision*, 58, 153; "The Dead Priestess Speaks," 59, 154; "Sigil," 154; "Advent," 60; "The Poet," 60, 155; "The Master," 60; "Hymn," 61; "The Mystery," 61; *Compassionate Friendship*, 62; 146–47; "Priest," 155; photo, 46
Hahn, Emily, 30, 35; 46
Halliday, Julius, *(Women in Love)*, 37
Hamalian, Leo, 9, 11, 12, 19, 20
Hannah *(Year Before Last)*, 102
Hannay, John, 127–28
Harris, Janice Hubbard, 104
Hannelle *(The Captain's Doll)*, 103
Hankin, C.M., 37, 40
Harris, Frank, 156
Hatlen, Burton, 108
Hayman, Ronald, 121
Heath, Stephen, 15, 16, 22
Hedges, Elaine, 75, 156
Helen, 55, 57–59, 154
Hemingway, Ernest, 102
Hepburn, Alexander and Evangeline *(The Captain's Doll)*, 102
Heseltine, Philip, 37
Hinz, Evelyn, 90–92, 94
Holbrook, David, 160
Holy Cow Press, 83
"Horse Dealer's Daughter, The," 104, 108, 145
Houghton, Alvina *(The Lost Girl)*, 93, 107, 128–29, 131–32
Hughes, Ted, 19, 115–16, 121, 158
Hugo (Guiler), 98
Huxley, Aldous, 152
Hyde, Virginia, 10
"Hyde Park at Night," 155

Ibsen, Hendrik, 27, 63
I Rise in Flame, Cried the Phoenix, 106
Ingersoll, Earl, 10, 14, 22, 150

James, Henry, 65–66, 67, 71, 75
Johnson, Greg, 160

Jong, Erika, 28, 148, 150
Jouve, Pierre Jean, 86
Julia *(Bid Me to Live)*, 49–50, 54, 60
Juliet *(Sun)*, 40, 80
Joyce, James, 18, 67, 71–72, 109, 142

Kalnins, Mara, 49
Kangeroo, 10, 48
Kazin, Alfred, 134, 155, 159
Keats, John, 158
Kenyon, Olga, 158
Kezia (Mansfield), 38, 42
Kierkegaard, Soren, 30
Kinkead-Weekes, Mark, 79
Kinnell, Galway, 25
Kizer, Caroline, 148
Klopfer, Deborah Kelly, 153
Knapp, Bettina, 156
Konner, Melvin, 30
Koteliansky, Samuel, 37
Kraft, Quentin, 150
Kristeva, Julia, 13, 31
Kroll, Judith, 157–58
Krook, Dorothea, Dr., 113
Kuntz, Paul Grimley, 157

Ladybird, The, 77, 96, 97
Lady Chatterley's Lover, 10, 14, 16, 37, 50, 52, 67, 71, 84, 91, 94, 96–99, 105, 114, 126, 132, 146, 154, 156
Laird, Holly, 77, 159
Laity, Cassandra, 155
Lake Garda, 102
Laurence, Patricia, 150
Laval, Pierre N., 25
Lawrence, Emma *(The Garrick Year)*, 125–26
Lawrence, Frieda, 27, 31, 35, 48–49, 70, 128, 151–52, 154, 158–59
Lawrence Among the Women, 9
Lawrence and the Women, 9
Lehmann-Haupt, Christopher, 157
Lessing, Doris, 10–17. *The Golden Notebook*, 14, 15, 22, 114, 146, 150, 158
LeSueur, Meridel, 12, 13, 19, 27, 28, 74–85; *The Ripening Seed*, 76; *Ripening*, 78, 82; "Wind," 79–80; "Harvest," 80; "Annunciation," 80–81; *The Girl*, 81–82; *Salute to Spring*, 81–82; "The Horses," 82; *Corn Village*, 82; *Rites of Ancient Ripening*,

83; *Little Brother of Wilderness,* 83; *Sparrow Hawk,* 83; "The Fetish of Being Outside," 84; photo, 74
Leavis, F.R., 15
Leslie, Kate *(The Plumed Serpent),* 40, 92–93
"Letter from Town," 77
Letters of D.H. Lawrence, 4, 43
Leuke, 58
Levertov, Denise, 12, 30, 47, 150
Lewis, Wyndham, 65
Lilly Library (Indiana University), 112
Lodge, David, 27
Loerke *(Women in Love),* 29
Lost Girl, The, 35, 66, 88, 92, 102, 128, 130–31
Love Ethic of D.H. Lawrence (Spilka), 14
"Love on the Farm," 116
Lowell, Amy, 45; *Some Imagist Poets,* 47, 50
Lucas, Robert, 159
Luhan, Mabel Dodge, 31, 151

Maata (Mansfield), 38–39
Macaulay, Rose, 68
Mackey, Nathaniel, 153
MacNiven, Ian, 157
Magalaner, Marvin, 153
Mailer, Norman, 19, 109
"Man Who Died, The," 27, 40, 52–53, 56–57; 76, 113, 140, 154
Mannheimer, Monica, 129
Mansfield, Katherine, 9, 12, 30, 34 (photo); 34–44; *Novels and Novelists,* 36, 42; *Maata,* 36; "Marriage a la Mode," 37; "Psychology" 38; "Rangataki Valley," 40–41; "The Awakened River," 41; "Sun and Moon," 41; "At the Bay," 41; "The Prelude," 42; *The Diary: Vol. Four,* 42; 114, 123, 146, 150–52
Marcus, Jane, 65
"Marriage a la Mode" (Mansfield), 37
Marsh, Edward, 120
Masters and Johnson, 16, 22
McClachy, J.D., 118
McClure, Michael, 47
McCullers, Carson, 12, 13, 114, 147, 150
McFarlin Library (University of Tulsa), 64

Mecklenburgh Square (London), 48, 54
Melisendra (Anaïs Nin), 88
Mellors, Oliver, 28, 84, 138
Melville, Ellen *(The Judge),* 68
"Mess of Love, The," 116
Meyer, Valerie, 126–27
Michaelis, 37
Midget *(Paint It Today),* 50
Millay, Edna St. Vincent, 75
Millett, Kate, 10, 11, 16, 19, 21, 22, 98, 151, 160
Miller, Henry, 88–89, 156
Milozzo, Lee, 134, 142, 159
Milton, Barbara, 158
Miranda Masters (Cournos), 61
Moi, Toril, 88
Moore, Harry, 15, 36, 50, 66
Moore, George, 70
Moore, Olive, 148, 150
Morel, Paul *(Sons and Lovers),* 68
Morrell, Lady Ottoline, 31, 35, 151
Morris, Library (University of Southern Illinois), 100
Moss, Howard, 42, 44
Munday *(Gentlemen, I Address You Privately),* 103
Murry, John Middleton and Katherine (Mansfield), 35–37, 38, 39, 43, 89, 150, 152
Meyers, Jeffrey, 37, 39, 152, 154
Moran, Mary, 125
Morris, Adalaide, 153

Nabokov, Vladimir, 29
Nathan, Rhoda, 152
Nekola, Charlotte, 84
Nettles, 89
Newman, Charles, 111, 158
New Directions Publishing Corp, 46
"New Heaven and Earth," 159
New Statesman, 68
New York Review of Books, 129, 155
New York Times (Book Review), 98–99; 123, 150
Nin, Anaïs, 9, 12, 19, 27, 28, 42, 86–99; *The Diary: Vol. III,* 86; *The Diary: Vol. VI,* 90; *In Favor of the Sensitive Man,* 86; 157; "D.H. Lawrence Mystic of Sex," 88; *The House of Incest,* 88, 96; "Nettles," 89; *D. H. Lawrence: An Unprofessional*

Study, 89–90, 94; *Delta of Venus*, 90–91; *Little Birds*, 91; *The Four-Chambered Heart*, 91, 95; "Hilda and Rango," 91; *The Novel of the Future*, 92; *Solar Barque*, 93; *The Seduction of the Minotaur*, 93; *The Children of the Albatross*, 94; "The Sealed Room," 94; "The Voice," 95; "The Sealed Room," 95; *Under a Glass Bell*, 96; "Hedja," 96; *This Hunger*, 97; *The Diary: Vol VII*, 97, 99; "Elena," 97; *A Spy in the House of Love*, 98; "Eroticism in Women," 98; *A Woman Speaks*, 99; 114; photo, 87

Nixon, Cornelia, 160
Novel: A Forum on Fiction, 21, 126; 146–47, 151
"November by the Sea," 159

Oates, Joyce Carol, 12, 13, 26, 30, 115–16, 121, 123, 133–45; *New Heaven, New Earth*, 133, 137, 159; *The Hostile Sun*, 134, 139–40, 142, 147, 159; *With Shuddering Fall*, 136; *Woman Writer*, 137; "Letter to Dale Boesky," 138; *Wonderland*, 138–39; *Do With Me What You Will*, 138–39, 145; "Lawrence's Gotterdammerung," 138; *Contraries*, 139; "Connection Between Men and Women," 140; "The Dead," 140, 159; "The Wheel," 140; *Solstice*, 140–41, 145; *American Appetites*, 142; *Because It is Bitter*, 142; *Marya*, 142; *Women in Love*, 143; *Angel Fire*, 143; "Firing a Field," 145; *The Fabulous Beasts*, 145; *The Lamb of Abyssalia*, 144; *Invisible Woman*, 144; "The Wasp," 144; "A Minature Passion," 144; *The Rise of Life on Earth*, 145; *The Time Traveller*, 145; "Peaches, Pineapples, Hazelnuts," 145; *The Profane Art*, 145, 151; "At Least I have Made A woman of Her," 145–46, 150–151, 159; "Bloodstains," 159; *Marriages and Infidelities*, 159; photo, 134
O'Connor, Flannery, 144
Old Wives' Tale, The (Bennett), 129, 131, 151
Olson, Charles, 120

"On That Day," 154
Orel, Howard, 67
Orpheus 48–49, 55; Lawrence as, 153
Ostriker, Alicia, 47

Parkin, Oliver *(The First Lady Chatterley)*, 84
Parachutes and Kisses (Jong), 28
Patmore, Brigit, 48
Pearson, Gabriel, 60
Pendennis (Death of a Man), 108
Pennings, Rhonda, 76
Persephone myth, 77–78; 116, 155–56
Phallic consciousness, 16, 89, 116–17, 134
Phillips, Robert, 133
Picasso, Pablo, 98
Plath, Sylvia, 12, 13, 19, 30, 111–21; "Johnny Panic and the Bible of Dreams," 115–16; *Colossus and Other Poems*, 116; "Pursuit," 116; "Two Sisters of Persephone," 116, 119; "Medallion," 117; *Journals*, 117; *Bell Jar, The*, 117; "The Eye-Mote," 117–18; "Elm," 118; "Two Sisters," 118; "Elm," 118; *Ariel*, 118–19, *Wreath for a Bridal*, 118; "Ariel," 119; 146–47, 158; *Letters Home*, 157; photo, 112
Plath, Warren, 114
Plumed Serpent, The, 40, 71, 83, 130
Point Counter Point (Huxley), 69
Pollnitz, Christopher, 48
Portland Villas (London), 38–39
Portrait of a Genius But, (Aldinton), 15
Pound, Ezra, 26, 45, 52, 55, 58, 62, 154–55
"Prelude, The" (Mansfield), 42
"Professions for Women" (Woolf), 13
Proust, Marcel, 67, 72, 86, 156
"Prussian Officer, The," 104
Psanek, Count, *(The Ladybird)*, 77
Psychoanalysis and the Unconscious, 117
Puritan ethic, 80, 123
"Purple Anemones," 156

Queens University Archives, 34
Quetzalcoatl, hymns of, 83

INDEX

Raeburn, Eve (*The Year Before Last*) 103
Rafe (*Bid Me to Live*), 50, 54
Rainbow, The, 9, 20, 37, 70, 76, 78–80, 92, 95–97, 117–18, 121, 127, 130, 140, 142, 152
Ramsden, Richard (*Miranda Masters*), 61
Rampion, Mark, 69
Rananim, 61
Rank, Otto, 99
Rasula, Jed, 47
Ray, Gordon, 67
Rexroth, Kenneth, 56
Richardson, Dorothy, 123
Rico (*Bid Me to Live*), 49–50, 60
Rico (*St. Mawr*), 104, 109
Rilke, Rainer, 25, 47–48
Roessel, David, 155
Roethke, Theodore, 120, 158
Ruderman, Judith, 10, 151
Rich, Adrienne, 25
Richardson, Dorothy, 12
Robinson, Janice, 48, 51–52, 58–59, 61, 154
"Rocking Horse Winner, The," 104
Root, Waverly, 86, 88
Rose, Ellen, 129
Russell, Bertrand, 39, 71

Sadler, Lynn, 126, 158
Sandburg, Carl, 85
Sartre, Jean Paul, 81
Sassoon, Richard, 113
Schaffner, Perdita, 46, 51, 154
Scheckner, Peter, 156
Schneider, Daniel, 150
Scholar, Nancy, 88, 157
Scholes, Robert, 15, 16, 20, 22, 158
Schreiner, Olive, 9
Schweik, Susan, 27, 154
Scott, Bonnie, 66–67, 73
Secker, Martin, 66
"Seven Seals," 55
Sexton, Anne, 120, 158
Sexual Fix, The (Heath), 15
Sexual Politics (Millett), 10
Sexual puritans, 17
Shaw, George Bernard, 63, 156
Sheehan, Martin ((*Year Before Last*), 102
Showalter, Elaine, 123, 128, 150

Siegel, Carol, 9–10, 22, 150, 153, 160
Silbert, Layle, 74, 87, 134
Simpson, Hilary, 89, 151
Skinner, Molly, 31
Sklar, Sylvia, 39
Sklenicka, Carol, 9, 11, 22
Skrebensky, Anton (*The Rainbow*), 20, 115
Sleeping Beauty theme, The, 96–97; 126
Smith, Ann, 151
"Snake," 117
Snyder, Gary, 47
Snyder, Robert, 88–89
"Soiled, Rose, The" 36
Somers, Harriet, 48
"Song of a Man Who Has Come Through, The," 79
Somers, Richard, 48
Sons and Lovers, 10, 29, 30, 31, 36, 65, 102, 115, 126–27
Spanier, Sandra, 106, 107, 109
Spaeth, Janet, 83
Spencer, Sharon, 156
Sportorno, 40
Spilka, Mark, 14, 22, 23, 146, 158–60
Stade, George, 114
Stephen, Julia, 13
Stesichorus, 53, 58
Stevenson, Anne, 113–15, 121
Stevens, C. J., 154
"St. Mark," 119
"St. Mawr," 54, 82, 104–5, 109, 118–19; 141–42
Storch, Margaret, 10, 151
Studies in Classic American Literature, 78
"Sun," 40, 80, 96, 153

Thatcher, Margaret, 132
Thompson, D.M. 21, 22
Times Literary Supplement, 66
Titus, Edward, 89
Todorov, Tzvetan, 28–29
Tomalin, Claire, 36, 43, 152
"Tortoise Shout," 111
Touch and Go, 39
"Trespasser, The," 63, 65
Turner, Reggie, 65–66
Turton, Oliver (*Touch and Go*), 39

Van Druten, John, 155
Van Eck, Petere, 155
Vane or Vanio, (Bid Me to Live), 51
Vence, 102
Vernon, Laurence (The Thinking Reed), 70,
Virgin and the Gypsy, The, 91, 126

Wagner-Martin, Linda, 111, 115–16
Wakoski, Diane, 25, 150
Walker, Alice 25
Wallace, Elizabeth, 10
Waller, G.F., 134, 142
Walsh, Ernest, 102–3
Weekley, Barbara, 154
Weekley, Ernest, 159
Weinstein, Norman, 155
Wells, H.G., 63, 65, 67, 69, 72, 144
Welty, Eudora, 146
West, Rebecca, 12; 63–73, photo, 64; The Return of a Soldier, 65, 67; Harriet Hume, 65; The Judge, 67; "Elegy" (A Carnival), 67, 155; The Strange Necessity, 69; D.H. Lawrence: An Elegy, 69; Ending in Earnest, 69, 72; Cousin Rosamund, 70; The Thinking Reed, 70; 73 Black Lamb and Gray Falcon, 72; A Train of Powder, 72, 114, 146; Court and the Castle, The, 155
Wharton, Edith, 75
White Peacock, The, 114
Whitman, Walt, 139

Widmer, Kingsley, 90
Widowing of Mrs. Holroyd, The, 65
Williams, Tennessee, 106
Williams, W.C., 55
Wilson, Angus, 158
Wilson, Edmund, 97
"Witch a la Mode, The," 153
Witt, Lou (St. Mawr), 104, 119, 142
Wolfe, Peter, 71
Woolf, Virginia, 9, 13, 22, 26, 43, 71, 111, 113, 121, 123, 128, 150–51, 157
Women in Love, 9, 20, 29, 30, 37, 38, 67–68; 70, 92, 95, 97, 98, 102–4, 107, 113, 115, 121, 125, 136, 138–40, 148, 152, 154
"Woman Who Rode Away, The," 20, 115–16; 139–40
Wordsworth, William, 124
Wrath, Anabel (Touch and Go), 39
Wulf, Anna, 14

Yaverland, Richard (The Judge), 68
Yeats, William Butler, 26, 134, 145
"Young Wife, A," 144
Yorke, Dorothy, ("Anabella"), 48

Zeller, Patricia English, 157
Zennor (Cornwall), 50, 54
"Zeppelin Nights," 59
Zinnes, Harriet, 93
Zinzindorf, Count (in H.D.), 61
Zola, Emile, 91
Zweig, Paul, 25

OHIO UNIVERSITY LIBRARY
Please return this book as soon as you have finished with it. In order to avoid a fine it must be returned by the latest date stamped below. All books are subject to recall after two weeks or immediately if needed for reserve.

RETURNED BY:

SEP 03 1996

DEC 1 5 2010

AUG 1 6 1996

AUG 0 1 1996